MEMOIRS

Illustrating the

HISTORY OF JACOBINISM

written in French by

AUGUSTIN BARRUEL

and translated into English by

THE HON. ROBERT CLIFFORD, F.R.S. AND A.S.

*Princes and nations shall disappear from
the face of the earth . . . and this* REVOLUTION
shall be the WORK OF SECRET SOCIETIES.
—Adam Weishaupt's *Discourse for the Mysteries*

Part II

THE ANTIMONARCHICAL CONSPIRACY

London
Spradabach Publishing
2021

Spradabach Publishing
BM Box Spradabach
London WC1N 3XX

Memoirs Illustrating the History of Jacobinism,
Part II: The Antimonarchical Conspiracy
originally published in English in 1798
© Spradabach Publishing 2021

First Spradabach edition published 2021

ISBN 978-1-9993573-2-0

British Library Cataloguing-in-Publication Data:
A catalogue record for this book is available from the British Library.

Table of Contents.

Preface of the Translator.

he Second Volume of the Memoirs of Jacobinism, containing the Antimo-narchical Conspiracy, is presented to the Public without the advantage which the First possessed in the flattering faction of Mr. Burke's favorable opinion; an awful event having deprived the world of that illustrious writer. In the first of his Posthumous Works however, we find him attributing the progress of the Frech Revolution to a Spirit of Proselytism: he calls it *"A Revolution of Doctrine and Theoretic Dogma*, bearing little analogy with any of those Revolutions which had ever been brought about in Europe, on principles merely political."

Our readers will be surprised at the coincidence of this Work with ideas if that eloquent Champion of Real Liberty. The very education of the Adept in Rebellion is described; the dangerous tendency of maxims which have been received in their abstract sense is explained; the means employed to pervert them into principles of rebellion is demonstrated; divers essays of their new doctrines delineated; and, finally, the union of men thus educated with the most formidable Sect of Antiquity, in the *Occult Lodges* of Freemasonry is illustrated. With such a regular progression in the training of youth, with such detestable Chiefs to lead them, what evil is there that may not be feared. Is not the public weal in danger? Is it not become a problem in the present state of Europe—WHETHER A SINGLE GOVENRMENT SHALL SUBSIST? Is not every State equally threatened with danger?

Should any readers have viewed with indifference the formidable though evident Conspiracy against Christianity, and have contented themselves with saying, that it was the business of the Clergy to guard against that; let them remember, that the ANTIMONARCHICAL CONSPIRACY approaches one step nearer to them—It will rob them of their laws, and plunge them into the horrors of civil war.—Such fears may perhaps awaken them, and spur them on to the study of principles fully detailed in this Volume (for it is a work of reflection and not of amusement); and if in treating of the *Occult Lodges*[1] of Masonry they find horrors scarcely credible, let them reflect on the proofs adduced, and shudder at the precipice yawning beneath them. It is the duty of every subject to avert the impending danger. Let the parent instruct the child, whose happiness may be endangered both in this life and the next. Let the Clergyman enlighten his flock on the perils with which it is threatened; for it is the duty he owes to his GOD and to his *Country*. Let the Magistrate watch over his district; for the laws call on him for his aid, and it is he that would fall the first victim of the popular fury. Let the honorable Mason read and learn the abuses to which the Lodges are exposed, and he will guard them against the impious and rebellious principles of *Occult Masonry*. In fine, in appealing to the most incredulous, we shall lay before them the words of the learned and military Commentator of Polybius (*Chevalier de Follard*), who, speaking of the revolt of the foreign troops against the Carthaginians, after many shrewd observations on Conspiracies in general, turns his mind towards the times in which he was then writing, and as early as the year 1727, makes use of the following remarkable expressions:

---

1   We repeat, that by OCCULT LODGES are meant those LODGES which were hidden from the generality of Fremasons themselves. They are not the common Lodges frequented by men too honorable to be tampered with, and too much attached to their God and country to hearken to the rebellious and impious plots of the ARRIÈRES LOGES.

A Conspiracy is forming at this present time, gradually gaining ground, and by means so subtile, that I regret my not having come into the world *thirty* years later to see the end of it. It must be owned, that certain politicians are very wise, and that the glasses of the European Powers are dim indeed. If ever *mathematical proofs* were acquired, it is at present.[2]

May my contrymen duly reflect on, and timely profit by this hint!

Tr.

---

2   *Histoire de Polybe*, vol II, page 329. The Chevalier de Follard died at Avignon, 1752.

Preliminary Discourse.

I n this Second Part of the *Memoirs illustrating the History of Jacobinism*, our object will be to show, how the *Sophisters of Impiety*, becoming the *Sophisters of Rebellion*, after having conspired against every altar, conspire against every throne. We shall demonstrate, that these men under the name of Philosophers, after having sworn to crush Christ and his altars, bound themselves in a second oath to annihilate all regal power.

We have said, in the former part of this work,[1] that the Sophisters of Impiety, when they were be-

Plan of this 2d part.

---

1   Preliminary Discourse, vol. I, p. xxxi.

come the Sophisters also of Rebellion, had leagued with a Sect, long since concealed in the occult lodges of Free-masonry, whose adepts, like the modern Philosophers, had sworn hatred to the altar and the throne, had sworn to crush the God of the Christians, and utterly to extirpate the Kings of the earth.

This two-fold object naturally divides our Second Volume into two Parts. The first will develope the rise and progress of the Conspiracy of the Sophisters, called Philosophers: The second, of that sect, which we have denominated Occult Masons (*Arrières Maçons*), to distinguish their adepts from the multitude of brethren who were too virtuous to be initiated in the occult mysteries, too religious, and too faithful citizens to associate in their plots.

After having treated separately of these two conspiracies, though both tending to the same object, we shall show them leaguing together; and by their united efforts accomplishing that part of the French Revolution which effected the overthrow of Religion and Monarchy, of the altar and the throne; in a word, which murdered, basely murdered, the unfortunate Louis XVI. on a scaffold.

Reflections on the conspiracy against Kings.

Confining ourselves to facts, and suppressing the powers of imagination, it seems incumbent on us to submit some few reflections to the reader, which, though naturally flowing from the subject, are yet requisite to enable him to follow the progress of the Sophisters in their second conspiracy, to show by what gradations they passed, or rather with what celerity they were hurried headlong, from the school of impiety to that of rebellion, by the inherent tendency of their principles.

While, under the direction of Voltaire, these pretended Philosophers had merely applied their principles of Equality and Liberty to matters of faith, and had thence conspired against the God of the Gospel, that each might be at liberty to form his own religion, or throw off every religious tie;— during that time, few were the obstacles they had to fear from those various classes of men, which it was chiefly their object to captivate.—During their war against Christianity, the passions proved their most powerful allies. There would be no great difficulty in deluding those unfortunate men, who combat the mysteries which they do not understand, merely to exempt themselves from the restraint of those precepts and the practice of those virtues which are unfavourable to their passions.

Sovereigns, seldom much versed in the science or history of religion; men who often, under the sanction of opulence and the splendour of rank, only seek to throw off all control on their moral conduct; others aspiring at fortune, and caring not by what unwarrantable means they acquire it; vain men panting after an empty name, and ready to sacrifice every truth to a sarcastic meteor, or some blasphemy mistaken for wit, and others who would have had little hope of celebrity had they not directed their genius against their God;—in short, all those men who, easily receiving sophisms for demonstrative proofs, never troubled themselves with the investigation of that *equality of rights*, and that *liberty of reason*, which the conspiring Sect represented to them as being incompatible with a religion revealed, and replete with mysteries.

Few even of the adepts had ever reflected on the absurdity of opposing the rights of reason to revelation; as if those pretended rights of our limited reason were to suspend the power of an infinite God who reveals himself, or were to depreciate the truth of his oracles, and of the mission of his Prophets and Apostles. They never had reflected, that the whole question of these rights of reason turned simply on this: to know whether God had spoken or not; and to believe and silendy adore whatever might be the nature of the truths he had revealed.

Men so little able to comprehend and to defend the rights of their God, could not have been very dangerous adversaries for the Sophisters, who are perpetually setting this liberty of reason in opposition to the Gospel.

But how different the case, when the Sect applying this same Equality and Liberty to the empire of human laws and to civil society, concludes, that after having crushed the altar, it was also necessary to overturn every throne, in order that men might be reinstated in their original Equality and Liberty! A conspiracy on such principles, and drawing after it such consequences, must naturally have been combated by the interests and the passions of the Royal Sophisters, of the protecting Princes, and of all those adepts of the higher classes, who were so docile to the accents of liberty, when those accents only menaced the destruction of the religion of their God.

Voltaire and d'Alembert could not expect to find Frederick, Joseph II., Catherine III.,[2] or Gustavus of Sweden, much disposed to subvert their respective thrones. It was very probable too, that many other protecting adepts, such as ministers or courtiers, nobles, or wealthy persons distinguished by their rank, would soon perceive the danger of depending on a multitude, who, having thrown off all obedience, would soon grasp at sovereignty itself, and, as the first essay of its power, would level every species of property, and strike off every head which rose above that multitude.

On the side of the Sophisters themselves, though gratitude could have had but little weight with them, yet their interest, their very existence might have abated their eagerness against the throne. D'Alembert lived on pensions from the Kings of France and Prussia; his very apartment in the Louvre was a gift from Louis XVI. The Empress of Russia alone supported Diderot's ruined fortune; and the Grand Duke pensioned the adept La Harpe.

---

2   Both the French and the English translation show Catherine III, but it seems Barruel might have meant Catherine II (Catherine the Great) of Russia; moreover, there has never been a Catherine III, so the entry has been indexed accordingly. —Ed.

Damilaville would have been a beggar, if discarded from his office. The Philosophic Sanhedrim of that French Academy composed of so many adepts owed its existence, its means, its counters (*jettons*) to the generosity of the monarch. There were few other scribbling Sophisters who did not either look up to a pension, or had not already obtained one by the intrigues of the protecting ministers.

Voltaire had acquired an independent fortune; but he was not, on that account, the less elated when M. de Choiseul gave him back the pension which, twelve years before, he had lost, on account of his impious writings.[3] Beside, nobody knew better than did Voltaire, that he was chiefly indebted for the success of his Antichristian Conspiracy to the royal adepts. He was too proud of numbering among his disciples Imperial and Regal Sovereigns, to conspire against their very existence on earth.

All these motives, therefore, gave quite a different turn to the conspiracy against the Throne, from that which we have already seen erected against the Altar. In the warfare against the Gospel, Equality and Liberty could have been but a shallow pretence; it was their hatred against Christ by which they were hurried away. It is hardly possible that they could have concealed from themselves that it was rather a war waged by their passions against the virtues of the gospel, than a warfare of reason against the mysteries of Christianity. In the Anti-

---

3   To Damilaville, 9 Jan. 1762, vol. 57, let. 152, p. 310.

monarchical Conspiracy, the pretext had grown into conviction. The Sophisters believed their principles of Equality and Liberty to be demonstrated, they did not even suspect an error in their principles. They believed the war which they waged against Kings to be a war of justice and of wisdom. In the former conspiracy, it was the passions inventing principles to combat the God of the Christians; in the latter, it was reason, misled by those same principles, seeking and glorying in the downfal of every crowned head.

Rapid had been the progress of the passions. From his very birth, Voltaire's hatred against Christ had been at its height. Scarcely had he known, ere he hated, scarcely hated when he swore to crush, the God of the Christians. Not such was the progress of the hatred against Kings. This sentiment had, like opinion and conviction, its gradations. The very interest of the Sophisters of Impiety thwarted for a long time the measures of those of Rebellion; many years were necessary to enable the sect to form its systems, to determine its plots, and resolve on its object. Were we to precipitate its steps, we should be guilty of misrepresentation. As faithful historians, it will be incumbent on us, to show this hatred against Kings in its infancy, that is, springing from the hatred against Christ, and successively applying those principles invented against the Altar, to the destruction of the throne. This hatred against kings had even in the chiefs of the conspirators its gradations: but their systems

will complete the delusion, and root it in the hearts of the adepts. It will bear absolute sway over their secret academy, and there will the same plots be contrived against the throne as Philosophism had framed against the Altar. The same means and the same success will combine the conspiracies. The same crimes and the same disasters will combine the revolutions.

CHAPTER I.

First Step in the Conspiracy Against Kings.

Voltaire and d'Alembert Passing from the Hatred of Christianity to the Hatred of Kings.

ur attention to truth and justice with regard to a man, who was so far from both with respect to religion, obliges us to begin this chapter by a declaration, which might make Voltaire appear to be the farthest from an enemy, much less from being the author of a conspiracy against the throne. If this man, the most unrelenting chief when conspiring against Christianity, had followed the bias of his own inclinations; or had he been able to sway his adepts in politics as he had in impiety, never would that oath of destroying the throne have issued from his school.

Voltaire at first friendly to Kings;

1

Voltaire loved kings; their favor and their ca-
resses were his delight; he was even dazzled with
their greatness. His sentiments cannot be mistaken, after having seen him glory in singing the
praises of Louis XIV. or Henry IV., kings of France;
of Charles XII., king of Sweden; of the czar Peter,
Emperor of all the Russias; of Frederick II., king
of Prussia; and of so many other kings both of ancient and modern times.

Voltaire had all the habits and manners of the
great, and at his court of Ferney acted the Grandee
perfectly well. He had too high an opinion of his
own abilities to assimilate himself, by Equality, to
that multitude which he contemptuously stiles, the
beggarly *canaille.*

He was not only partial to kings, but even to the
monarchical form of government. When he gives.
a loose to his own sentiments, and in his historical writings, we see him invariably preferring the
dominion of one to that of the many. He could
not endure the idea of having so many masters
as there were counsellors in the parliament;[1] how
then could he adopt that liberty and sovereignty
of the people which would have given him as joint
sovereigns, the towns and suburbs, the peasantry
and his own vassals. He who so much delighted in
reigning in his own castle, who was so jealous of
his prerogatives in the midst of his estates which

---

1   To the Due of Richelieu, 20 May, 1771, vol. 61, let. 281, p. 490;
     and 20 July, let. 293, p. 515.

he called his little Province, how could he wish to sanction an Equality and Liberty which was to level the castle with the cottage?

Beside, Voltaire's principal object was to annihilate Christianity; and he feared nothing so much as to be thwarted by the kings in his undertaking, on pretence that he equally aimed his blows at the throne as he did against the Altar. It was for this reason that he perpetually warns the adepts of what consequence it was, that the Philosophers should be considered as faithful subjects. When assuring Marmontel how much he (Voltaire) was protected by Choiseul and the courtezan Pompadour, he writes, that they may send him any thing without danger. *jealous of the title of faithful subject.*

> They know that we love the king and the state. It was not among us that such people as Damiens heard the voice of rebellion. I am draining a bog, I am building a church, and *I pray for the king*. We defy either Jansenist or Molinist to have a greater attachment for the king than we have. My dear friend, the king must be acquainted that the Philosophers are more attached to him than all the fanatics and hypocrites in his kingdom.[2]

It was the self-same motive which induced him to write to Helvétius (that Sophister whom we shall see so unrelenting in his hatred to kings),

---

2   To Marmontel, 13 Aug. 1760, vol. 56, let. 183, p. 352.

It is the king's interest that the number of Philosophers should augment, and that of the Fanatics diminish. We are quiet, and they are all disturbers of the peace; *we are citizens,* they are the children of sedition . . . . *The faithful servants of the king,* and of reason, shall triumph at Paris, at Voré, and even at the Délices.[3]

Apprehensive, however, that the Philosophers might be suspected, notwithstanding all his protestations, he had already written thus to d'Alembert: "Do you know who the bad citizen is that wishes to persuade the Dauphin that France is overrun with the enemies of religion? They will not pretend to say, I hope, that Peter Damiens,[4] Francis Ravaillac, and their predecessors were Deists and Philosophers." Nevertheless, he ends his letter by saying, "I fear that Peter Damiens will be a great detriment to Philosophy."[5]

Finally, if any thing can paint in strong colours Voltaire's attachment to kings, it will be the

Defends the authority of Kings.

---

3   To Helvétius, 27 Oct. 1760, vol. 56, let. 220, p. 438.

4   There was an Auguste-Pierre Damiens de Gomicourt (1723 - 1790), who was a journalist, but in this context, it seems the person Voltaire may have had in mind was Robert-François Damiens (1715 - 1757), a mentally unstable domestic servant who, blaming on the king the uproar following the Catholic Church's refusal to grant the holy sacraments to members of the Jansenist sect, made an assassination attempt on Louis XV. François Ravaillac (1578 - 1610), in turn, was a Catholic zealot , domestic servant and school teacher, and the assassin of Henry IV, whom he thought had launched a war against the Pope when invading the Spanish Netherlands. —Ed.

5   To d'Alembert, 16 Jan. 1757, vol. 68, let. 18. p. 31.

method in which he treats those of the adepts who dared attack the authority of the sovereign. The adept Thiriot had sent him a work on the Theory of Taxation, and Voltaire answers,

> *Received the Theory of Taxation*, an obscure theory, and apparently to me an absurd one. All such theories are very ill timed, as they only serve to make foreign nations believe that our resources are exhausted, and that they may insult and attack us with impunity. *Such men are very extraordinary citizens indeed, and curious friends to man.* Let them come where I am on the frontiers, and *they will presently change their opinions. They will soon see how necessary it is that the king and the state should be respected. Upon my word, at Paris people see every thing topsy-turvy.*[6]

The staunchest Royalist could not have insisted in a clearer manner on the necessity of supporting the Royal authority; nevertheless, he had already let fall many expressions which little denoted any zeal for the cause of kings. He had not adopted, as yet, that Philosophism of rebellion, of Equality and Liberty, which was to fanaticise the French people, and raise Robespierres and Marats in succession to the fanatics Ravaillac and Damiens.—There were times even when he would have treated the Mirabeaux, La Fayettes, and Baillys, as he used sometimes to treat those mad Œconomists, who,

---

6   To Thiriot, 11 Jan. 1765, vol. 57, let. 7, p. 14.

attacking the authority of kings, saw, through their pretended theory, every thing in a wrong light. But this love for his king was but a remnant of his first education, which Philosophism had often belied, and of which the very trace would soon be erased from the heart of the Sophister.

Declines towards Liberty and Equality.

Had Voltaire, either from his own sentiments, or for the interest of the Sect, been still more desirous of being looked upon as a good citizen, or a faithful subject of the king, yet the adepts could have retorted the arguments he had perpetually repeated to stir them up against Christianity, in too powerful a manner against his arguments in favor of kings, for him to have been able to withstand them. It was but natural that men who had been taught to oppose their Equality and Liberty to the God of revelation, to his ministers and prophets, should also oppose them to the kings of the earth. Voltaire had taught them that the Equality of rights and Liberty of reason were incompatible with that power of the church and of the gospel commanding a submission to and a belief in mysteries which were inconceivable by reason. The adepts, as the next step, declare that the Equality of men, the Liberty of nature, were equally incompatible with any submission to the empire and laws of *one* man, or even of many, whether called parliaments or senates, lords or princes, pretending to the dominion over a whole nation, and dictating laws to the multitude, who had neither made them, discussed them, nor wished for them.

These principles, so forcibly insisted on by Voltaire when combating Christianity, might naturally be objected to his propositions respecting submission to the sovereign; and they were so. The adepts urged the consequences, and the premier chief was unwilling to lose the pre-eminence over his own school in what he called Philosophy. The process by which he was led from the Sophistry of Impiety to that of Rebellion, is too much blended with the progress of his anti-religious Philosophism, not to be worthy of investigation.

Voltaire had been actuated by no other passion than that of hatred against Christ, when in the year 1718 he caused to be publicly recited in his tragedy of Œdipus those two famous verses, which alone comprehend the whole of that anti-religious revolution which was to be accomplished seventy years afterward:

> Priests are now what they seem to vulgar eyes.
> In our credulity their science lies.[7]

These two lines only proclaim that Equality of rights and Liberty of reason which, disavowing the authority or mission of the clergy, leave the people at full liberty to form their religious tenets on whatever they may please to call their reason. But many years elapsed before Voltaire could form a

---

7 *Les prêtres ne sont pas ce qu'un vain peuple pense;*
  Notre credulité fait toute leur science.

correct idea of that Equality and Liberty which was to divest the monarch of his rights, as he had divested the church of hers. It even appears that he had not at that time any idea of deducing from this Equality and Liberty principles so fatal to monarchy; that he was perfectly ignorant of what Equality and Liberty, applied to civil society, meant, when he published his epistles or discourses on Equality and Liberty in 1738. The first lessons he received on the subject were from his *élève* Thiriot, whom he had left in England, and from whom he wished to learn what opinion the adepts had formed on those epistles. Or, as is more probable, Thiriot, knowing his master's bias for aristocracy, only wrote that he had not sufficiently *gone to the point*, and that he was not in complete possession of the true principles. Piqued at such a reproach, Voltaire, like a man who did not care to see himself outdone by his disciples, writes, "A word on the Epistles. Where the devil do you find that they do not go to the point. There is not a single verse in the first epistle, which does not show the *Equality of conditions*, nor one in the second which does not prove *Liberty*."[8]

Notwithstanding this reply, the disciple was in the right. He might have rejoined, that throughout the whole of the Epistles there was not a single verse which, philosophically speaking, was not a misconstruction; since, in the first, all that Voltaire aimed at proving was, that in all stations of life the

---

8   To Thiriot, 24 Oct. 1738, vol. 53, let. 35, p. 88.

sum total of happiness was nearly the same; and in the second, Liberty is considered much more as a physical faculty, than as a natural, civil, and political right. The inference drawn from the first is, that it is useless for man to trouble himself about the difference of stations as the same portion of happiness is nearly allotted to each; the second does not even mention that liberty which the adepts so much insist on against kings, and only asserts that liberty which so well demonstrates the distinction of right and wrong, and which the sect always looked upon as too favorable to religion.

Without seeming to submit to his disciples, Voltaire, nevertheless, gradually adopted their sentiments; vexed at having asserted the rights of free agency, he counteracted all the influence that doctrine might have had, and gave his definition of liberty[9] such a turn, that Predestinarians them-

---

9   If we are to believe this definition, *Liberty* consists in *the power of doing what we will.* A true metaphysician would say, *The power itself, the faculty of willing or not willing,* that is to say *of determining one's will, of chusing and willing any thing, or the contrary.* These two definitions are very different. It is not the power but the will which is culpable. A righteous man has frequently the same power of committing the same crime as the wicked man; but one wills it, while the other does not. The wicked man is at liberty not to will it, as the upright man is at liberty to will it; otherwise, there can be no moral difference between the good and the bad man. For how could the latter be culpable, if he had not had it in his power to will the contrary? Suppose three men—the first can commit a bad action, but his will *freely rejects it;* the second can accomplish the same, and he *freely wills it.* The third not only can but he *irresistibly wills it.* The first of these men will be a virtuous man, the sec-

selves could not have cavilled at it. In a word, he no longer asserted any other liberty than that which has proved such a powerful weapon against sovereignty in the hands of the Sect.

The corrections he made in his Epistle on Equality, had a more direct affinity to the system of the political revolution. In the first edition of that Epistle we read,

Equal the state, in men the difference lies.[10]

The Sect wished him to have said,

Equal are men, in states the difference lies.[11]

At length Voltaire understood their meaning, and blushed at finding that his own disciples had made a greater progress in the knowledge of Equality than he had himself; and to avoid their future criticisms he changed both his doctrine and his verses. He corrected, and almost reconstructed his Epistle on Equality; nor did he let his poetic genius rest, till he had shown the adepts that

---

ond a wicked man, the third a mere brutal machine, a madman who is neither master of his will nor of his reason. The wicked man and the mad one could and did will the same action. The difference did not lie in the power of the action, but in the will itself more or less free to will or not to will. But Voltaire and his sophistical school had their reasons for not making such distinctions.

10   *Les États sont égaux, mais les hommes différent.*

11   *Les hommes sont égaux, et les états différent!*

he understood the equality of man as well as they did, and that they could no longer reproach him with not *going to the point*. It was then that he wrote the following verses, which contain all that the revolutionary populace have alledged against the wealthy, the nobility, and kings, in proof of its equality.

> With calm indifference let my friend survey
> The pomp of riches and despotic sway;
> This world's a ball, where his undazzled eyes
> Pierce thro' each silly actor's vain disguise.
> My Lord, your Highness, are the masks that hide
> Their little beings and exalt their pride;
> *But, men are equal*; pride do what you can,
> *The mask may differ but the same the man.*
> The five weak senses by us all possest,
> Of good, of evil, are our only test.
> A slave has five, *six can the Monarch claim?*
> The same his body and his soul the same.[12]

This is precisely what the democratic rabble of Paris was wont to say, less elegantly indeed, when

---

12   *Tu vois, cher Ariston, d'un œil d'indifférence*
     La grandeur tyrannique, et la fiere opulence.
     Tes yeux d'un faux éclat ne sont point abusés;
     Ce monde est un grand bal, où des fous déguisés.
     Sous les risibles noms d'Éminence et d'Altesse,
     Pensent enfler leur être et hausser leur bassesse.
     En vain des vanités l'appareil nous surprend;
     Les mortels sont égaux, le masque est différent.
     Nos cinq sens imparfaits, donnés par la nature,
     De nos biens, de nos maux sont la seule mesure.
     Les Rois, en ont-ils six? et leur âme et leur corps
     Sont-ils d'une autre espece? ont-ils d'autres ressorts?

it asked whether kings and nobles were not made of the same clay as the simple clown? Whether those who enjoyed large fortunes had two stomachs? And of what use were all those distinctions of Sovereigns, Princes, or Chevaliers, since *all men were equal?*

It was with reluctance, it must be confessed, that Voltaire became the Apostle of Equality. For without having a body or soul of a different species from that of Pompignan, Fréron, or Desfontaines, or of so many other men whom he was perpetually overwhelming with his sarcasms, he nevertheless was aware that in the same species, and with the same nature, there existed no small inequality among men; that without being endowed with a sixth sense, he felt the great distance there was between himself and the rabble he so much despised. At length he submitted to the criticisms of the adepts, and after having declared

Equal the state, in men the difference lies,[13]

he writes in absolute opposition,

The mask may differ but the same the man.[14]

Becomes a Republican;
As to that liberty which commences in the love of Republicanism, and ends in the hatred of Kings,

---

13   *Les États sont egaux, mais les hommes différent.* (1st and 2d Edit.)

14   *Les mortels sont égaux, le masque est différent. (See the variations, edit, of Kell.)*

it is probable that Voltaire would never have adopted it, had it not been necessary to establish that liberty which was essential to the hatred of Christ; but he had found himself too much thwarted by the authority of Kings in his first publications against Christianity. In Holland he enjoyed a greater liberty for printing his blasphemies; and it was to that circumstance, that he owed his bias for Republicanism. Those who have read his correspondence while in Holland, and particularly the following letter to the Marquis d'Argenson, dated from the Hague, will not have a doubt that this was the case. "I am," says he,

> better pleased even with the abuses of the liberty of the press here, than with that sort of slavery under which the human mind is kept in France. If you continue on that plan, the simple remembrance of the glorious age of Louis XIV. will be all that will remain. This degeneracy almost inclines me to settle in the country I am now in . . . . The Hague is a charming residence; *liberty alleviates the rigors of the winter. I like to see the Rulers of the State no more than plain Citizens.* There are factions, it is true, yet they must exist in Republics: But faction does not damp patriotism, and I see great men contending with great men . . . . On the other side, I see, with equal admiration, the chief members of the state walking on foot without servants, living in houses worthy of those Roman Consuls who dressed their own roots . . . . you would like this government extremely, notwithstanding

THE ANTIMONARCHICAL CONSPIRACY

> all those imperfections which are unavoidable in it. *It is entirely municipal, and that is what you admire.*[15]

All these expressions naturally denote a man declining towards a Republican Equality and Liberty, and who impatiently bore the yoke of Kings. A few years after, we may observe this passion much more predominant in Voltaire, especially in a letter which he is supposed to have written to an Academician of Marseilles, and mentioned in Mr. de Bevis's Memoirs. "I should accept your invitation, were Marseilles still a Grecian Republic; for I greatly admire Academies, *but am much more partial to Republics.* How happy are those countries where our masters visit us, and are not affronted when we do not return to wait on them!"

In all this, however, we see nothing more than a partiality for Republics; it was not positively a hatred of Kings, nor an imputation of tyranny and despotism in the regal government. But a few years after this, that same rancour is directed by Voltaire against the throne, which he had already conceived against the altar. Such at least is clearly the purport of a confidential letter which he writes to d'Alembert, wherein he says, "As to Luc (the King of Prussia), sometimes biting sometimes bitten, he must be a most unhappy mortal; *and those men who put themselves in the way of a*

His secret on Kings;

---

15   To d'Argenson, 8 Aug. 1743, vol. 53, let. 221, p. 455.

musket or a sabre for such gentry, are most abominable fools. Don't betray my secret either to Kings or Priests."[16]

This, however, could be no secret to those who had observed the modern Sophisters trying to cast all the odium of war and its miseries on Kings and the nature of their governments, and wishing to persuade the people that their only way of acquiring happiness, and everlasting peace, was to take the government into their own hands by wresting it from their Royal Masters. This proposition, so evidently contradicted by that perpetual state of warfare, interior or exterior, so common to Republics, evinces that Voltaire had no care about proof, when he decided in so peremptory a stile, that those who were persuaded they were fighting for their country when rallied under the standard of their king, were most abominable fools.

We should particularly remark in this letter, how much his secret with regard *to Kings* is connected with that respecting *the Priesthood*; and he had more than once publicly divulged them both. The latter he had expressed in the verses already quoted from his Tragedy of Œdipus,

> Priests are not what they seem to vulgar eyes,
> In our credulity their science lies.[17]

---

16   To d'Alembert, 12 Dec. 1757, vol. 68, let. 36, p. 60.

17   *Les prêtres ne sont pas ce qu'un vain peuple pense;*
      Notre credulité fait toute leur science.

and as to the former, we see Voltaire by the same means teaching the people what they are to think with regard to Sovereigns, their rights, and their origin; or with regard to the Nobility, who are perpetually led and spurred on to the defence of their country in emulation of those services by which their ancestors distinguished themselves. It would be in vain to excuse the poet: it is a hatred of Kings, and not the genius of poetry, which inspires such artful turns, and makes the dramatic actor speak the sentiments of the Sophister. It certainly was not the love of Monarchy which dictated the following verses, and caused them to be spoken on the stage of a nation under the dominion of a King, and proud of the achievements of its Nobility. In his Tragedy of Mérope, he says,

His principles against Kings.

> Some lucky soldier was the first of Kings;
> Who serves the state, no matter whence he springs.[18]

When Voltaire taught this doctrine to the French people, the Antimonarchical Revolution had made as great a progress in his mind, as the Antichristian formerly had, when the verses already quoted had been spoken against the Clergy. But nothing short of the most abandoned Jacobinism could testify applause when Voltaire continues, *Do you wish to be happy? Never own a master.*[19]

---

18 *Le premier qui fut Roi, fut un soldat heureux,*
   Que sert bien son Pays, n'a pas besoin d'aïeux.

19 Dialogues of the Philosophers on Happiness.

It was thus that Voltaire, carried away by his System of Liberty opposed to the Altar, daily cherished the sentiments of that liberty which was to combat the throne. Nor was it inadvertently that these maxims escaped from his poetic genius. In his correspondence with d'Alembert, his intention appears clearly when he points out to his confidant all those verses which may teach the subject to rise in judgment against his King, or even to become his assassin or executioner, should he ever chuse to view his Prince in the light of a tyrant or a despot. Exactly such are the passages which he wishes d'Alembert to notice, when he writes, "Last year I hurried over a Play called *The Laws of Minos*, which presently you will see hissed. In those *Laws of Minos*, Teucer says to Merion the Senator,

> Our laws a change, our state a King requires.[20]

The Senator answers:

> Of me, my treasures, and my life dispose;
> But should the pow'r this sovereign rank bestows
> Be turn'd against our laws and native land,
> Then shall my arm that guilty pow'r withstand.[21]

---

20 *Il faut changer de loix, il faut avoir un maitre.*

21 *Je vous offre mon bras, mes trésors et mon sang;*
    Mais si vous abusez de ce suprème rang,
    Pour fouler à vos pieds les loix et la patrie,
    Je la défends, Seigneur, au péril de ma vie.
    To d'Alembert, 13 Nov. 1772, vol. 69, let. 81, p. 131.

Had Voltaire ever met with such verses in the writings of a Clergyman, he would immediately have attacked him as an assassin and a traitor; he would have exclaimed, Behold the subject who raises himself in judgment against his Sovereign, who takes upon him the right of deciding between his King and the Laws, the right of attacking and combating his King, and of turning his sword against him, every time it may please him to believe, or to persuade the people, that the death of the Prince would restore energy to the laws.—Voltaire would have immediately added, there we see the people decidedly created both judge and sovereign over their Kings; such are the maxims which form Rebels, and produce Revolutions with all their concomitant horrors of democratic anarchy.

What Voltaire would very properly have said on this affectation of their making a distinction between the King and the Country, history may as properly apply to Voltaire himself; more particularly as nobody knew the consequences and danger of such maxims better than he did; nor did he even make any secret of their dangerous tendency when writing to his friends. He begins his letter to the Count d'Argental on sending him some of those seditious publications, by saying,

His secret and indirect attack against the throne.

> In the first place, promise me upon oath, that you never will let my *petit pâtés* out of your

hands, that you will send them back to me, and inform me whether they are too highly seasoned, or whether the general taste of the day is more depraved than my own. *The forcemeat of my* petit pâtés *is not quite palatable to a monarchy, but you told me that a dish of Brutus* had been lately served up at the Count de Falkenstein's (the name under which Joseph II travelled), and that none of the guests had left the table.[22]

Such language is not very enigmatical; but it paints Voltaire in very different colours from those we have seen him in, when reproaching his Parisian brethren with seeing every thing *topsy-turvy* in their attack on the King's power. It denotes an author who dares not yet show his sentiments so opposite to that power, but who wishes to go as far as possible without exposing himself to danger. We see him flattering himself that he has not been too daring, as Joseph II had been imprudent enough *to let a dish of Brutus be served up at his table;* that is to say, that monarch had heard broached at his table, without shewing his displeasure, doctrines the most dangerous and threatening to the fives of Sovereigns.

There are many other letters extant, which indicate how deeply this Antimonarchical liberty had rooted itself in the heart of Voltaire, and even how much he despised that love for their Sovereign at that time so universally prevalent among the

He wishes for and foretells the Revolution.

---

22   To d'Argental, 27 Juin, 1777, vol. 63, let. 220, p. 377.

French people. There is one in particular, in which he complains most bitterly, that strangers perfectly conversant in the catechism of liberty, and equal to the task of teaching it to the Parisians, are obliged to carry their systems elsewhere, before they have succeeded in teaching them to the French people; that if man was created to serve God, *he was also created to be free.* In short, what displeased Voltaire more particularly was, that while he was making such progress in this catechism of liberty, the French people, whom he calls his *Vetches,* did not keep pace with him.[23] When the Historian shall treat of the progress which Voltaire was making in the arts of liberty, he shall not extenuate his error, by saying that Voltaire was not aware of the fatal consequences of a revolution, or that he would have started back from his purpose could he by possibility have foreseen them. Certainly his soul could not be so ferocious as to have aspired after the bloody reign of a Robespierre; but he complacently foretells, and offers up his prayers for a revolution, which he knows to be big with bloodshed and surrounded with firebrands; and, however disastrous such revolutionary scourges may appear to him, he nevertheless deems those persons happy, who, from their juvenility, may live to see them. He writes to the Marquis de Chauvelin,

> Every thing is preparing the way to a *great revolution,* which will most *undoubtedly take*

---

23   Letter to Damilaville, 23 May, 1764, let. 196, p. 361, *et passim.*

place; and I shall not *be fortunate enough to
see it*. The French arrive at every thing slowly,
but still they do arrive. Light has so gradually
diffused itself, that on the first opportunity the
nation will break out, *and the uproar will be
glorious. Happy those who are now young, for
they will behold most extraordinary things.*[24]

Let the reader notice the date of this letter,
which is twenty-five years anterior to the French
revolution. During the whole of that long period
we shall never observe Voltaire reproaching the
adepts with seeing every thing *topsy-turvy*, when
they attack the Royal prerogative.

Whether it was that the victories he had obtained over the altar gave him more confidence in
his attacks against the throne; or that the success of
his sarcastic attacks gradually made against kings
with impunity, had persuaded him that they were
not so formidable as he had believed them, either
to himself or to his adepts; which of these was the
true reason we cannot now determine. This however is certain, that so far from being startled at
the principles of insurrection inculcated throughout the writings of his disciples, he hugs himself in
the idea that their productions were becoming the
catechisms of all nations.

When Diderot published his *System of Nature*,
it was neither his attacks nor his frantic declamations against kings, that the Philosopher of Ferney
sought to combat; but a kind of metaphysics the

24   To Chauvelin, 2 April, 1764, vol. 58, let. 171, p. 315.

absurdity of which he feared would reflect on Philosophy. Yet, notwithstanding this absurdity, and the violent declamations against sovereignty, we find him exulting with d'Alembert in the success of that abominable work, and bragging of its being *so greedily read throughout all Europe, that people snatched it* from each other. When he saw the courtiers and princes encouraging new editions of Helvétius's work ON MAN AND HIS EDUCATION,[25] notwithstanding the seditious and antimonarchical principles it contained, and which will be noticed in the course of this work, Voltaire, so far from fearing the indignation of kings, which such writings would naturally draw down on his school of Philosophers, smiles exultingly with d'Alembert at the great success of the work, and receives it as a proof that *the flock of sages silently increased.*[26]

Thus it is that all his fears of irritating sovereigns, by this apostleship of Equality and Liberty gradually subside, and are succeeded by that thirst of revolution, of *riot*, and of those tempestuous scenes which were to accompany the downfal of emperors and kings, in a word, of all sovereigns, or, in their philosophical cant, of tyrants and despots.

D'Alembert's sentiments against the throne.

Our readers, and future ages, will naturally inquire, whether d'Alembert walked in the footsteps of his dear master; whether, as zealous as Voltaire

---

25 *A Treatise on Man, His Intellectual Faculties and His Education* (London: B. Law and G. Robinson, 1777). —Ed.

26 Letter to d'Alembert, 3 July, 1773, vol. 69, let. 114, p. 195, et passim.

for the Antichristian Liberty, he also adopted that liberty so inimical to royalty. Let d'Alembert speak for himself: his answer is contained in a letter already quoted, but which may throw new light on this question.

> You love REASON AND LIBERTY, my dear and illustrious brother; and a man can hardly love the one without loving the other. Well then, here is a worthy *Republican Philosopher* whom I present to you, who will talk with you on PHILOSOPHY AND LIBERTY: it is Mr. Jennings, chamberlain to the king of Sweden, a man of great merit and enjoying a high degree of reputation in his own country. He is worthy of your acquaintance, both for his own merit, and for the uncommon esteem he has for your writings, *which have so much contributed toward disseminating those two principles among persons worthy of feeling them.*[27]

What an avowal is this for a man like d'Alembert, who was extremely cautious in his expressions, and always on his guard, lest he should utter any thing that might expose him to danger. *You love Reason and Liberty; and a man can hardly love the one, without loving the other.* A few lines lower, we find this *Reason* to be Philosophy; and the subsequent *Liberty* to be that of a Republican Philosopher; who nevertheless lives under a monarchy, loaded with the favors, and enjoying the confidence of his sovereigns. It is d'Alembert then who avows, that

---

27   From d'Alembert, 19 Jan. 1769, vol. 69, let. 3, p. 7.

one can hardly love his pretended Philosphy, without loving Republicanism, or *that liberty* which he believes not to exist under Monarchy.

It is d'Alembert again who selects from among the numerous claims which may entitle the sophistical courtier to Voltaire's or his own esteem, that of his love for Republican Philosophy; though he certainly could not cultivate such a disposition, without secretly wishing to betray the cause of his King.

In short, it is d'Alembert who extolls the writings of his dear and illustrious brother, as peculiarly adapted to disseminate *those two principles of Republican Liberty and Republican Philosphy among persons worthy of feeling them*; or, in other words, as peculiarly adapted to fulfil the wishes of those pretended sages, who can find no liberty under the government of Kings, and who detest Monarchy in proportion to their love for Republics. He who believes himself worthy of feeling this twofold sentiment, he who acknowledges no Philosphy as true if void of these two sentiments, could he, I ask, demonstrate in a more forcible manner, how ardently they glowed in his heart, or how much he panted after those revolutions which were to crush the throne, and establish Republicanism on its ruin?

In drawing these inferences, let not the reader suppose that we mean to confound in all cases a bias for Republics, or the love of Liberty, with the hatred of Kings, and the desire of subverting every Throne. We are perfectly aware, that there exist many worthy Republicans, who, while they love their own Government, are not unmindful of the respect due to those of other nations. Nor are we ignorant that true Civil Liberty is no less compatible with Monarchies than with Republics: indeed, it might not be difficult to prove, that the subject frequently enjoys a more real and extensive Liberty under a Kingly, than under a Republican Government, especially if a Democracy. But when we behold the Sophisters perpetually complaining of the Government of Kings under whom they live, styling their Sovereigns Despots, and sighing after the Liberty of the Republican Philosopher, we are certainly entitled to view their love for Liberty and Republicanism as blended with the hatred of Kings. If their blasphemies against Christ, if what they call their Philosophy be by any means thwarted, impatient of the rein, they burst forth into complaint, and they exclaim that *Reason is shackled*; that Despotism, *Decius like, perpetually persecutes them*; or, that *man is unfortunate indeed* when he lives under the eye of a Monarch, or of his Ministers.[28]

But to confine ourselves to d'Alembert, let us recal to mind, that in the warfare against the altar, he acted the part of the fox. We shall see him employing the same cunning in his attack against the Throne. He will excite and stimulate others, he will even guide their pens; but he carefully avoids every thing by which he might himself be eventu-

28   See Voltaire's and d'Alembert's Correspondence *passim*.

ally endangered. It is thus that he lauds Voltaire, that he extols the zeal with which his dear brother propagates the Republican Liberty and Philosophy; and fearing lest this zeal should sometime abate, he adds, "Continue to fight as you do, *pro aris et focis*; as for me, *my hands are tied by ministerial and sacerdotal tyranny*; I can only follow the example of Moses, and raise up my hands to heaven while you contend in fight."[29]

Again, we find him informing Voltaire of the eagerness with which he reads and devours all those writings in which that Premier Chief had combined his attacks against the Altar and the Throne. We see him applauding his sarcastic wit, and thus addressing him:

> I am almost angry when I learn from public report, that without informing me of it you have given a slap to Fanaticism and Tyranny, and that without detriment to the swingeing blows which you apply in so masterly a manner on other occasions. You enjoy alone the privilege of covering with odium and ridicule those two pests of society.[30]

During this warfare, it was not the good fortune of all the adepts to gain the applause of d'Alembert. They had not, like Voltaire, the art of pleasing or amusing Kings, who did not perceive that the sarcastic wit and satire of his romances and historical

---

29 From d'Alembert, 19 Jan. 1769.

30 From d'Alembert, 14 July, 1767, vol. 68, let. 213, p. 446.

productions fell on their own heads, though seemingly aimed only at the persons of other Kings.

It was not every one of the adepts that had the art of throwing the living into contempt, by striking at the dead; of flattering the person of the Sovereign, and rendering sovereignty odious; nor shall we find d'Alembert equally pleased with all those who appear in array against the Royal cause. Some of them, too eager, said too much; others were awkward in their attacks, and these he styles *bunglers who are to be found every where.*[31] Others again were not sufficiently bold. He will allow them wit, but he wishes *them to be less favorable to Despotism*; and the reader will easily conceive what he would have written himself if his *hands had not been tied*, when he confidentially writes to Voltaire, *I hate Despots almost as much as you do yourself.*"[32]

It would be futile to object, that the hatred of Despotism does not infer the hatred of Kings. We know that; but who are the Despots implied by our Sophisters, if not the Kings under whom they lived. Were the Emperor of the Turks, or the Grand Mogul, who had nothing to do with our Philosophers, the objects of their repeated complaints and hatred? Such objections are unworthy of being noticed. Their language is known; and sufficient proofs will occur to show, that with the Sect *Despots or Tyrants* and *Sovereigns or Kings* are synonymous terms. The very affectation of confound-

---

31   From d'Alembert, 24 Jan. 1778, vol. 69, let. 190, p. 313.

32   From d'Alembert, 25 Jan. 1770, vol. 69, let. 17, p. 34.

ing them together shows that the hatred of the one and of the other were blended in the hearts of the Chiefs and of their Adepts.

In short, the compliments of d'Alembert are not the sole proofs with which the Adepts have furnished us of the great part Voltaire had taken in that Revolution so fatal to Monarchy, and which he so exultingly foresaw. Had he never aimed his sarcastic wit, so much admired by the sophisters, at the persons of Kings, still he would have been the man, at least in the eyes of his school, who had smoothed the way, who had sealed the rampart, to assail the Throne and shiver the Scepter of the pretended Tyrants; in a word, to contrive what the French Revolution has since accomplished, both with respect to the crown and person of the unfortunate Louis XVI.

Avowal of the Sect concerning Voltaire.

These important services are thus appreciated by Condorcet:

> Shall (says he) men who would still have been slaves to prejudice if Voltaire had not written, accuse him of betraying the cause of Liberty!— They cannot understand that if Voltaire had inserted in his writings the principles of the elder Brutus, that is to say, those of the American Act of Independence, neither Montesquieu nor Rousseau could have published their works. Had he, as the Author of the System of Nature did, obliged all the Kings of Europe to support the ascendancy of the Clergy, Europe would still have remained *in the bonds of slavery and buried in superstition.* They will not reflect, that in our writings, as in our actions,

we are to make no more than a necesssary display of courage.[33]

Condorcet, in writing this, seems to have considered himself as having displayed a sufficient courage, as he did not think it necessary to say, that the throne would have remained unshaken, if Voltaire had not begun by eradicating religion from the minds of the people. His brethren the hebdomadary adepts, criticized the panegyrist as not having sufficiently extolled the services which Voltaire had rendered. At that period the French Revolution was at its summit, Louis XVI. was reduced to a mere phantom of royalty in his palace, or rather prison, of the Thuilleries. The literary part of the *Mercure* was conducted by La Harpe, Marmontel, and Champfort; and these reviewers undertake to inform the unfortunate Monarch of the hand which had wrought the downfall of his throne. In giving an account of the life of Voltaire, written by the Marquis de Condorcet, the hebdomadary Philosophers speak in the following terms:

> It appears that it would have been possible to show in a clearer light, *the eternal obligation which human nature has to Voltaire.* Circumstances were favorable. *He did not foresee all that he has done, but he has done all that we now see.*—The enlightened observer and the able historian will prove to those who are capable of reflexion, *that the first Author of the*

---

33   *Life of Voltaire*, edit. Kell.

great Revolution, which astonishes all Europe,
which infuses hope into the hearts of nations,
and disquiet into courts, was, without doubt,
Voltaire. He was the first who levelled that formidable rampart of Despotism, the religious
and sacerdotal power. Had he not broken the
yoke of Priests, that of Tyrants never could have
been shaken off; both equally weighed upon our
necks, and were so intimately interwoven, that
the first once slackened, the latter must soon
have lost its hold. The human mind is no more
to be impeded in the career of independence
than it is in that of slavery; and it was Voltaire
who shook off the yoke, by teaching it to judge,
in every respect, those who kept it in subjection.
It was he who rendered reason popular; and if
the people had not learned to think, never would
it have known its own strength. The reflexions
of the sage prepare *Political Revolutions*, but it
is the arm of the people which executes them.[34]

Result
of these
avowals.

Had I no other object in view than to demonstrate that these men, styling themselves Philosophers, and glorying in the school and name of
Voltaire, chiefly aimed at the overthrow of Monarchy when they attacked religion; that it was to the
successful warfare which Voltaire had carried on
against the religion of Christ that they peculiarly
attribute their success against the Throne; that by
the appellation of Tyrant and Despot they point at
the best of Kings and most rightful of Sovereigns:
had this been my only object, I say, it would have

---

34   *Mercure de France*, Saturday, 7th August, 1790, No. 18, p.
xxvi.

been useless to continue these Memoirs on the Antimonarchical Conspiracy, or that of the Sophisters of Rebellion against every King.

And who are these Sophisters that declare so openly and so expressly the secret of the Sect? First view Condorcet, the most resolute Atheist, the dearest of the brethren, the steady support of Voltaire's hopes, the most intimate confidant of d'Alembert.[35] It is he who sets out by declaring, that, if Voltaire had not combated Religious prejudices, or that if he had attacked Regal authority in a more direct manner, France would have remained enslaved.

Next on the list we find the Journalists La Harpe, Marmontel, and Champfort, who, in the most celebrated journal of the Sect, complain that Condorcet has not shown sufficient courage, and that he is not sufficiently explicit on the pretended *eternal obligations* which mankind have to Voltaire, who by shaking Religion to its foundations has overturned the Throne, who by the ruin of the Pontiff has struck the Tyrant.

And who is the Tyrant, the Despot over whom they so loudly triumph? A King whose very name echoes to that of justice and goodness; a Monarch almost adored by his people, and who loved them to a degree of weakness; for he very often repeated, that he would not suffer one drop of his subjects blood to be spilt in his defence.

Will history believe, that the unfortunate Lou-

---

35   See the first part of these *Memoirs.*

is XVI. was the Despot over whom they triumph? And yet if any King upon earth should believe that he is not comprehended in the general subversion aimed at by the conspirators, let him hearken: It is not of France alone that they speak, but of all mankind: it is a mankind that they pretend to behold enslaved under Kings; and that hope which they had infused into the heart of man, is the same which they joyfully observe expanding itself through all nations! If now tranquil on his throne, let him remember, that he is destitute of the prudence which even the Conspirators suppose him to be endowed with. They believe *disquiet to be infused into every Court*; for they well know, that their principles and their lawless attempts openly menaced monarchy. Yes, that their conspiracy was universal, is already evident; history needs no farther proof: But before they dared proclaim it, that conspiracy had its gradations; its means are to be laid open. The first step is that hatred against the throne, flowing in the hearts of the chiefs, from the hatred they had conceived against their God. The second will be found in the investigation of those systems devised by the adepts to overthrow regal authority, and substitute another in its stead. The teachers of the Sect had applied the vague principles of Equality and Liberty to Religious tenets; and hence originated the hatred of Christ and his Church. From the same principles applied to politics arose those theories and systems of subversion, with which the Sect assails every Throne.

CHAPTER II.

Second Step of the Conspiracy Against Kings.

Political Systems of the Sect.

D'Argenson and Montesquieu.

A mong the adepts who must have fore- D'Ar-
seen the consequences which natu- genson's
rally ensued from the application of system.
a pretended equality of rights, and of
an irreligious liberty, to politics, none
could have done so more intuitively than the Marquis d'Argenson. This man, minister of the foreign
department, had lived during the greater part of
his life near the person of his Sovereign, and enjoyed that favour, to which he was thought to be
entitled by having consecrated his life to the Royal
service. Yet he was the man who, during the reign
of Louis XV., drew the outlines of those Sophisticated Systems, which were to oppose Regal au-

thority, and gradually metamorphose the French Monarchy into a Republic.

We have seen Voltaire, as early as the year 1743, extolling the affection which this Marquis bore to Equality, to Liberty, and to the Municipal Government. These praises of the Premier Chief evidently show, that Mr. D'Argenson had already conceived his Municipalizing System, and all those wild plans, which the future rebels, under the title of a Constituent Assembly, were to adopt as one of the leading features of their Royal Democracy, at once the most senseless and most seditious as well as the most heterogeneous form of government that could be conceived, and more especially for Frenchmen: They also prove, that he made no secret of his plans to his confidents and co-operators.

His system consists in the division and subdivision of the Provinces into small States, first called *Provincial Administrations* by Necker, and afterwards termed *Departments* by Target and Mirabeau.

According to d'Argenson's plan, resumed and corrected by Turgot and Necker, each of those petty states was, under the inspection of the King, to be charged with the interior administration of its districts, and the levying of taxes; to superintend the different plans adopted for the relief of the people; to inspect the hospitals, the high roads, the establishments useful to commerce, and other such objects. The administrators could not determine on any subject of importance without the orders of his Majesty, and this was judged a sufficient fence to the Royal prerogative, especially as at the first formation of these provincial administrations, one half of the members were to be nominated by the King, which half when assembled chose the remaining moiety. The distinction of the three orders, of the Clergy, the Nobility, and the third Estate, was preserved, as it used to be in the States-General.[1]

The towns and boroughs, and even the villages were to have their respective municipalities, all acting on the same plan, and under the direction of the Provincial Administrations, in their secondary districts.

Though at first sight this system appears extremely advantageous, yet, on examination, we shall find, that its sole tendency was to apply Republican forms, as much as circumstances would permit, to a Monarchical government; that its object was to cramp the authority of the Monarch, to clog and weaken it; and to annihilate the power of his officers, or direct agents, the intendants of provinces.

Natural effects of this system.

Soon was France by means of these assemblies and their committees, or permanent offices, to be filled with ambitious men starting forth in the new political career; men indeed who, in the first instance, would have recognized the authority of a

---

1   See d'Argenson's plans, See *On the Nature of Governments.*
     [In the original: *Projets d'Argenson, ses Considérations sur la nature des Governments.* —Ed.]

King, but who would soon have considered themselves better informed of the wants of the people (being nearer to them) than his ministers, and therefore more fully acquainted with the means of alleviating their distresses. Remonstraces and philosophic reasonings would soon have followed, and sufficed to justify disobedience. The people, under a fond persuasion, that these provincial administrators supported their interests against the court, would easily have been brought to believe them the bulwark of their liberties and privileges, assigning every happy event to them, and attributing every misfortune to the King and his ministers. Each municipality coalescing with the administrators, a hundred petty Republics start into existence, ready to league against their Sovereign, who, under the title of King, would scarcely have retained the authority of a Doge.

In time we should have seen a swarm of politicasters, or petty tribunes, sallying forth from these administrative bodies, who would have left no means untried to persuade the populace that such a King was rather a burden than an advantage to the state; that it would be proper to lay him aside, since he was unnecessary; that the provincial and municipal administrations would then be able to follow up in a more effectual manner, the salutary measures they had conceived for the good of the people: and thus, step by step, the Monarchical government would have been overthrown, and a municipal administration established, with the freedom of which Voltaire and d'Argenson had been so fascinated in Holland. The man who could not readily foresee that such would be the consequence of this municipalizing system, must have been very ignorant of the character of Frenchmen, and especially of French Philosophers when drawn into the vortex of modern politics.

Even the admission of the clergy into these provisional administrations must have proved a fatal boon to the church, as it necessarily tended to change the spirit of its ministers. Priests and bishops were admitted, or rather called upon, to form a part of their administrations, so foreign to their sacred functions, for the conspiracy had not yet attained sufficient force to cast them off. The zeal for salvation was to be superseded by the wild ambition of moving in a sphere so contrary to their calling. Already were several prelates distinguished by this new title of Administrators. Soon should we have seen them become rather the disciples of d'Argenson, Turgot and Necker, than of Christ; soon seen the bishoprics conferred upon none but Morellets and Beaudeaux, with whom religion would have been a very subordinate object, when compared to the glorious enterprize of system-making, or of resisting the Ministers and the Sovereign. This was a sure method of ruining the church, by robbing her of the real bishops, and substituting petty politicians, who would easily be carried away by the torrent of impiety and ambition, and join with heart and hand a Brienne or an Expilli.

Whatever might have been the consequence to the church, it is very evident that all these new forms of administration tended directly to republicanize the state. Each of these petty administrators would soon have swelled himself into the representative of the province, and the aggregate would have styled themselves the Representatives of the Nation. The bare appellation of National Representative, combined with Modern Philosophism, sufficed to crush the Monarchy.

D'Argenson did not live to witness the experiment of his system; some may suppose that he had not foreseen its consequences. But it plainly appears, that if he even had foreseen them, so great an admirer of municipalized Republics would not have been much alarmed. At a time when the Sophisters had not sufficiently erased the love of religion from the hearts of the French to efface their affection for their Monarch, this system appeared to make but little impression; but we shall see the Sophisters afterward making it the particular object of their dissertations, to accustom the people to the idea of governing themselves.[2]

Montesquieu.

To the great misfortune of France, a man far more capable than d'Argenson of giving to any system the appearance of deep thought and erudition engaged in these political speculations.—The love of the commonweal may appear to have directed him toward this study; but the real cause is to be found in the restlessness of Philosophism,

---

2   Suppl. to *Social Contract*, Part 3. chap. 2, by Gudin.

and in that liberty of thinking which is disgusted with every thing around it, and which would continue restless even after having attained the object of which it was in search. This man, who by so many claims commands the public veneration, was Charles Secondat, Baron de la Brede and De Montesquieu. He was born on the 18th of January, 1689, in the Chateau de la Brede, within three leagues of Bourdeaux; and in 1716, became president *à mortier* of that parliament. We have already mentioned, that his first productions were those of a young man who had no fixed principles of religion; and this is clearly perceptible in perusing the *Lettres Persannes*. At a riper age his duty called him to the study of the laws; but not content with the knowledge of those of his own country, and desirous of making himself conversant in those of foreign nations, he made the tour of Europe, stayed sometime in England, and then returned to France full of those ideas which he has developed in the two works that have chiefly contributed to his fame. The first is entitled, *Considerations on the Causes of the Grandeur and Decline of the Roman Empire*, and was published in 1733; the latter was *The Spirit of Laws*, which appeared in 1748.

It was obvious, on the first appearance of his work on the Romans, that Montesquieu had not acquired from his travels an additional esteem for the government of his own country. One of the prime causes to which he attributes the éclat of the Romans, is their love of a Liberty which be-

Montesquieu's first attacks on the Throne.

gins by dethroning all Kings. The Sophisters, who were still less favorable to Monarchy, did not fail to adopt this idea, to make it the leading principle, and to inculcate it in all their discourses.[3]

Both Montesquieu and his panegyrists would have been more correct, had they traced back to this love of liberty all those scourges and intestine broils which harrassed Rome, from the expulsion of its Kings until the reign of the Emperors.—Liberty perpetually convulsed the people, and the senate could only free themselves from their clamours by habitual war and foreign pillage. This perpetual state of hostility rendered the Roman the most warlike of all nations, and gave them that immense advantage which they enjoyed over all other people. To the man who has read the Roman history, nothing can be more evident.—But if such be the merits of that liberty which expelled the Kings of Rome, that antisocial spirit, which, sowing discord in the interior economy of families, drives them from their homes, inures them to fatigue and the inclemency of the weather, and gives them all the advantage and strength of robbers, by forcing them to live on plunder, after having denied them the sweets of social life,—the antisocial spirit, I say, must needs possess the very same advantages.

His Paradoxes on the Kings of Rome.

Montesquieu was so strangely misled by his admiration for liberty, that he did not perceive the strangely paradoxical positions that he advanced. After having spoken of the public edifices, *which*

---

3   *Éloges de Montesquieu*, by d'Alembert.

even to this day give us a great idea of the power and grandeur of Rome under its kings, after having said, "that one of the causes of its prosperity was, that its Kings were all great men; and that no country could ever shew such *a continued series of statesmen and great generals;*" he adds, nearly in the same page, "that on the expulsion of the Kings it must necessarily follow, either that Rome would change its government, or remain a poor and petty monarchy."[4] In a word, that if Rome arrived at that very high pitch of greatness, it was owing to his having *substituted annual Consuls* to the dethroned Kings.

This work teems with satyrical remarks on Rome, when again brought under the dominion of a Monarch; and his frequent expressions of regret for the loss of the Republican Liberty, could not but tend to diminish that love, that admiration, that enthusiasm so natural to Frenchmen for their king. One might really suspect that he wished to instil into the minds of the people a belief, that what sovereigns call establishing order, is another term for riveting fetters on their subjects.[5]

But the work that we have been considering was merely a prelude to the doctrines which he was about to teach (in his *Spirit of Laws*) to all nations governed by a monarch. Let us premise, and with great sincerity we say it, that had we to perform the task of a panegyrist, causes for admi-

His *Spirit of Laws.*

4   *Considerations* &c. *See* On the Romans.

5   Chap. 13.

ration would abound; had we to answer those critics who reproach Montesquieu with having taken the motto, *prolem sine matre creatam*, and giving his work as if it were an original, though he may appear to have followed the footsteps of Bodin, celebrated for his work on Republics, we nevertheless think we may triumphantly answer, that the dross he may have borrowed from others cannot alloy the sterling value of his own production; and that in spite of the errors contained in the *Spirit of Laws*, it will for ever continue to be considered as the work of a wonderful genius.[6]

But it is not for us to assume the character, either of the critic or of the panegyrist. Our object is to investigate how far Montesquieu broached

---

6   We may safely assert, that if Montesquieu has borrowed such dross as the *System of Climates* from Bodin, he has thrown aside many articles which by no means coincided with his ideas. For example, the definition of a Sovereign given by Bodin could never agree with Montesquieu's notions of a free people, or of its representatives. The former is exaggerated. In Bodin's language, we might say, that the covenant by which the Sovereign is constituted, gives him the right of disposing at pleasure of the fives and fortunes of every citizen: That the sole distinction between the Tyrant and the lawful King is, that the former exercises his authority for the subjugation, while the latter exerts his for the happiness of the people. The generality of Montesquieu's principles appear not to recognize a sufficient Sovereignty in the real Monarch; but the opposite excess into which Bodin had fallen may, by disgusting Montesquieu, have driven him into the opposite extreme. In short, whether this criticism be correct or not is of little consequence, our object being to represent Montesquieu's ideas exactly as he has expressed them, in whatever part of the work they may be found.

or influenced revolutionary ideas. It is the misfortune of a great genius, that his very errors are too often converted into oracles. Truth must often submit to error, when that error is supported by a celebrated name! That victory which he would have disclaimed, resulted merely from the celebrity of his name, and the weight of his authority. The distinction which he makes between the principles of monarchy and those of republicanism may convince the reader. In an ordinary writer, the whole of that part of the *Spirit of Laws* would have been looked upon as the sport of imagination playing upon words. But from Montesquieu they are received as the result of profound thought, sanctioned by the great name of history. Let us examine whether the notions branding monarchy with disgrace can originate from any thing but the abuse of terms.

Honour, in the general acceptance of his countrymen, was the fear of being despised, and a horror particularly of being looked upon as a coward. It was the sentiment of Glory and of Courage. When a more moral sentiment attached itself to *honour*, it was converted into the shame of having done, or of hearing oneself reproached as having done, some act unworthy of an honest man; for instance, as having broken one's word. Montesquieu, observing the despotic influence which this word exercised over his countrymen, adopted *honour* as the first principle, the main spring, the prime mover of monarchies, and flatters republics with having virtue for

His distinction between the principles of Monarchies and of Republics.

their first principle.[7] The chivalry of the French, pleased with the idea, applauds Montesquieu, but does not perceive that in adopting the word he falsifies the sentiment and metamorphoses it into *a false honour, a prejudice, a thirst of fame, an ambition for distinctions or for favor*; in a word, into all the vices of the courtier.[8] This was bewildering honour, it was telling those bold knights, so zealous for their king, that they were no more than effeminate courtiers, ambitious men, and slaves to a prejudice the source of all the vices of courts: an assertion the more evidently false, as many a Frenchman replete with true honour was entirely free from any of those vices. Such a distinction was not only odious and disgraceful, it was also delusive, and the delusion seems to have prevented Montesquieu from perceiving that hereafter Philosphism would adopt the principle, but would only repeat the word honour as the opposite *to virtue, the principle of republics*, and brand the royalists with all the false prejudices, the ambition, and other vices, which he had artfully ascribed to *honour*.

This first error therefore was the offspring of delusion. Though, in one sense, as much may be said of the pretended principle of democracies. In another point of view, however, this principle may be introduced with more correctness; and this latter sense appears to be that to which Montesquieu at first alluded. It is undeniable, that virtue ought to

7   *Spirit of Laws*, book III. chap. 3, and following.

8   *Ib*. chap. 7, & *passim*. Book III and V.

be more particularly the principle of democracies than of any other form of government, they being the most turbulent and the most vicious of all; in which virtue is absolutely necessary to control the passions of men, to quell that spirit of cabal, anarchy, and faction inherent to the democratic form, and to chain down that ambition and rage of dominion over the people, which the weakness of the laws can scarcely withstand.

But it would have been satyric in the extreme to have adopted this latter sense; and Montesquieu's great admiration for the ancient democracies would never permit him to give such an explanation of the principle. He therefore generalizes or particularizes his definitions as suits his purpose. At one time this virtue, the prime mover of Republics, is *the love of one's country—that is to say, of Equality—is a political, and not a moral virtue*.[9] *At another, this political virtue is a moral one*, as it is directed to the public good.[10] In one place it is not *the virtue of individuals*,[11] though in another it is every thing that can be understood by good morals, or by the virtue of a people *who are preserved from corruption by the goodness of their maxims*.[12] Again, it is the most common virtue in that state where "theft is blended with the spirit of justice; the hardest servitude with excess of Liber-

9   Advertisement of the Author to the new Edition.

10   Note to chap. 5, book III.

11   *Ibidem.*

12   Chap. 2, book I.

ty, the most atrocious sentiments with the greatest moderation;" in short, it is the virtue of that state where "natural sentiments are preserved without the tie of son, husband, or father, and where even chastity is denuded of modesty and shame."[13]

Whatever idea the reader may have formed of virtue through the mist which appears to have enveloped the genius of Montesquieu in enigmatic darkness, let us ask, which principle will he adopt, or which will he conceive to be the most clearly expressed? If asked, whether virtue was not also to be found in Monarchies, he will answer, "I know that virtuous Princes are no uncommon sight; but I venture to affirm, that *in a Monarchy* it is extremely difficult for the people to be virtuous;"[14] and this sentiment, so odious and so injurious to all Royalists, will in the end be the most clearly deduced of all the new opinions he has broached upon Monarchical Government. Whether such were his intentions or not, a day will come, when the Sophisters, repeating his assertions, will say to the people,

> You only love your King because you have not a sufficient sense of Philosophy to raise yourselves above the prejudices of ambition and of false honour, because you are destitute of those moral virtues which direct to the public good; because you are not inflamed with the love of your Country; because you admire that form of

13   Chap. 6, book IV.
14   Chap. 5, book III.

Government, where it is *extremely difficult for the people to be virtuous.* You would admire *Democracy* were your *morals good,* and were you fired with the *amor patriæ*—but, destitute of virtue and unacquainted with Philosphy, you are only capable of loving your Kings.

Such, as every reflecting reader must perceive, is the real explanation of these principles. The Revolution has only brought them into practice. We have heard a Robespierre and a Sieyès, proclaiming to the people, that in crushing the Scepter, murdering their King, and constituting France a Republic, they had *only put virtue on the order of the day.* In the midst of massacres and bloodshed, they profaned the sacred name of virtue; and with virtue in their mouths they plunged the people into the most horrid scenes of vice and debauchery. But have we not seen Montesquieu teaching them how to blend virtue with the *most atrocious* sentiments, and how it may reign amidst the *hardest servitude, or the excess of Liberty?* To attribute such intentions to this celebrated writer would most certainly be doing an injustice to his memory; but still it is our duty to speak unreservedly on what he has written, and to shew what sentiments nations may have imbibed from his writings. It is awful (whatever may have been his intentions) to reflect on the terrible ravages which his opinions, suported by the authority of his name, have operated in the minds of men. Error is in its infancy with Montesquieu; but it is the same error that was afterwards, in the state of manhood, adopted by Robespierre. Montesquieu would have shrunk back with horror had he heard that Democratic villain place virtue *for the order of the day* with his sanguinary Republic; but what could the astonished master have replied, on being told, *that it was extremely difficult for the people to be virtuous under a Monarch*, or under Louis XVI.?

Let genius shrink back with horror at seeing its errors traverse the immense interval between Montesquieu and Robespierre; let it tremble at its despotic influence over the public opinion. Without designing any convulsion, by its very name it may raise the most dreadful storm. At first, its errors may be tender shoots; but, daily gaining bulk and strength, will they not in the form of massive limbs be wielded by a Condorcet, a Pétion, or a Sieyès?

During a long period Montesquieu's opinions on the principles of Monarchies and Republics were entirely overlooked, and they might have remained in oblivion at any other time, when Philosophism was less active in its research after every means of rendering the Throne odious.—Almost as much may be said of that *Equality* which, he believed, "in Democracy limited ambition to the sole desire of doing greater services to our country, than the rest of our fellow-citizens:"[15] a virtue far too sublime for Monarchies, "where nobody aims at Equality; it does not so much as enter their thoughts; they all aspire to superiority. People of the very lowest

---

15   Chap. 3, book V.

condition desire to emerge from their obscurity only to lord it over their fellow-subjects."[16] Genius may have been so led away, as not to perceive how powerful a weapon it was forging for the Jacobin, who, extolling the merits of this Equality, and persuading the people that it was impracticable under the dominion of the Monarch, would also paint in glowing colours *that ambition of serving the country*, arising from the ashes of the Throne and the destruction of the Nobility. But there appeared another system in the *Spirit of Laws*, deeper laid, and replete with weapons more directly pointed at the Throne. They were the first on which Philosophism seized, while others adopted them through ignorance, from want of reflection, or from imprudence. They were too fatal in the hands of the first rebels not to claim a place in these Memoirs.

To form a correct idea of the Revolutionary tendency of Montesquieu's system, we must revert to the time at which it was published. Whatever may have been the Legislative forms in the primitive days of the French Monarchy, it is certain that at the time of his publication (and he avows it) not only the King of France, but most of the crowned heads united in their persons the rights of executing the Laws, of enacting those which they conceived necessary or conducive to the welfare of the State, and of judging those who had infringed the law.[17]

State of the French Monarchy, when his system on the distinction of Powers appeared.

16 Chap. 4, book V.
17 Chap. 6, book XI.

The reunion of this Triple Power constitutes an *absolute Monarch*, that is to say, a real Sovereign who in his person concentrates the whole power of the law. At that period the French were far from confounding this absolute power with the arbitrary power of the Tyrant or the Despot. This power was to be found in Republics and in mixt States. Here it existed in the Senate, or in the assembly of Deputies; there in the compound of the Senate and the King. The French nation beheld it in their Monarch, whose supreme will, legally proclaimed, was the utmost degree of political authority.

Difference between an absolute and an arbitrary power.

This supreme will, construed into law by the requisite forms, was equally binding on the King and on his subjects. It is not only Henry IV. and his Minister Sully, who declare *that the first law of the Sovereign is to observe them all*; but it is Louis XIV., that Prince whom the Sophisters affectedly style the Despot, who at the height of his glory openly proclaims this obligation in his edicts: Do not let it be said," are his words,

> that the Sovereign shall not be subject to the laws of the state. The rights of nations proclaim the contrary truth, which has sometimes been attacked by flattery, but which all good Princes have defended as the guardian of their states. How much more accurate it is to say, that to constitute the perfect happiness of a kingdom, it is necessary in order that the Prince should be obeyed by his subjects, *that the Prince should*

obey the Laws, and that those laws should be
just and directed to the public good![18]

This obligation alone in the Sovereign immediately destroys all despotic or arbitrary power.—
For, in the idiom of modern languages, the Despot
is the man who rules only by his passions and caprice; under whom no subject can be at ease, as
he is ignorant whether his master will not punish
him to-day for having executed the orders he had
received from him yesterday.

In short, it may be justly said, that Political Liberty consists in two points:

1 st. That every Citizen should be free to do all
that is not forbidden by the law: 2dly, That the law
should prescribe or forbid any particular action
for the public good only. Experience will vouch for
the correctness of this definition. And where could
the honest and upright man, obedient to the laws
of his country, enjoy greater security and freedom
than he did in France?

It may indeed be objected, that there existed
many abuses, but did not they originate from the
genius of the French, or from an excess rather
than a want of liberty? Were the conspirators to
exclaim against the immoral and impious Minister for having abused the power with which he
was entrusted, when these Sophisters had during many years conspired against the morals and

---

18   Edict of Louis XIV., 1667; also the Treatise of the Queen's
Rights on Spain.

piety of the whole nation? No; they had no right to complain that the law was often sacrificed to private passions; the exact observance of the law should have been their prayer, but they only sought after ruin and revolution.

On *Lettres de cachet* and their abuse.

One real abuse had crept into the French Government, which savoured much of Despotism.— This was the use of *Lettres de cachet*.[19] Undoubtedly they were illegal. On a bare order from the King the subject lost his liberty. I will not defend such an abuse by saying, that none but the higher classes or seditious writers were exposed to the effect of this arbitrary power. But, perhaps, few are acquainted with the origin of those Letters. It was to the moral character of the French, and to the notions particularly of the higher classes, that this abuse owed its origin; and it was necessary either to do away those notions, or to leave so formidable a power in the hands of the Monarch.

Such was the received opinion in France, that a family would have thought itself dishonored, if any child, brother, or near relation were brought to justice. Hence it was that families, fearing the arm of the law, applied to the King to obtain an order to imprison any profligate youth whose irregular conduct might disgrace the family. If any hopes of reformation could be conceived, the *Let-*

---

19   *Lettres de cachet* were letters signed by the king of France, countersigned by one of his ministers, and closed with the royal seal, that contained the king's direct orders, often to enforce arbitrary actions and judgments beyond appeal. —Ed.

tre de cachet was only temporary, and served as a correction; but where the offence was criminal and infamous, the culprit was imprisoned for life.

The reader must not be misled to suppose, that these Letters were granted on a mere request and without any inquiry into the case. After Mr. de Malesherbes' administration, the petitions sent to the King were transmitted to the Intendant of the Province, who immediately ordered his sub-delegate to call a meeting of the relations and witnesses, and to take minutes of their proceedings. On these informations, which were forwarded to the Ministers, his Majesty granted or refused the *Lettres de cachet*.[20]

Under such restrictions it was evidently rather the authority of a common parent, which the King exercised over his subjects, than that of a despot enslaving them. With the notions which the French nation had adopted, it was the necessary means of

---

20 Although these *Lettres de Cachet* did not generally regard the commonalty, yet the King, when petitioned, did not always refuse them to the lower classes. I was once ordered to attend one of those meetings as interpreter for an honest German, who, though low in life, had requested his Majesty to grant a Lettre de Cachet for his wife, who, violent and choleric, had attempted to stab him, but fortunately he had stopped her hand. The poor man, unable to five in peace or safety with this woman, and unwilling to bring her before a tribunal, had recourse to the King, who ordered the Intendant to take all the proper evidence. The relations and witnesses were secretly assembled. I saw the Subdelegate examine the facts with the greatest humanity. The whole being verified, the minutes were laid before his Majesty, and the *Lettre de Cachet* granted. The lady was confined; but in a few months she was permitted to return,

preserving the honour of different families; and few were victims to this authority but those who were dangerous either to private or public society. From the use to the abuse of a thing, however, the distance is but small: a profligate minister might exercise this power against the citizen or the magistrate who had fulfilled his duty with the greatest integrity. Nor was it unexampled, that a minister, solicited by powerful men, rather consulted their private animosities, than public justice, or general utility. But a profligate minister abusing his authority does not make his King a despot. The morals of the higher classes being perverted, as we have seen, by Philosophism, the abuse of this prerogative might loudly call for reform; but are the Sophisters thence justifiable in seeking to overthrow the Monarchy?

The French attached to their King, at the time the *Spirit of Laws* was published.

In short, whatever may have been the cause of these abuses at the period when *The Spirit of Laws* appeared, it had never entered the minds of Frenchmen, that they lived under a despotic government. Let us hear Jean-Jacques Rousseau lay down the law, he who created systems to overthrow it; and let the candid reader judge how far the Sophisters are authorized to represent the French government as arbitrary, oppressive, and tyrannical.

> What (says Jean-Jacques) is the true end of a political association? Is it not the preservation and prosperity of its members? And what is the most

---

and was ever after a model of gentleness and submission.

certain sign that they are preserved, and that
they prosper? Is it not the increasing population?
We need seek no further for the sign in dispute;
but pronounce that government to be infallibly
the best (provided there is no particular circumstance to make it stand an exception to a general
rule) under which, without the application of any
improper means, without the naturalization of
strangers, without receiving any new colonists,
the citizens increase and multiply: and that to
be the worst under which they lessen and decay.
Calculators, it is now your affair; count, measure,
and compare them.[21]

—The same author adds,

It is a long continuance in the same situation
that makes prosperity or calamity real. When a
whole nation lies crushed under the foot of despotism, it is then that the people perish; and it
is then that their masters can hurl destruction
among them with impunity, *ubi solitudinem
faciunt, pacem appellant* (and call peace, the silence of the desert they have created). When the
factions of the chief men of France had arisen to
such a height as to agitate the kingdom, and the
coadjutor of Paris judged it necessary to carry a
dagger in his pocket every time he went into the
parliament, the French people lived free and at
ease, and they were happy and their numbers increased. The prosperity of a nation and its population depends much more on *liberty* than on
peace.[22]

---

21 *Social Contract*, chap. 9, book. III.
22 *Ib.* in the note.

Thus, without taking on himself the task of calculator, Jean-Jacques confesses that the French people, even in the midst of civil broils, *lived free and at ease.* But let us attend to one of his most faithful disciples, who undertook to calculate, and that at a time when the Revolution had done away every idea of exaggerating the happiness of the French people under the government of their Kings. The revolutionist Gudin, in his annotations on the above text, and in his *Supplement to the Social Contract*, has examined and calculated, year by year, the state of the population, the deaths, births, and marriages of all the principal towns in the kingdom during the course of this century, and then proceeds:

> The author of the *Social Contract* spoke a grand truth when he exclaimed: Calculators, it is now your affair; *count, measure, and compare.* His advice has been followed; we have calculated, measured, and compared, and the result of all these calculations has demonstrated that the population of France is really twenty-four millions, though it had always been supposed to be under twenty; that the annual births amount to one million; and *that the population is daily increasing.*
>
> Hence we may conclude, after Rousseau, that the government was very good. It really was better than it ever had been at any period since the destruction of that which the Romans had established in Gaul.

Such are the words of the same author, and according to his calculations it was *in the reign of Louis XIV.*, whom the Sophisters represent as the haughtiest of despots, *that the population of France began to increase regularly and univerally throughout the whole kingdom*, notwithstanding all his wars.

"The long reign of Louis XV. (another alledged despot, under whose reign the Antimonarchical Conspiracy was begun and indefatigably conducted) was not exposed to such calamities; and it is certain," continues the revolutionist Gudin,

> that during the whole monarchy there has existed no period when population increased in a more constant and uniform progression throughout the whole kingdom, than during that reign. It increased to that amazing height, that from twenty-four to twenty-five millions of souls were spread over a surface of twenty-five thousand square leagues, which makes about a million souls to a thousand square leagues, or a thousand inhabitants to every square league, *a population so unparalleled in Europe, that it might be almost looked upon as a prodigy.*

Let us hear the same author on the state of France at the time when the Revolution broke out, which he is perpetually extolling; and let us remark, that the work whence we have extracted our documents was so acceptable to the Revolutionary Assembly, that by a particular decree of the 13th of November 1790, *it accepted the homage of it*: a stronger contrast cannot be sketched between that Revolution and its authors, whether distant or immediate, and the necessity of those plans by which they pretended to work the happiness of the Empire. The same author continues:

> The French territory is so well cultivated, that its annual produce is estimated at four thousand millions.
>
> Its currency amounted to two thousand two hundred millions, and the gold and silver employed in plate and jewels may be estimated at a similar amount.
>
> The Records of the Assinage Office in Paris attest, that the annual consumption or rather waste of refined gold, in gilding furniture, carriages, pasteboard, china, nails, fans, buttons, books, in spotting stuffs, or in plating silver, amounted to the enormous sum of eight hundred thousand livres.
>
> The profit on trade was annually computed at between forty and fifty millions.
>
> The taxes paid by the people did not exceed six hundred and ten or twelve millions, which does not amount to one third of the circulating medium nor to one sixth part of the gross territorial produce, and which probably cannot be computed at more than one third of the neat produce, a sum which in that proportion could not have been exorbitant if every one had paid according to his means.[23]

---

23 As this last sentence alludes to the privileges and exemptions of the Clergy and Nobility, I cannot but refer my reader to a work attributed to Mr. Sénac de Meilhan, and which is very satisfactory on this point. It contains the following passage:

In this kingdom were annually born upwards of 928,000 children; in short, nearly a million. The town of Paris contained 666,000 inhabitants. Its riches were so great, that it paid annually one hundred millions into the King's coffers, about one sixth of the whole taxation of France.

But even this immense taxation did not overburthen Paris. Its inhabitants lived in affluence. If its daily consumption amounted to one million, at least from eighty to one hundred millions were necessary for its interior circulation.

In short, calculators have estimated, that during the reign of Louis XV. the population of the country was increased by one ninth, that is to say, by two millions five or six hundred thousand souls.

"Mr. Necker at length, in a moment of pique against his ungrateful children, disclosed the whole truth, and declared before the National Assembly, that the exemptions of the Clergy and Nobility, which had been represented in so odious a light, did not exceed seven millions of livres (381,181l. that the half of that sum belonged to the privileged persons of the *Tiers État*—and that the tax on enregistering (*droit de contrôle*) which only bore on the two first orders, amply balanced the privileges they enjoyed with regard to the ordinary taxes. These memorable words were spoken in the face of all Europe, but were drowned in the cries of the victorious demagogues. The Clergy, the Nobility, and the Monarchy, all have perished,"—and perished under the pretence of an inequality of privileges (an empty assertion), which was more than amply compensated by a single tax on the privileged orders. This was the tax on all public acts. It was rated in proportion to the sum specified in the act, or to the titles inserted. "Thus the Most High and Puissant Lord, Marquis, Count or Baron, was rated according to his birth, or rank, while a citizen only paid in the ratio of his obscurity." *Vid. that work, and note to chap. 6.*

Supple-
ment to
the *Social
Contract.*
See note
*Popula-
tion.*

Such was the state of France and of Paris at the time the Revolution took place; and as no other state in Europe could exhibit such a population, nor boast of such revenues, it was not without reason that *it passed for the first kingdom on the Continent.*

The revolutionist Gudin, to whom we are indebted for all these particulars, concludes by saying,

> I thought it necessary to state in a precise and exact manner the population and riches of the kingdom at the period when *so grand a Revolution took place.* I apprehended that this investigation would shew the future progress of the nation, and serve as a table by which we might calculate the advantages that will accrue from the constitution when brought to perfection.

Without doubt our author has by this time formed his opinion on the advantages of that constitution; but we can plainly see by his enthusiastic admiration of the revolution, and of the Philosophers to whom he attributes the honor of having effected it;[24] that he was very far from wishing to exaggerate the liberty and happiness of France under the Monarchy. By the foregoing long extract we have no other object in view, than that of furnishing the historian with the proper materials (all extracted from the greatest admirers or chief authors of the French Revolution) to enable him to judge of those systems in which the Revolution originated, and to

---

24   Book III. Chap, on the Philosophers.

appreciate properly the wisdom or the imprudence of its authors.—But to return to Montesquieu.

Precisely at that period when *L'Esprit des loix* was published, the French were so happy and so pleased with their King, that the surname of well-beloved (*bien aimé*) had resounded from one extremity of the nation to the other. And, unfortunately for Montesquieu, it is from this publication that we are to trace all those Philosophical reveries on Equality and Liberty, which at first only produced disquiet and doubt, but which soon after created other systems, that misled the French people in their ideas on government, that weakened the tie of affection between the subject and the monarch, and generated at length the monster of Revolutions.

There is an essential difference to be perceived between Voltaire and Montesquieu. Voltaire, as we have shown, would willingly have endured a Monarch that should have connived at his impiety. He would have thought himself sufficiently free, had he been allowed publicly to blaspheme; and, generally speaking, he was more partial to the forms of Monarchy, or of Aristocracy, than to those of Democracy. It was his hatred to religion (and he hated religion more than he loved Kings) which plunged him into the municipalizing system.

With Montesquieu it was far otherwise. Though he was not indifferent on the subject of religious liberty, it was nevertheless Monarchy itself that he meant to investigate. He pro-

His admiration for sovereign laws. His systems inapplicable to his country.

61

posed to regulate all kingly power and authority according to his ideas of political liberty. Had religious liberty been carried to excess, still he would have looked upon himself as immersed in slavery in every state where the public authority was not subdivided, according to his system, into three distinct powers, *the Legislative, the Executive, and the Judiciary*. This distinction was new to the French nation, which had been accustomed to view its Monarch as the central point of all political authority. The peaceful ages they had passed under their Legislative Kings little inclined them to envy the boisterous liberty of a neighbouring country, perhaps more celebrated for its civil broils in quest of liberty, than for the wisdom of its constitution, which, at length fixing every mind and every heart, had scarcely terminated a long struggle between the Monarch and the People.

Without doubt we may admire, as much as Montesquieu, the wisdom of that nation which has known how to model its laws according to the experience it had acquired during those struggles. Laws indeed, congenial to the manners which characterize it, to its local situation, and even to its prejudices. But is that constitution, the most perfect perhaps existing for a nation surrounded by the ocean, to be equally perfect when transplanted into a continental state? Has not nature, by diversifying the soil, varied its culture? Are men so heterogeneous in their characters, men that may be viewed under so many different points, are they, in order to attain happiness and freedom, to be reduced to one only mode of government? No; it would have been madness to adopt the English constitution in France. The genius of the French ation must have been totally changed before a Frenchman would believe himself free where the Englishman does not even perceive the yoke of the law; before the former would refrain from abusing that liberty which the latter will scarcely taste of; and particularly before the Frenchman could be kept within those limits where the Englishman rests content.

We are willing to believe, that Montesquieu had never made these reflections, when, carried away by his admiration for foreign laws, he was inventing new principles, and presenting as constant and general such truths, as would make his countrymen view their Sovereign in the light of a real Despot, and the mild government they lived under, though so conformable to their interests and their genius, as that of a most horrid and shameful slavery.

It is painful to apply such a reproach to this celebrated writer; but can history refrain from observing the fatal impression which such doctrines must have made on a people so long accustomed to say, *si veut le Roi, si veut la loi* (as the King wills, so wills the law); the doctrines, I say, of him who dared assert as a demonstrated truth, that "when the legislative and executive powers are united in the same person or in the same body of magis-

His systems alienate the French from their King.

trates, there can be no liberty; because apprehensions may arise lest the same Monarch or Senate should enact tyrannical laws, to execute them in a tyrannical manner."[25] But in laying down this principle, he had taken care to say immediately before, "the political liberty of the subject is a tranquillity of mind, arising from the opinion which each one has of his safety. In order to have this liberty, it is requisite that the Government be so constituted, as that one man need not be afraid of another."[26]

Either Montesquieu must have believed the French reader incapable of uniting those two ideas, or else he meant to say, "Frenchmen! You believe that under the government of your King you are in safety, and enjoy liberty. Your opinion is erroneous, it is shameful. Amidst that calm which you seem to enjoy *there is no liberty*, and none can exist so long as you repeat *si veut le Roi, si veut la loi*; in short so long as the Legislative and Executive Powers are united in the person of your King. He must be deprived either of the one or the other; or else you must submit to live in the perpetual terror of *tyrannical laws, tyrannically executed*."

This language is not held out to the French alone, but to every people governed by Kings, even to most Republics, where, as he himself remarks, these powers were often united. The whole universe was then in a state of slavery, and Montesquieu was the apostle sent to teach them to break their

25   Chap. 6, book XI.
26   Chap. 6, book XI.

chains, chains so light that few were even sensible of their existence! A general Revolution was then necessary, that mankind might assert its liberty! I could wish to exculpate Montesquieu; but if on the one side I am afraid of attributing intentions to him which he never had, on the other I dare not revile genius by separating it from reason; by saying that he had laid down new principes without even perceiving their most immediate consequences. It is a hard task to represent Montesquieu brandishing the torch of discord between nations and their Kings, between the subjects even of Republics and their Senates, or their Magistrates; but would it not be something more or less than kindness, to behold the torch, and the man who wields it, without daring to intimate the intention of kindling a blaze? How chimerical must have been that terror of tyrannical laws tyrannically executed in a country where the legislator himself is bound by pre-existing laws, whose sole object is the preservation of property, liberty, and the safety of the subject!— What a phantom such a supposition must be in a country where the King was omnipotent in the love of his subjects, and null in tyranny; in a country where, if the representations of the Magistrates were insufficient, the Monarch could never resist those of the people, whose very silence was sufficient to disarm him, and he would abrogate any number of laws to make them return to their noisy acclamations. Montesquieu, who attributes so much influence to climates, might very well have taken into consideration the manners, the character, and the received opinions, acting so much more powerfully among his countrymen than in any other nation. But the fact was, that the French laws enacted by their Legislative Monarchs were not to be surpassed either in wisdom or mildness by the laws of any country; under those Legislative Kings they had seen their liberties, so far from being contracted, ascertained and extended, and facts are better authorities than systems.[27]

His errors on the Judiciary Power.

The same error, the same delusion shows itself when Montesquieu believes every thing to be ruined, if the Prince who has enacted a law has the power of judging the man who transgresses it. Such a fear might be reasonable in a country where the Legislative Monarch could be both judge and plaintiff, thus sitting in judgment on his own cause, and over those of his subjects of whom he might have reason to complain; or where the Legislative King becomes sole Magistrate and sole Judge, or violates the accustomed forms requiring a certain number of Magistrates and votes to condemn or

---

27 On the occasion we may cite Mr. Garat, a lawyer, whose opinion cannot be mistrusted, having with many others of his brethren distinguished himself by his philosophical zeal for the Revolution; and before that period he was one of the most obstinate sticklers for the sovereignty of the people.—Nevertheless he says, "at present all laws emanate from the supreme will of the Monarch, who no longer has the whole nation for his council. But his throne is so easy of access, that the wishes of the nation can always reach it." *Garat's Report: de Jurisprud. art.* Souverain.

absolve a subject. This was a chimerical terror in every true Monarchy, where, as in France, the first law is to observe those of nature, which will always preclude either Sovereign or Magistrate from sitting in judgment on their own causes, and on their private differences with the subject. A terror still more futile wherever, as in France, the King might be cast in his own tribunals, and where equally with any subject he was bound by the law. Hence nothing could ever have made the French unite the idea of Despotism to that of a Monarch the judge of his subjects. With what romantic ideas and tender affection they were wont to paint those happy days when Louis IX., surrounded by his subjects as if they had been his children, would, under a shady oak, hear and determine their differences, with all the authority and justice of the first magistrate of his kingdom![28] How new must it then have been for the people to hear Montesquieu assert, that

> there is no liberty, if the power of judging be not separated from the Legislative and Executive Powers! Were it joined with the Legislative, the life and liberty of the subject would be exposed *to arbitrary control*, for the Judge would then be the Legislator. Were it joined to the Executive Power, the Judge might behave with all the violence of an oppressor. There would be an end of every thing, were the same man, or the same body, whether of the Nobles or of the people, to exercise those three powers, that of enacting

---

28   See Joinville's *Memoirs*.

THE ANTIMONARCHICAL CONSPIRACY

laws, that of executing the public resolutions, and that of judging the crimes, or determining the disputes of individuals.[29]

Montesquieu appears to have felt the danger of such lessons, when he really seeks to console nations by telling them, that "most kingdoms in Europe enjoy a moderate government, because the Prince who is invested with the first two powers leaves the third to his subjects." But such a distinction can little avail; of what consequence can it be, that the Prince should leave this third power to his subjects, when about twenty lines higher Montesquieu has laid down as a constant principle, that when the two first powers are united in the same person *there can be no Liberty?* And why does he immediately add, "In Turkey, where these three powers are united in the Sultan's person, the subjects groan under the weight of the most frightful oppression?"[30] Is it not very well known, that the Sultan generally leaves the judiciary power to the tribunals? Could the illustrious author have meant to address his countrymen in saying,

> You who in every age of your history behold your Kings exercising this power, such as Hugues Capet judging Amould de Rheims; as Louis the Younger, the Bishop of Langres, and the Duke of Burgundy; as Louis IX. administering justice to all those of his subjects who had recourse to him;

29 Chap. 6, book XI.
30 Chap. 6, book XI.

as Charles V. judging the Marquis of Saluces, or Charles VII. condemning the Duke of Alençon; as Francis I. pronouncing on the Connetable de Bourbon, and Louis XIII. judging the Duke de La Valette; in fine, all you, I say, who behold your Monarchs exercising the judiciary power learn that there was *an end of every thing* under such Princes, who were real Sultans, by whom the subject was made to groan under the most *frightful despotism*, and that you are in danger of seeing it revived every time your Kings shall exercise the same powers.[31]

Would it not have been wiser and more correct if Montesquieu had said, that what constituted the despotic power in the Sultan was the power of capriciously and instantaneously pronouncing on all points, following no other guide but his passion and his momentary interest? He sends the bowstring and it is an order to die; but can such an order be deemed a judgment. He sends it because he wills it, little regarding the letter or decisions of the law; and it little imports whether such a will be

---

31   It might be objected, that some of the Kings, as in the case of Francis I., who sat in judgment on trials for High Treason were judges in their own cause. But in reality those are causes which interest the whole state. It might as well be objected, that a French Parliament could not judge a traitor to the state, because it is the cause of every Frenchman. This was an objection made against Francis I. in the case of the Marquis de Saluces. It was quashed by the Attorney General. But its having been made is sufficient to prove that the King was no despot, since the laws of the country and a court of justice were to decide, whether he could exercise his power in that particular case.— (*Report: de Jurisprud. art. Roy, par M. Poluerel*).

assented to by a senate which may bear the title of judges, or whether he wills it alone, and in direct opposition to such a body of Magistrates. Such is the power which creates a Sultan, and which constitutes Despotism. But is it not chimerical to suppose, that in France the power of making a law and then pronouncing according to the decisions of that law antecedently made and promulgated, could constitute Despotism?

This erroneous assertion of so celebrated a writer is the more extraordinary, as we find it fully refuted in that part of his work where he treats of those ancient Dukes and Counts who, under the ancient government of the Franks, exercised the three powers.

> It may be imagined perhaps, (he says) that the government of the Franks must have been very severe at that time, since the same officers were invested with a military and a civil power, nay, even with a fiscal power over the subjects, which in the preceding books I have observed to be distinguishing marks of Despotic Authority. But it is not to be believed, that the Counts pronounced judgment by themselves, and administered justice in the same manner as the Bashaws do in Turkey. In order to judge affairs, they assembled a kind of assizes where the principal men appeared. The Count's assistants were generally seven in number, and as he was obliged to have twelve persons to judge, he filled up the number with the principal men. But whoever had the jurisdiction, whether the King, the Count, the *Grafio*, the *Centenarian*, the Lords,

or the Clergy, they never judged alone; and this usage, which derived its origin from the forests of Germany (as also did the *beautiful system* of the admirable constitution), was still continued even after the fiefs had assumed a new form.[32]

He was not then to come and tell the French people, whose Kings did not judge alone in modern more than they had done in former times, that all was over with them, that Liberty was at an end, because the judiciary power was not separated from the legislative and executive powers.

It is easy to see what disquiet such principles must have created in the minds of his countrymen, and how they exposed the Royal Authority to odium and mistrust. But, alas! this work contains the origin of far greater evils.

Further error, which begets the States-General.

Forewarned by experience of the trouble which accompanied the States-General, the French seldom recalled them to mind but to enjoy the peace and glory they had acquired under Monarchs, who by their wisdom had supplied the want of those ancient States. Montesquieu not only spread his false alarms on the legislative and executive powers of the Sovereign, but he was unfortunate enough to lay down as law to the people, that every state that wishes to believe itself free must only confide in itself, or its representatives, for the enacting of its laws. He was the first who said,

---

32   Chap. 18, book XXX.

71

> *As in a free State every man, who is supposed a free agent, ought to be his own governor,* so the legislative power ought to reside in the whole body of the people. But since this is impossible in large States, and in small ones is subject to great inconveniences, *it is fit that the people should execute by their Representatives what they cannot execute by themselves.*[33]

This is not the place to observe what a multitude of errors these assertions contain: the chief is that of having converted into a principle what he had observed in England, without considering that often what has conducted one nation to Liberty, may lead another into all the horrors of Anarchy, and thence to Despotism. On seeing this opinion laid down as a general principle, the French believed, that to become a free state it was necessary for them to return to their former States-General, and vest them with the legislative power. And in order to throw the fiscal power also into their hands Montesquieu adds,

> If the legislative power were to settle the subsidies, not from year to year, but for ever, *it would run the risk of losing its Liberty,* because the executive power would no longer be dependent; and when once it was possessed of such a perpetual right, it would be a matter of indifference whether it held it of itself, or of another. The same may be said, if it should fix, not from year to year, but for ever, the sea and

---

33   Chap. 6, book XI.

land forces with which it is to entrust the executive power.[34]

When we consider how little such a doctrine was
ever thought of in France before Montesquieu had
written; when we behold that swarm of scribbling
copyists, who all repeat that Liberty is at an end
wherever the people do not exercise the legislative
and fiscal powers, either by themselves or by their
representatives; when we compare this doctrine
with that of the first revolutionary rebels, whether
under the denomination of *Constitutionalists or
Monarchists*; when we reflect that it was on such
principles that Necker, Turgot, Barnave, Mirabeau,
and La Fayette founded their systematic rebellion,
do we not immediately infer (an awful truth indeed for Montesquieu, but which History can never hide), that it is to Montesquieu the French must
trace that system which disjoints the sceptre and
throws the Monarch into the hands of the people,
who by means of their representatives proclaim
their pretended laws; that system which recalls the
States-general, who soon, styling themselves National Assembly, leave nothing to their King but the
theatrical show of royal pageantry, until, carrying
their consequences still further, the people assert
their unbounded sovereignty by dragging the unfortunate Louis XVI. to the scaffold?

History will be astonished when it beholds
Montesquieu, ignorant of his system having been

---

34   *Ibid.*

precisely that which the most inveterate enemies of his country had formerly adopted, in hopes of diminishing the lustre and grandeur which it enjoyed under the dominion of its kings. For ever will the memory of those servile copyists, the Constitutionalists and Monarchists, be odious to their country, when it shall be remembered that their main object was to subject their Monarch to the authority of the States-General, and thus consummate the very plan concerted by the foreign enemy.

His systems coincide with those of the greatest enemies of the State.

All these wonderful men, who were so well versed in the English constitution, might during their researches have learned what every English school-boy was acquainted with, who, in his most tender years, on receiving Salmon's Geography must have read the following passage:

> January 16th, 1691, at the Congress of the Hague, consisting of the Princes of Germany, the Imperial, English, Italian, Spanish and Dutch ministers, a declaration was drawn up, wherein they solemnly protested before God, that their intentions were never to make peace with Louis XIV., until the Estates of the kingdom of France should be established in their ancient liberties; so that the Clergy, the Nobility, and the Third-Estate, might enjoy their ancient and lawful privileges; nor till their kings for the future should be obliged to call together the said estates *when they desired any supply*, without whom they should not raise any money, on any pretence whatever, and till the parliaments of that kingdom and *all other his sub-*

jects were restored to their just rights. And the confederates invited the subjects of France to join with them in this undertaking for restoring them to their *rights and liberties*, threatening ruin and devastation to those who refused.[35]

It is thus that, after thirty years of the most learned discussion and research on the part of Montesquieu, and forty years of new discussion on the part of his learned disciples, the Constitutionalists and Monarchists, that they adopt that plan for restoring their country to liberty which every

---

35 Edit. 1750. Page 309. [The exact text reads: "January 16.] At the Congress of the Hague, consisting of the Princes of Germany, the Imperial, English, Italian, Spanish and Dutch ministers, a declaration was drawn up, wherein, 1. they solemnly protested before God, that their intentions were never to make peace with Louis XIV., until he had made Reparation to the Holy See, for whatever he had acted against it; and till he had annulled and made void all thofe infamous Proceedings against the Holy Father Innocent XI. 2. Nor until he had restored to each Party all he had taken from them since the Peace of Munster. 3. Nor till he had reftored to the Protestants of France all their Possessions and Goods, and an entire Liberty of Confcience. 4. Nor till the Estates of the Kingdom of France should be establisjed in their ancient Liberties; so that the Clervy, the Nobility, and the third Estate might enjoy their ancient and lawful Privileges; Nor till their Kings, for the Future, should be obliged to call together the said Estates, when they desired any Supply, without whom they should not raise any Money on any Pretence whatsoever; and till the Parliaments of that Kingdom, and all other his Subjects, were restored to their just Rights. And the Confederates invited the Subjects of France to job with then in this Undertaking, for restoring them to Rights and Liberties; threatening Ruin and Devastation to those who refused." Taken from the 1758 edition, pages 309-10. —Ed.]

English school-boy knew to have originated in the mind of the enemy, who wished to overturn the Throne, and tarnish the lustre which France had acquired under its Legislative Monarchs.

Had I already said it, I should nevertheless repeat, that the object here in debate is, not what the ancient constitution of France has been, nor whether their kings enjoyed the legislative power, (which has been very ill discussed by our modern politicians); still less are we disposed to agitate the question, which is the most perfect constitution in itself? Nobody will deny that government to be the best, under which the people are happiest at home, and most formidable abroad; and such a reflection will suffice to show how baneful the doctrines broached by Montesquieu and repeated by the Sophisters of Rebellion must have proved to France: they who came to stun their countrymen with the pretended fears of despotism, alienating their minds from their own constitution to excite their admiration for foreign laws, and that at a time when the love of the subjects for their king was carried to enthusiasm after the tranquil ministry of the Cardinal Fleury, and the brilliant campaigns of the Marechal de Saxe in Flanders.

It may be difficult to decide how far this imprudent doctrine is to be looked upon as the error or as the perversion of genius; were we to appeal to the testimonies of his greatest admirers, we should not hesitate at the latter decision, and rank him among the Sophisters of Rebellion, as the sect appears to have done. D'Alembert rather accuses than defends him, when, answering those who complained of the obscurity of the *Spirit of Laws*, he says,

> All that may appear obscure to common readers is not so to those whom the Author had particularly in view. Beside, *a voluntary obscurity* ceases to be obscure. Mr. de Montesquieu, often wishing to advance certain important truths, which, boldly and absolutely expressed, might have given offence to no purpose, *very prudently disguised them, and by this innocent artifice* hid them from those who might have been offended, without destroying their intended effect on the sage.[36]

It is difficult to pass over this *voluntary obscurity* in a man who has advanced principles so subversive of the laws and government of his country. His pretended *innocent artifices* would almost convince the reader, that all those protestations of Montesquieu were hypocritical and sophistical, when we see him, after having strained every nerve to prove to most nations that they are perfect strangers to liberty, and that their kings are real despots, seeking every means to dispel any suspicion of his being of that disquiet, morose, and seditious temper which thirsts after revolutions.

Nor is the suspicion removed by d'Alembert when he compliments him as having "diffused that general light on the principles of government

---

36 Montesquieu's Elogy by d'Alembert, at the head of the 5th volume of the Encyclopedia.

which has rendered the people more attached *to what they ought to love.*" What can be the signification of "what they ought to love" in the mouth of this artful Sophister? Why should he not have said more attached to their King and the Government of their country? But we have already seen how little this Sophister was attached to either the one or the other.

It is equally unfortunate, that his panegyrist, now that the name of Encyclopedist is so justly covered with opprobrium, should extol his zeal for that monstrous digest, whose object remains no longer a secret, or when the most revolutionary among the Sophisters positively assert, that *Montesquieu would not have written* had not Voltaire written before him. Condorcet, by advancing such a proposition, clearly means, that if Voltaire had not succeeded so well in his Antichristian Conspiracy, Montesquieu would not have contributed so powerfully towards the political revolution;—that if the one had been less daring against the Altar, the other would have dared less against the Throne.

In solving this unfortunate problem, what "damning proof" would be acquired against Montesquieu if the authenticity of a letter which appeared in one of the London papers could ever be ascertained! Voltaire and d'Alembert conspired against the Jesuits, because they believed that society to be one of the firmest props to religion; Montesquieu, if the letter be genuine, presses for heir destruction, because he thought them too much attached to the Royal authority. "We have a Prince," says he,

> who is good, but weak. That society employs every art to transform the Monarch into a Despot. If it succeeds: I tremble for the consequences, civil war will rage, and streams of blood will inundate every part of Europe.—The English writers have thrown so great a light upon Liberty, and we have so great a desire of preserving what little of it we enjoy, that we should make the worst slaves in the world.

Were those violent and extreme measures which we have since witnessed already taken? This letter would indicate as much; beside, it is entirely written in the style of a conspirator. It is full of such expressions as these: "If we cannot write freely, *let us think and act freely.* We must wait patiently, but never cease working for the cause of Liberty. Since we cannot fly to the pinnacle, let us climb."

Could it be possible that Montesquieu had already formed the plan of driving out the Swiss guards, and of calling forth the national guards of the revolution? The following lines strongly denote such a plan: "What a point should we have gained, if we could once get rid of those mercenaries and foreign soldiers! *An army of natives* would declare for Liberty, at least the greater part of them would. But that is the very reason why foreign troops are maintained."[37] However difficult it may appear to

---

37 It is earnestly requested of all persons who may have any

79

vindicate Montesquieu from being a conspirator, if it be true that he was the author of the above letter, still I must say what may absolutely excuse him. This letter may have been written in a moment of anger, and be the effect of one of those fantastical contradictions from which the greatest genius is not always exempt. Montesquieu had bestowed the highest encomiums on the Jesuits in his *Spirit of Laws*;[38] but that did not hinder them from condemning several of his propositions. The resentment of the moment might have induced him to wish for their destruction. It is generally known, that he was much more tender to criticism than could be supposed for a man of his superior genius. All his love of Liberty could not hinder him from applying to the Marquise de Pompadour to obtain the despotic order for suppressing and even for burning Mr. Dupin's Refutation of his *Spirit of Laws*.[39]

We may observe various traits in this celebrated genius which are irreconcileable. He was very

---

further knowledge of that letter, or are in possession of the Newspaper in which it was published, that they will be kind enough to give such information to the Author, at Mr. Dulau's, bookseller, No. 107, Wardour-street. He cannot question the veracity of the Abbé le Pointe, who gave him the translation of it, taken from an Evening Newspaper about the latter end of 1795; but, not attaching the same importance to the letter which the Author would have done, the Abbé neither remarked the title nor the date of the paper which he translated it from, and that the Author hopes will plead his excuse for troubling his readers.

38   Chap. 6, book IV.

39   See Feller's *Historical Dictionary*.

intimate with the Encyclopedian Deists and Atheists, but always desirous that his friends should die good Christians, and that they should receive all the rites of the church. At that awful period he was an Apostle or Divine, he would exhort and insist until the sick person assented; he would run, though it were at midnight, to call the clergyman whom he thought the most proper to complete the conversion; at least such was his conduct with respect to his friend and relation Mr. Meiran.[40]

His works are equally fantastical. He speaks of religion in terms of the highest panegyric; nevertheless we have to guard against many an attack which he makes against it. In defending Christianity against Bayle, he tells us, that perfect Christians

> would be citizens infinitely more enlightened with respect to the various duties of life. That the more they believed themselves indebted to religion, the more they would think due to their country; that the Principles of Christianity deeply engrave on the heart should be infinitely more powerful than the false honour of Monarchies, than the human virtues of Republics, or the servile fear of Despotic States.[41]

And yet he lays aside that religion, and continues to make this false honour and these human virtues the prime movers of Monarchies and Republics! He represents the Christian religion as the most

---

40 *Ibid.*
41 Chap. 6, book XXIV.

consonant to Monarchy;[42] and he has said before, "There is no great share of probity or virtue necessary to support a Monarchical Government—That in well regulated Monarchies, they are almost all good subjects, and very few good men—That in a Monarchy it is extremely difficult for the people to be virtuous,"[43] that is to say, that the Christian religion is the most consonant with Monarchies,—but that it is the most difficult for the people to follow under that government. He writes in the midst of a people then the most distinguished for its love to its Sovereign, and his whole system appears to be calculated for a nation enslaved under the severest Despotism, and of which Terror is the prime agent. Certainly, either the beloved Monarch is not a Despot, or fear is not the prime agent of Despotism. Might not all this be comprised under what d'Alembert calls *innocent artifices?* but another cause may be surmised.

Montesquieu declared in his last moments, that if he had hazarded any expressions in his works which could cast a doubt on his belief,

> it was owing to a taste for novelty and singularity; to a wish of passing for a transcendent genius soaring above prejudice and common maxims; to a desire of pleasing and of obtaining the plaudits of those men who directed the public opinion, and who were never more lavish of their praise than when one appeared to author-

---

42   Chap. 3, book XXIV.

43   Chap. 3, book XXIV.

ize them to throw off the yoke of all dependence and restraint.[44]

This avowal would lead us to infer, that there was a greater taste for novelty and singularity in his political systems than in his religious ideas. He always preserved a sufficiency of his religious education to respect Christianity, though not enough to guard against those political systems which might and really did gain him that applause which he so much sought for, I mean that of the modern Sophisters, who, with their new-fangled ideas of Equality and Liberty, thought themselves authorized to shake off the yoke of all dependance. I cannot believe that he conspired with them; but that he forwarded their plans is too certain. And such will be our opinion, till the before-mentioned letter can be authenticated.[45] He did not conspire by setting up his systems, but his systems formed conspirators. He created a school, and in that school systems were formed, which, improving on his, rendered the latter more fatal.

---

44 See *Historical Dictionary.*

45 It is certainly a most extraordinary coincidence, that while our Author, though obliged to state the revolutionary principles laid down in Montesquieu's works, does all he can to exculpate him from any evil intention, Bertrand Barère, the sanguinary Reporter of the successive Committees of General Safety which have butchered France, and who was himself at length

involved in the downfal of Robespierre, after having been his agent during his whole reign of terror, should have been writing precisely at the same time a long declamatory pamphlet under the title of *Montesquieu peint par lui-même*, claiming the honours of the Pantheon for him, as one of the Doctors of Democracy and a Progenitor of the French Revolution. He even declares his object to be no other than to form an Edition of Montesquieu for the use of Republicans. Could it be possible that men of Barrère's stamp were the persons whom d'Alembert meant to design when he said, "All that may appear obscure to common *readers is not so to those whom the author had particularly in view*; besides, a voluntary obscurity ceases to be obscure"?—Tr.

Jean-Jacques Rousseau's System.

owever cautiously Montesquieu may have expressed himself, the grand principle of all Democratic Revolutions was nevertheless laid down in his writings. He had taught in his school, "that in a free state, every man who is supposed a free agent ought *to be his own governor.*"[1] This axiom evidently implies, that no man nor any people can believe themselves free, unless they are their own legislators; and hence it was natural to conclude, that there hardly existed a nation on earth that had a right to believe itself free, or that

Consequences not observed, or passed over by Montesquieu.

---

1   Chap. 6, book XI.

had not some bonds to burst in order to extricate itself from slavery.

Scarcely could England even flatter itself with the real enjoyment of this liberty; and we see Montesquieu not venturing to assert it when he adds, "It is not my business to examine whether the English actually enjoy liberty or not. It is sufficient for my purpose to observe, that it is established by their laws, and I inquire no farther."[2] Though this may have satisfied the master, it might not be sufficient for all the disciples; and some one of them might answer, that according to his principle the English laws were far from granting that liberty inherent to a people governing itself.

It is evident, that to believe in their own freedom the English were obliged to deny this principle as too general, and certainly they were entitled to reply, "With us liberty consists in the right of freely doing all that the law does not forbid; and every Englishman, whether rich or poor, is equally free, whether he have the requisites for being an elector or not, whether he make the law by his direct vote, or by his deputies; or even if he does not in the least contribute toward it. For in all these cases he is certain of being judged by the same law. The Foreigner even is as free among us as ourselves, when he is willing to observe our laws, for he may do as freely as ourselves all that is not forbidden by the law."

If England could justly reproach Montesquieu with the generality of his principle, what must have

---

2   Chap. 7, book XI.

been the case with other nations, such as France, Spain, Germany, or Russia, where the people do not partake either by themselves or by their representatives, of the power of enacting laws? What was to be said of all those republics, either in Switzerland or Italy, where the three powers are united in the senate, where, to use Montesquieu's expression, the power being one, he thinks *he discovers and dreads at every step a despotic Prince?*

It was a necessary consequence, either that this principle must have been done away; or that all Europe, persuading itself that it groaned under slavery, would attempt, by a general Revolution in all Governments, to cast off the yoke. Some great genius must have arisen who, could have counteracted the fatal shock given by this illustrious author. But for the misfortune of Europe the very reverse came to pass.

Montesquieu was not only admired and extolled, as he deserved, in consideration of many parts of his *Spirit of Laws*; but he was more especially venerated for those passages in which, by means of his principles on Liberty, Equality, and Legislation, he aspersed the existing governments with the imputation of Slavery. The Sophisters easily overlooked his restrictions, *his protestations, his obscurities and his innocent artifices,* because they conceived it to be sufficient that he had opened the path, and shown how far it might lead.

The first who undertook to widen this path was Jean-Jacques Rousseau, that famous citizen of

Jean-Jacques following up Montesquieu's principle and more daring in his consequences.

87

Geneva, whom we have already seen so powerfully forwarding the conspiracy against the altar. He was in every shape the man of whom the Sophisters of rebellion stood in need to conduct them in their attack against the Throne. Born a citizen of a Republic, he imbibed with his milk, as he says himself, *the hatred of Kings*, as Voltaire had done that of Christ. He was better versed than Montesquieu in that dangerous talent of propagating error with the tone of importance, or of presenting paradox as the result of deep thought. He possessed, above all, that boldness which neither admits principles by halves, nor shrinks at their consequences. He surpassed his master, and in his political theories greatly outstripped him.

The Spirit of Laws appeared in the year 1748, and *The Social Contract* in 1752. Montesquieu had revived the ideas of Equality and Liberty; but Jean-Jacques construes them into supreme happiness. "If we examine," says he,

> in what the *supreme happiness of* ALL consists, which ought to be the grand object of every legislature, it will appear to center in these two points, LIBERTY AND EQUALITY. In Liberty, because all private dependence is so much strength subtracted from the body of the state; in *Equality*, because Liberty cannot subsist without it.[3]

Man everywhere in slavery according to Jean-Jacques.

Montesquieu had not dared to decide whether the English were free or not; and at the very time

---

3   *Social Contract*, chap. II, book II.

when he was passing the most severe criticism on other governments, he sheltered himself under the intention of not wishing to *vilify* or *debase* any one. Jean-Jacques was above such cautions; he begins his work by saying, *Man is born free, and yet we see him every where in chains.*[4]

Montesquieu had surmised, that to believe himself free it was necessary that *man should be his own governor*; that he should act according to his own laws, and according to his own will. But he judged the means of execution to be difficult in a small state, and impossible in a large one. Jean-Jacques would have believed that principle false had he found it impossible in practice. But he believed the principle, as laid down by Montesquieu to be true in theory; and to surpass his master he had only to demonstrate its possibility, and to facilitate its execution. This constitutes his favorite problem:

To find a form of association which

Object of Jean-Jacques system.

> will defend and protect with the whole aggregate force the person and property of each individual; and by which every person, while united with ALL, *shall obey only* HIMSELF, *and remain as free as before the union*; such is the fundamental problem, says Jean-Jacques, of which the Social Contract gives the solution.[5]

This was in other terms precisely seeking to realize Montesquieu's principle; to give to each man who

4   Chap. 1, book I.

5   Chap. 6, book I.

feels himself a free agent the means of being his own governor, and of living under no other laws than those which he has himself made.

His object erroneous. How a man, after having entered into the Social Contract, is to find himself as free as if he had never engaged in it, is not easily conceived; or, how a man who has subjected himself to the will of the majority can be as free as when his actions were to be directed solely by his own will, is equally inconceivable. This was precisely saying, that the object of civil society is to preserve that Liberty which is anterior to government, or of the state of nature; though the Social Contract, according to all received ideas, expressly imports the sacrifice of part of that Liberty to preserve the rest, and to obtain at that price peace and security to one's person, property, and families; in short, all the other advantages of civil society.

The solution of this problem became more difficult when Jean-Jacques asserted, that "it is evident, that the first wish and intention of the people must be, that the state should not perish."[6] According to their second maxim, it was not essentially necessary to be one's own governor, or to act always according to one's own will, and to live under laws enacted by oneself; but to have good laws, whoever might have been the legislator, and to be governed so as to save the State.

I. Consequence. The people sole legislators. But contradictions could not thwart Jean-Jacques in his career. He wished to realize Mon-

---

6   Chap. 6, book IV.

tesquieu's principle. He sets off on the supposition, that every man, a free agent, is to be his own governor; that is to say, that every free people are to obey those laws solely which they have themselves enacted: and in future he never views the law in any other light than *as the act of the general will*. Such a proposition immediatly annuls all laws which had ever been enacted by any King, Prince, or Emperor, without the participation of the multitude; nor does Jean-Jacques hesitate in saying,

> It is unnecessary to inquire to whom belongs the function of making laws, because the laws are but the acts of the general will. The legislative power belongs to the people, and can belong only to them. Whatever is ordered by any man of his own accord is not law. For the people, to be subjected to laws, must enjoy the right of making them.[7]

Such was the first principle which Jean-Jacques deduced from his master's distinction of the three powers. The second was not less flattering for the multitude. All Sovereignty, according to Jean-Jacques, resided in the power of Legislation. In giving this power to the people, he concluded *the people were Sovereign*; and so much so, that they had not the power *of submitting to another Sovereign*. All submission on the part of the people is represented in this new school as a violation of the very act by which every people exists; and to vio-

II.
The people sovereign.

---

7   Chap. 6, book II.

late this act was to annihilate their own existence; and as a further consequence he concludes, that all submission on the part of any people is null in itself, for this great reason, that *by nothing nothing can be performed.*[8]

Lest he should not be understood, we see Jean-Jacques frequently repeating both the principle and the consequences.

> The Sovereignty, he says, being no more than the exercise of the general will, can never alienate itself. If therefore a people promise unconditionally to obey, the act of making such a promise dissolves their existence, and they lose their quality of a people; for at the moment that there is a *master* there is no longer a Sovereign; and the body politic is destroyed of course.[9]

It was impossible to say in a clearer manner to all nations, Hitherto you have been governed by Kings whom you looked upon as Sovereigns; if you wish to cease being slaves, begin by taking the Sovereignty to yourselves, that you may enact your own laws; and let your Kings, if you wish to keep them, be no more than servants, to obey your laws, and to see them observed by others.

III. The people infallible in their laws.

Montesquieu feared that a legislative people would not be sufficiently enlightened for the discussion of laws and affairs in general; but this fear had not made him relinquish the principle. Jean-

---

8   Chap. 7. Book I.

9   Chap 1. Book. II.

Jacques, insisting on the principle, could see nobody more proper than the people to carry both principle and consequence into practice. In this new system, the general will of the people was not only to frame the laws, but in the making of those laws it became infallible. For he says, "the general will is always right, and tends always to the public advantage. The people can never be bribed, yet they may be deceived."[10] But in whatever manner they may be deceived, this *Sovereign people, by its nature, must, while it exists, be every thing that it ought to be.*[11]

To compensate for the incapacity of the people in the framing of laws, Montesquieu proposed representatives, or men who should make the laws for them. Jean-Jacques would not allow these men to be representatives in any thing but in name: He contended, that Montesquieu, in causing deputies to be chosen, placed the people under attornies and barristers, that is to say, under men who were to plead their cause as a guardian does that of his ward. But neither attornies nor guardians could be looked upon as real representatives. That these men, whose judgment the people would be obliged to receive as law, might differ both in will and opinion from the people; in fine, it was giving absolute legislators to the people, and thereby divesting it of the legislative power. He further observes, that the will of the people could be no more represented by

IV.
Sole represent-ative.

10   Chap. 3. Book II.

11   Chap. 7, book I.

these deputies than that of a ward by his guardian. And he adds, in spite of his master,

> *The Sovereign*, (the people) *which is only a collective being, cannot be represented but by itself; the power may be transmitted, but not the will.* Besides, the Sovereign power may say, 'my will at present agrees with the will of such a man, or at least with what he declares to be his will;' but it cannot say, 'our wills shall likewise agree to-morrow,' as it would be absurd to think of binding the will for any time to come.[12]

V.
The people above the laws.

From these reasonings certain qualities and rights are inferred, which Montesquieu would not perhaps have refused to the Sovereign people, but which he had not dared to express. This Sovereign made the law; and, whatever might be the law made by the people, it could not be unjust, as no person can be unjust towards himself.

The Sovereign people make the laws, but no law can bind them. "For, continues Jean-Jacques, in every case the people are masters, to change even the best laws: for, if that body is disposed to injure itself, who has a right to prevent it?"[13]

VI.
Assemblies of the people.

In short, the great difficulty which Montesquieu found in free men being their own governors and legislators lay in the impossibility of holding, especially in great states, the assemblies of this legislative people. These inconveniences, or even impossi-

---

12   Chap 1. Book. II.

13   Chap. 12. Book II.

bilities, vanish before Jean-Jacques, because he felt that either the principle was to be abandoned, or the consequences to be followed up; and neither Parliaments nor States-General could suffice for him; he wished for real assemblies of the whole people.

> The Sovereign, having no other force but the legislative power, acts only by the laws; and the laws being only the authentic acts of the general will, the *Sovereign can never act but when the people are assembled.* Some will perhaps think, that the idea of the people assembling is a mere chimera: but, if it be so now, it was not so two thousand years ago; and I should be glad to know whether men have changed their nature? The limits of possibility, in moral things, are not so confined as many are apt to suppose them: it is our weakness, our vice, and our prejudice, that narrow the circle. The abject mind distrusts the very idea of a great soul; and vile slaves hearken with a sneer of contempt when we talk to them of Liberty.[14]

However confidently Jean-Jacques may have laid down this doctrine, still the examples which he adduces to corroborate it were far from demonstrating that these assemblies of the Sovereign had ever existed. The citizens, for instance, of Rome or Athens were perpetually flocking to the forum; but those citizens, especially the people of Rome, were not the Sovereign people and every where Sovereign. The Empire was immense, and the people in

Examples of a sovereign people false.

---

14   Chap. 12, book. III.

this immense Empire, so far from being Sovereign, were a people enslaved by a Despotic Metropolis, by an army *of four hundred thousand soldiers* called Citizens, always ready to burst forth from an entrenched camp called Rome, to crush any town or province which should dare to assert its own liberties. Athens followed the same conduct with respect to its colonies and allied towns.

These examples adduced by Jean-Jacques only showed what the French Revolution has, since, so well demonstrated: that when the inhabitants of an immense town, like Rome or Paris, take up their arms, they may style their Revolutions by the names of Equality and Liberty, but all the real distinction is, that in place of one King whom they may have banished or murdered, the inhabitants are transformed into four or five hundred thousand Despots and Tyrants over the Provinces, while they in their turn are tyrannized by their tribunes. Are not the ashes of Lyons, are not the unfortunate people of Rouen or Bourdeaux the unhappy examples that may be cited to show what fate awaited the miserable town that might attempt to shake off the yoke of the suburbs of Saint-Marceau, Saint-Antoine, or of the citizens of Paris? And has not that immense town paid its tribute to a Robespierre at one time, and at another to the five Kings?

At some times, however, Jean-Jacques was sensible of these inconveniences. But he would not on that account abandon his grand principle of the

Sovereignty of the people, nor even the general assemblies. He would, after Montesquieu's example, have recourse *to the virtue* of Republics or of the Sovereign people; but he would even reproach Montesquieu with a "frequent *want of precision* in not making the necesssary distinctions, and not perceiving, hat, the Sovereign authority being every where the same, the same principle must prevail in every well constituted state." Then he would add, "that there is no government so subject to civil wars and internal agitations, as the democratic or popular one;" (that is to say, as the state of which virtue is the basis) "because there is not one which has so strong and so continual a tendency to change its form, which can only be preserved by the vigilance and courage employed to maintain it."[15]

He even then confesses, that "if there were a nation of Gods, *they* might be governed by a Democracy; but so perfect a government will not agree with men."[16] Yet then, lest, after Montesquieu's example, he should be wanting in precision, he proscribes all great empires from the sweets of liberty; he would allow of none but small states,[17] of one town in each state; and capitals are in his plan particularly excluded.[18]

His doctrine on this point is precise enough, when he says, "no city, any more than a nation,

Jean-Jacques reproaches Montesquieu.

VII. Division of states.

15 Chap. 4, book III.

16 *Ibid.*

17 *Ibid.*

18 Chap. 13, book III.

can be lawfully subjected to another, because the essence of the body politic consists in the perfect union of obedience and liberty, and because the words *Subject* and *Sovereign* are the identical co-relatives whose meaning is united in the word *Citizen*."[19] That is to say in a plain style, that all the Sovereigns and Subjects of a given state are only the burgesses of the same town. That a *Citizen*, subject and sovereign of London, has no authority at Portsmouth or Plymouth, and the citizens, subjects and sovereigns of these latter or any other towns cannot be subject to a sovereign which inhabits another town. And Jean-Jacques continues,

> It is always wrong to unite many cities in one (that is to say in one empire); it would be absurd to speak of the abuses prevalent in great states, to those who would wish to form only small ones. But is it proper to consider, how sufficient strength can be communicated to small states, to defend them from the attacks of great ones? The reply here is, that they must follow the footsteps of the Grecian cities, which formerly resisted the power of the great King; and of Holland and Switzerland who more recently withstood the house of Austria.[20]

All which meant, that in this system of Liberty and Equality applied to the sovereign people it was necessary to subdivide the greater states into small

---

19   Chap. 13, book III.
20   *Ibid.*

federative democracies.

> In fine, if it be impossible to reduce a state within proper limits, (notwithstanding his admiration for Rome), there is still one measure to be adopted—that of not allowing a capital, or settled seat of government, but moving it in rotation to every city, and assembling the states of the country alternately in the same manner.[21]

Lest it should be objected to our Philosopher, that to form these litde democracies, would only be subdividing the larger states into so many lesser provinces, which would be for ever a prey *to civil war and intestine divisions*, and always *tending to change their form,* which he declares to be the lot of all democracies, he is pleased to grant existence to aristocracies. These, and particuarly "the Elective Aristocracy, which is the true one, are the best of all governments."[22] But whether Democracy, Aristocracy, or Monarchy be adopted, the people always remain sovereign; the general assemblies of the overeign are always requisite, and they were to be frequent, "and so ordered as to assemble of course at the stated period, without being formally convened, not leaving it in the power of any Prince or Magistrate to prevent the meeting *without openly declaring himself a violator* of the laws, and an enemy to the state."[23]

---

21 Chap. 13, book. III.

22 Chap. 5, book III.

23 Chap. 18, book III.

VIII.
Ques-
tions to
be made
at the as-
semblies
of the peo-
ple.

Jean-Jacques, more consequent than his master, follows up the principle he had borrowed from Montesquieu, and continues,

> at the opening of these assemblies, whose object is the maintenance of the social treaty, two questions should always be proposed, and never on any account omitted; and the suffrages should be taken separately on each—The first should be, Does it please the Sovereign (the people) to preserve the present form of government? And the second, Does it please the people to leave the administration with those who are at present charged with it?[24]

That is to say, to continue the Magistrate, the Prince, or the King, whom they had chosen.

These two questions in the system of the sovereignty of the people are only consequences of the great principle laid down by Montesquieu, *that every man feeling himself a free agent ought to be his own governor.* For this man, or people, feeling themselves free agents, might not chuse to be governed to-day after the same manner they were governed yesterday. If they were unwilling, how could they be free agents, when obliged to maintain that government and those chiefs which they had formerly chosen.

IX.
Kings only
provision-
al.

Such a consequence would have made any Philosopher less intrepid than Jean-Jacques abandon the principle. Without pretending to Philosophy,

---

24   Chap. 18, book III.

one might have told him, "that every people which foresaw the misfortunes that perpetual revolutions in their government exposed them to, might without vilifying or enslaving themselves, have chosen a Constitution and sworn to maintain it. They might have chosen Chiefs, Magistrates, or Kings, who were bound by oath to govern according to that Constitution: a compact which it would be no less criminal to violate, than the most sacred oath (and equally so to-morrow as to-day). If the people are supposed to sacrifice their Liberty by a compact of this nature, you will call every honest man by the degrading name of slave, who shall think himself bound by the promise he made yesterday, or the oath he took to live according to the laws of the state?" But such reasonings would have had little weight with Jean-Jacques. In his opinion, it was a great error to pretend, that a Constitution equally binding for the people and their chiefs was a compact between the people and the chiefs they had chosen; because, (says he) "it would be absurd and contradictory to suppose, that the Sovereign should give itself a superior; and that, to oblige itself to obey a master, would be to reinstate itself in the fullness of Liberty."[25]

Such was the consequence naturally flowing from the idea of the sovereignty of the people, of the people essentially sovereign, who to be free must be their own governors, and who must retain, notwithstanding all their oaths, the right of

---

25   Chap. 16, book III.

annulling to-day those very laws, which yesterday they swore to maintain. This conclusion, however strange it may appear, is nevertheless that in the application of which the Revolutionary Sophister particularly exults when he says, "when it happens therefore that the people establish an hereditary government, whether it be Monarchical in family, or Aristocratical in one order of Citizens, *it is not an engagement which they make*, but a provisional form given to Administration, until it shall please the Sovereign to order otherwise."[26] That is to say, until it shall please the people to expel their Senate, Parliament, or King.

Let not the reader be astonished at seeing me insist so much in these memoirs on the exposition of such a system. The application of the causes to the effects will be more evident when the Historian treats of the acts of the French Revolution. But should he wish to know more particularly, how much our Philosopher of Geneva influenced the warfare which the Revolution had kindled against every throne, let him examine how this Sophister applies his principles to Monarchies, and the lessons that he teaches to all nations respecting their Kings.

X.
Every
Monarchy
a real De-
mocracy.

Here again it was Montesquieu who had laid the ground-work, and Jean-Jacques raised the superstructure. He, walking in the footsteps of his master, admits the absolute necessity of separating the Legislative from the Executive Power, but, always

26   Chap. 18, book III.

more daring than Montesquieu, he scarcely leaves to Monarchy its very name.

> I therefore denominate every State a Republic which is regulated by laws, under whatever form of administration it may be; for then only the public interests governs, and the affairs of the public obtain a due regard.—*To be legitimate*, the government should not be confounded with the Sovereignty, but be considered as its administrator; and then the Monarchy itself would be a Republic.[27]

These last words seem to imply, that Jean-Jacques recognized at least the legitimacy of a King who would receive the law from the people, and who, acquiescing in their sovereignty, would submit to be a simple administrator, in a word their slave. For, according to this system, the only free man is he who makes the laws, and the only slave he who receives them. The people were to make the law, the King to receive it; the King therefore is only the slave of the sovereign people.

On such conditions Jean-Jacques consents to recognize a King in great empires; but he teaches the people at the same time, that it is owing to their own faults if a King be necessary in such a state. They would have learned to govern themselves without one if they had reflected, that *the greater the enlargement of the state, the more Liberty is*

XI.
To govern without Kings if possible.

---

27   Chap. 6, and Note to Book II.

diminished;[28] that their real interest would have been to occupy a space of ground a hundred times less extensive, in order to become a hundred times more free; that if it be difficult for a large state to be properly governed, it is still more so for it to be *well governed by one man.*

XII.
Kings
mere
Officers
which the
people
may de-
pose.

In fine, whatever states these may be, we are never to forget, according to this Philosopher, that the whole dignity of those men called KINGS *"is certainly no more than a commission,* under which, simply as officers of the sovereign power, they exercise in the name of the Sovereign the power delegated to them, and which may be limited, modified, or recalled at the will of the Sovereign."[29]

Even on these conditions, had Jean-Jacques succeeded according to his wishes, Kings, though reduced to mere Officers or Commissioners for the Sovereign people, would not have had a long existence. This wish is clearly expressed throughout the whole of his Chapter on Monarchy.[30] There he has heaped up every argument against Royalty, whether hereditary or elective; there, extolling the supposed virtues of the multitude, he beholds the throne invaded by Tyrants, or vicious, covetous and ambitious Despots. Nor did he fear to add, that if we were to understand by KING him who governs *only for the welfare of his subjects,* it

---

28   Chap. 1, book III.

29   *Ibid.*

30   Chap. 6, book III.

would be evident that *there had never existed one from the commencement of the world.*[31]

The direct consequences of this whole system evidently were, that every nation desirous of preserving its rights of Equality and Liberty, was in the first place to endeavour to govern itself without a King, and to adopt a Republican Constitution; that nations who judged a King necessary were cautiously to preserve all the rights of Sovereignty, and never to lose sight, in quality of Sovereigns, of their inherent right of deposing the King they had created, of shivering his scepter, and of overturning his throne, whenever, and as often as they pleased. Not one of these consequences startled the Philosopher of Geneva. He was obliged to admit them, lest it should be objected (as he had done against Montesquieu) that *he sometimes wanted precision!* and once more to leave the word a prey to slavery. Had it been objected, that it was precisely among those nations who carried their ideas of Equality, Liberty, and Sovereignty to the greatest lengths, that the greatest number of slaves were to be found, he would have contented himself with answering, "Such, it is true, was the situation of Sparta.—But as to you, people of the present day, you have no slaves, *but are yourselves enslaved.*—You purchase their Liberty at the expence of your own. Forbear then to exult in a presence which discovers, in my opinion, more of indolence than of humanity."[32]

XIII. All nations slaves at present.

---

31 Note to chap. 10, book III.
32 Chap. 15, book III.

It is evident that Rousseau, always more lively and more daring than his master, could not suppress any of the consequences which flowed from the principle laid down by Montesquieu. He brands every nation, even the English, with slavery, declaring them all to be slaves under their Kings.

His religion Deism.

To have surpassed his master in politics was not sufficient. Montesquieu is often lax, even insinuates error, and, notwithstanding all the eulogy he bestows on Christianity, appears sometimes to sacrifice the religious virtues to politics; yet he appeared too timid to his disciples. Jean-Jacques, more dogmatic, declares openly that he knows of no Religion *more destructive of the social spirit* than that of the Gospel; and he paints a true Christian as a being always ready to bend his neck under the yoke of a Cromwell or a Catiline.

Montesquieu had mentioned the *Catholic Religion* as particularly adapted to moderate Governments and Monarcy; *the Protestant Religion* as appropriate to Republics.[33] Jean-Jacques will neither allow of the Catholic nor of the Protestant Christian, and finishes his system with Bayle's famous paradox that Montesquieu had refuted. He conceived no Religion but Deism to be worthy a Sovereign, equal, and free people; and in order to undermine every throne, he banishes from the state every altar where the God of Christianity was adored.[34]

---

33   *Spirit of Laws*, chap. 5, book XXIV.

34   See *Social Contract*, chap. 8, book IV.

This conclusion alone raised Jean-Jacques far above Montesquieu in the eyes of the Sophisters. Time was to decide which of these two systems should bear away the palm of victory. Let the historian compare the effects of each, observing their nature and the successive progress of opinion. He will then be less surprized at beholding that school triumph which is regardless of the sanctity of the Altar and of the authority of the Throne.

.

CHAPTER IV.

Third Step of the Conspiracy.

The general Effect of the Systems of Montesquieu and Jean-Jacques.

Convention of the Sophisters.— The Coalition of their Plots against the Throne, with their Plots against the Altar.

I n comparing the two Systems that we have just exposed, it is easy to remark, that the respective authors of those Systems have been biassed in their application of the ideas of Liberty and Equality to polity by the different stations which they held in life. The first, born of that class in society that is distinguished by riches and honours, participated less of those ideas of Equality which confound every class of citizens. Notwithstanding his great admiration for ancient Republics, he observes, that

Why Montesquieu aims at Aristocracy.

> In every state there are always persons distinguished by their birth, riches, or honours; but

109

were they to be confounded with the common people, and to have only the weight of a single vote like the rest, the common liberty would be their slavery, and they would have no interest in supporting it, as most of the popular resolutions would be against them.[1]

It was this system which was at an after-period to induce the Jacobin Club to style Montesquieu the *Father of Aristocracy*, and it appears that he was led to the adoption of this idea by the supposition that the class of citizens (the parliament) to which he belonged, would become legislators and thus, enjoying his distinctive mark of liberty, would be their own governors, and would never obey any but their own laws. The care he had taken not to generalize his ideas, excepting when treating of the island where he had learned to admire them, screened him from all censure, and removed any imputation of his wishing to overturn the constitution of his country, in order to introduce that of another. But such a precaution did not repress that desire which he had kindled in the breasts of many of his readers, a desire of seeing that constitution, which he so much extolled, established in their own country, a desire also of the only laws congenial to liberty, those of a country where each person is his own governor.

The French at that period, little accustomed to political discussions, rather enjoyed the advantage

Why his system is extolled, and by whom.

---

1   *Spirit of Laws*, chap. 6, book XI.

of their government under the laws of their Monarch, than cavilled at his authority. They were free under their laws, nor did they lose their time in disquisitions on the possibility of being so, though they had not participted in the making of them. The novelty of the subject irritated the curiosity of a nation with whom the bare title of *Spirit of Laws* was sufficient to captivate their suffrages. Besides, it contained an immense fund of learning; and in spite of many witty reflections, even bordering on epigram, a strong feature of moderation and candour laid further claim to the public esteem. The English also admired it.—Notwithstanding Montesquieu's reserves, it was but natural for them to extol so great a genius, whose chief error lay in having believed that their laws and their constitution were sufficient to impart Liberty to all nations, whatever might be their moral or political position on the globe.

The esteem in which a nation, perhaps at that time its most worthy rival, had always held Great Britain, added much to the high repute of the *Spirit of Laws*. It was translated into several languages; and it would have been a disgrace for a Frenchman not to have been acquainted with it. I hope the expression I am going to make use of will be forgiven; that poison, that true source of the most democratic of all revolutions, infused itself without being perceived. The ground-work is entirely comprized in the principle, that *Every man who is supposed a free agent ought to be his own gover-*

nor, which is absolutely synonimous with another, viz., *"it is in the body of the people that the legislative power resides."* Those members of the aristocracy who admired Montesquieu, had not sufficiently weighed the consequences of this grand axiom. They did not perceive that the Sophisters of rebellion would one day only change the terms, when they proclaimed that the law was but the *expression of the general will*, and hence conclude, that it is a right inherent in the people or multitude to enact or abrogate all laws; and that should the people change and overturn every thing at pleasure, they would do no more than exercise a right.

He forwards democracy.

When Montesquieu passed over these consequences, or rather pretended not to see them; when, viewing the different Monarchies of Europe, he finds himself obliged to confess that he knew of no people, one excepted, who exercised the pretended right of governing themselves, and of making their own laws; when he adds, that the less they exercised that right, the more *the Monarchy degenerated towards Despotism*; when, declaring that Liberty was at an end wherever those powers which were generally concentrated in the person of the Sovereign, were not distinct, he seems to console nations, by flattering them with a greater or smaller portion of Liberty, for which they were indebted to what he calls prejudices, to their love *of the Subject's, the State's, and the Prince's glory;*[2] in what cloud could he have enveloped himself?

2   Chap. 7, book XI.

After having laid down principles which stigmatize all nations as in a state of slavery, will he pretend to appease their minds by speaking of what little Liberty prejudice may have left them? Are not these some of the voluntary obscurities which d'Alembert styles innocent artifices? Or, are we to join with Jean-Jacques in accusing Montesquieu *of not being precise, and being often obscure?*

Be this as it may, such were Montesquieu's principles, that it was impossible to adopt them either in France or elsewhere, without inviting those weful revolutions which, snatching the most important branch of the Royal prerogative from the Monarch, invest the people with his spoils. After the *Spirit of Laws* only one thing was wanting to operate such a Revolution; and that was, a man who, sufficiently daring, would assert these consequences without fear, perhaps even complacently, because he beheld in them a means of annihilating all titles or distinctions, which decorate stations of life superior to his own. The son of a poor artizan, in a word Jean-Jacques Rousseau, bred in a watchmaker's shop, proved to be this daring man. He grasped the weapons which Montesquieu had forged to assert the privileges of the multitude, and ascertain the rights of legislation and sovereignty in the poor workman as the former had in the rich man; in the commoner as in the nobleman. The whole aristocracy of Montesquieu was no more than a scaffolding for the Sophisters of rebellion; and if he ever uses the word *Aristocracy* as expressing the best government, it was only in its original signification; he does not understand by it the government of the wealthy and noble classes, but that of the *best* of each, whether rich or poor, who were to be chosen magistrates by the people; and then in the very aristocracy he constitutes the people Legislators and Sovereigns.

Montesquieu believed the Nobility to be necessary intermediates between the King and the People. Jean-Jacques detested these intermediate bodies, and thought it absurd that a sovereign people should stand in need of them. Montesquieu parcels out the authority of Kings, to adorn the aristocracy of riches and nobility with one of its fairest branches. Jean-Jacques, pennyless, shivers the scepter of his King, and proscribes the prerogative of nobility or wealth, and to assimilate himself to the Peer or Nobleman he invests the Sovereignty in the multitude. Both forboded Revolutions; both taught nations that they laboured under the yoke of slavery, whatever may have been their protestations to the contrary; both led nations to believe, that the liberty of the subject could never be ascertained until they had adopted new Constitutions and new Laws, and had chosen chiefs, who, more dependent on the people, would ensure the liberty of the subject at the expence of their own.

Both, in giving their ideas upon Liberty, instructed nations in what they ought to do to acquire this supposed Liberty. Public opinion, like the two systems, was to be restrained within cer-

Comparison and natural effects of the two systems.

tain limits with Montesquieu, or expand itself to any lengths with Jean-Jacques, according to the strength, preponderance or multitude of disciples which interest might have enrolled under the banners of either of these modern politicians. Every reflecting person could already foresee, that all the rebels of aristocracy would follow Montesquieu as their chief, but that all the lower classes, and all the enemies of aristocracy, whether from hatred or jealousy, would fight under Jean-Jacques.

Such must have been the natural effect of these two systems according to the progress they made in the public opinion. This effect, it is true, might have been counteracted by opinions still predominant among many nations, whom these false ideas of Liberty had not misled so far as to make them believe they lived in slavery because they were governed by the laws of their Princes.

All these revolutionary principles must have been fruitless in nations whose religious tenets teach and ordain submission to their lawful Sovereign, in nations where the Gospel was followed and respected, a Gospel which equally proscribes injustice, arbitrary and tyrannic power in the Prince, and rebellion in the Subject, which, teaching the true worship of the King of Kings, does not instil pride into nations by stunning them with the repeated proclamation of their sovereignty.

But the Sophisters of Impiety had undermined the foundations of the religion of the Gospel, and numerous were their impious adepts. Many had been led to impiety by their ambition, and by the jealousy they had conceived against those who enjoyed distinctions or exercised power, and they soon perceived that by means of these two systems, the same ideas of Equality and Liberty, which had proved such powerful agents against Christianity, might prevail also against all political Governments.

The Sophisters conspire and adopt the system against Kings.

Till this period, the hatred which the school of Voltaire, or the brethren of d'Alembert, had conceived against Kings was vague and without any plan. In general, it was a mere thirst after Equality and Liberty, or a hatred of all coercive authority. But the necessity of a civil government stifled all their cries. Here they were convinced, that to destroy was not sufficient, and that in overturning the present laws, it was necessary to have another code to replace the former. Their writings teemed with epigrams against Kings, but they had not attacked their rights; Despotism and Tyranny were represented in the most fantastic light, though they had not yet decided that every Prince was a Despot or a Tyrant. But this was no longer the case when these two systems had appeared; Montesquieu taught them to govern themselves, and make their laws in conjunction with their Kings; and Jean-Jacques persuades them to expel all Kings, and to govern and make their laws themselves. The Sophisters no longer hesitate, and the overthrow of every throne is resolved on, as they had before resolved on the destruction of every altar. From that period the two conspiracies are combined and form but one in the school of the Sophisters. It is no longer the isolated voice of a Voltaire, or of any particular adept who, following the explosions of his brain, raises a sarcastic cry against the authority of Kings; it is the combined efforts of the Sophisters leagued in plots of rebellion and impiety, aiming all their hatred, their means, their wishes and their artifices, at teaching all nations to destroy the throne of their Kings, as they had formerly excited them to overturn the altars of their God.

Such an accusation is important, it is direct; and the proofs are taken from the words of the conspirators themselves. It is not only the simple avowal of the Conspiracy, but the exulting pride of the Sophister who glories in his crime. He paints the hypocrisy, the wickedness, the hideousness of his crime in as glowing colours as if he had delineated the triumph of genius and wisdom, in a word of true Philosphy, in the cause of the happiness of mankind. Let us attend, and we shall hear them tracing the history of their plots, which they represent as the climax of human understanding in Philosophical learning.

The French Revolution had hurled the unfortunate Louis XVI. from his throne, when the most unrelenting conspirator, that monster Condorcet, thinks it incumbent on him to celebrate the glory of Philosophism, and trace the progress of this fiend which had kindled the torch of discord and had reared the Republic on crime, bloodshed, and the

Proofs of the conspiracy.

ruins of the throne. Lest the school whence these horrid deeds had issued, should not be known, he describes it from its origin, and historifies all the monsters of iniquity and rebellion which each century had produced. He then descends to the new Republican æra. That history may carefully weigh his evidence and appreciate his avowal, his words shall suffer no alteration: without interruption from us he may extol his school and its pretended benefactions. He supposes us at the middle of this century, considers his reader as arrived at that period when the delirium of superstition is dispelled by the first rays of modern Philosophy. Then it is that he developes the following plot as the history and triumph of his false Philosophy.

Avowal of Con-dorcet.

There was a class of men which soon formed itself in Europe with a view not so much to discover and make deep research after truth as to diffuse it: whose chief object was to attack prejudices in the very asylums where the Clergy, the Schools, the Governments, and the ancient Corporations had received and protected them; and made their glory to consist rather in destroying popular error than in extending the limits of science: this, though an indirect method of forwarding its progress, was not on that account either less dangerous or less useful.

In England Collins and Bolingbroke, in France Bayle, Fontenelle, Voltaire, Montesquieu, and *the schools formed by these men*, combated in favour of truth. They alternately employed all the arms with which learning and Philosophy, with which wit and the talent of

writing could furnish reason. *Assuming every
tone, taking every shape*, from the ludicrous
to the pathetic, from the most learned and extensive compilation to the novel or the petty
pamphlet of the day, covering truth with a veil,
which, *sparing the eye that was too weak, in-
cited the reader by the pleasure of surmising it*,
insidiously caressing prejudice in order to strike
it with more certainty and effect; seldom menacing more than one at a time, and that only in
part; sometimes flattering the enemies of reason *by seeming to ask but for a half toleration
in Religon or a half Liberty in polity; respecting Despotism when they impugned religious
absurdities, and Religion when they attacked
tyranny; combating these two pests in their
very principles, though apparently inveighing against ridiculous and disgusting abuses;
striking at the root of those pestiferous trees,
whilst they appeared only to wish to lop the
straggling branches; at one time marking out
superstition, which covers despotism with its
impenetrable shield, to the friends of Liberty,
as the first victim which they are to immolate,
the first link to be cleft asunder; at another denouncing it to Despots as the real enemy of their
power*, and frightening them with its hypocritical plots and sanguinary rage; but indefatigable
when they claimed *the Independence of Reason
and the Liberty of the Press* as the right and
safeguard of mankind;—inveighing with enthusiastic energy against the crimes of Fanaticism
and Tyranny; reprobating every thing which
bore the character of oppression, harshness, or
barbarity, whether in Religion, Administration,
Morals or Laws; commanding Kings, Warriors,

Priests and magistrates in the name of nature to spare the blood of men; reproaching them in the most energetic strain with that which their policy or indifference prodigally lavished on the scaffold or in the field of battle; in fine, adopting *reason, toleration*, and humanity as their signal and watch-word.

Such was the Modern Philosophy, so much detested by those numerous classes whose existence were drawn from prejudices—Its chiefs had the art of escaping vengeance, though exposed to hatred; *of hiding themselves from persecution, though sufficiently conspicuous to lose nothing of their glory.*[3]

Result of this avowal.

Had rebellion, impiety, and revolt wished to trace their means and ascertain their object, could they have made a better choice than the pen of Condorcet to delineate the actors, describe their detestable plots, and fix the epoch of their double conspiracy, which, first aiming at the altar, is afterward directed and pursued with fury against all Kings and Rulers of nations? How could their means and plots have been rendered more manifest? How could the hero of the plot, or the adept most intimately initiated in the mysteries of the conspiracy, have more evidently pointed out the object, the double tendency of the Sophisticated school; or shown in a clearer light the wish of destroying the throne springing from the league which they had formed against the altar?

Let the historian seize on this avowal or rather on this eulogy of plots. He will find concentrat-

---

3   Chap. 7, book XI.

ed and flowing from Condorcet's pen, every thing that the most daring and the deepest initiated conspirator could have let fall, to characterize the most authenticated and most universal conspiracy, planned by those men called Philosophers, not only attacking the persons of particular Kings but of every King, and not Kings only, but the very essence of Royalty and all Monarchy. The commencement of this conspiracy was when Collins, Bolingbroke, Bayle, and other masters of Voltaire, together with that Sophister himself, had propagated their impious doctrines against the God of Christianity.

We see it fast rising into eminence when Montesquieu and Jean-Jacques, nearly his contemporary, applying their ideas of Equality and Liberty to Polity, had given birth to that disquiet spirit which sought to investigate the rights of Sovereigns, the extent of their authority, the pretended rights of the free man, and without which every subject is branded for a slave—and every King styled a Despot. In fine, it is that period when their systems, by means of empty theories, furnish the Sophisters with a means of supplying the want of Kings in the government of nations.

Until that period the sect seemed to have carried their views no further, than to the establishment of Philosophic Kings, or Kings at least who would let themselves be governed by Philosophers, but, despairing of success, they league in the oath of destroying all Royalty, the very isntant they shall have found in any system the means of governing without Kings.

The persons who compose this school of conspirators are strongly marked. They are the authors and adepts of this *Modern Philosophy*, who, before they resolved on the destruction of Monarchy, began by raising their heads against Religion; who, before they depicted every Government in the colours of Despotism and Tyranny, represent fanaticism and superstition as the sole growth of Christianity.

The extent, the means, the constancy of the conspiracy all are shown in the clearest light—Our conspiring Sophisters pretend to *ask but for a half-toleration in Religion or a half-Liberty in Polity; respecting* the authority of Kings *when they impugned Religion, and Religion when they attacked* Royalty. They pretend *to inveigh only against abuses*; but both Religion and the authority of Monarchs *are but two pestiferous trees*, at whose very *roots they strike*. They are the two giants whom they combat in their principles, that every vestige of their existence might be annihilated.

They assume every tone, they take every shape, and artfully flatter those whose power they wish to destroy. They spare no pains to deceive the Monarch whose throne they undermine. They *denounce* Religion *as the real enemy of their power*, and never cease reminding their adepts, that it is Religon which covers Kings with an *impenetrable shield: That it is the first victim to be immolated, the first link to be deft asunder*, in order to succeed in shaking off the yoke of Kings, and in annihilating Monarchy, when once they should have succeeded in crushing the God of that Religion.

The whole of this wicked game is combined among the adepts; their action, their union cannot be better delineated. Their watch-word is *Independence and Liberty*. They all have their secret, and during the most vigorous prosecution of their plots they *sedulously conceal them. They nevertheless pursue them with an indefatigable constancy*. What can be called conspiracy, if this is not conspiring against all Kings; and how could the Philosophers more clearly demonstrate, that the war which they waged against Christ and his Altar, against Kings and their Thrones, was a war of extermination?

I still fear its being objected, that the Philosophers did not mean to point at Royalty by the words *Despotism and Tyranny*. I have already said, that the Despots and Tyrants whom the Sophisters were to destroy could be no other than those Monarchs under and against whom they did conspire; and if the unfortunate Louis XVI. was a Tyrant and a Despot in their eyes, the mildest and the most moderate of Monarchs must have been guilty of Tyranny and Despotism. But let it not be thought that these conspiring Sophisters were always restrained by a sense of shame from casting aside the veil of Despotism and Tyranny with which they had shrowded the hatred they had conceived against Royalty. The same Condorcet who may be supposed (at the head of the Sophisticated bands) to have attacked only Tyranny and Despotism, leaves us no room to doubt.

Scarcely had the original rebels called Constitutionalists left the name or phantom of a Monarch to France in the unfortunate Louis XVI., so greatly had they abridged the regal authority; and most unjustly could that unfortunate Prince, in his degraded state at least, be accused of Despotism or Tyranny; nevertheless the designs of the Sophisters had not been fulfilled, and it is Condorcet who undertakes to shew the extent of their views. Royalty was still preserved as to the name, and Condorcet now no longer exclaimed, "Destroy the *Tyrant*, the *Despot*," but "*destroy the* KING." Speaking in the name of the Philosophic Sect, he proposes his problems on Royalty in the most direct language. He entitled them *Of the Republic*; and the first question he proposes is. *Whether a King is necessary for Liberty?* He answers it himself, and declares that Royalty is not only unnecessary and useless *but even contrary to Liberty*, that it is irreconcileable with Liberty; and after having solved this problem, he continues:

> As to the reasonings which may be brought against us, we will not do them the honour of refuting them; much less shall we trouble ourselves to answer that swarm of mercenary writers, who have such good reasons for believing that a Government cannot exist without a civil

list, and we will give them full liberty to treat
those persons as madmen who have the misfortune to think as the sages of every age and
nation have done before them.[4]

It is thus that, from the mouth of that Sophister,
who was the most deeply initiated of the adepts, we
learn, without the least subterfuge, the extent of
their plots; such were the wishes of his pretended
sages. It is not only Despotism but Royalty itself, it
is even the empty name of an imprisoned King, that
is incompatible with Liberty. What then is necessary to accomplish their last views with respect to
Kings as well as to the Priesthood? These views are
not confined to France alone, no, not even to Europe; but they extend to all nations, to the whole
globe, to every region on which the sun shines.
It is no longer a wish, it is a hope, it is the confidence of success, which makes the same Sophister,
adopting the prophetic strain, announce to Kings
and the Priesthood, that, thanks to the union, toils,
and unrelenting warfare of the Philosophers, "the
day will come when the sun shall shine on none
but free men, a day when man, recognizing no
other master than his reason, when Tyrants and
their Slaves, when Priests, together with their stu-
pid and hypocritical agents, will have no further
existence but in history or on the stage."[5] At length
the whole extent of their plots is revealed, and re-

---

4   *Of the Republic*, by Condorcet, an. 1791.

5   *Of the Republic*, by Condorcet, epoch 10.

vealed by that adept who was at the head of the Sophisticated school; by him, whom the original masters had judged to be the most proper person to succeed them and as most strongly fired with their spirit; by him, in fine, who proves to be their *greatest consolation* in their last moments, as they leave a chief to their school worthy of themselves.[6] That their conspiracy might be complete, the *Royal Authority and the Priesthood* were not to exist but in history or on the stage. In the former, as the subject of calumny and all the imprecations of the Sect; on the latter, as an object of public derision.

Evidence of many other adepts.

Condorcet is not, however, the only one of the Sophisters, who, exulting in the success of their double conspiracy, lay open its source and shew it springing from that concert and understanding of the Sophisters, uniting their means, their labours, and directing them at one time against the throne, at another against the altar, with a common wish of crushing both the one and the other. Condorcet is, without doubt, the Sophister who betrays the greatest vanity on the subject, because he is the adept who, scoffing at all shame and disclaiming every moral sentiment, would blush the least in describing those artifices which he so complacently relates; for it was he that could with the least embarrassment reconcile that atrocious dissimulation, those tortuous plans, those snares laid at once for Priests, Kings, and Nations, to the rules of honour, probity, and truth; while the

---

6   To d'Alembert, 27 March, 1773, vol. 69, let. 101, p. 170.

whole conduct of his school exhibits a concatenation of guilt and cunning, unworthy of the Philosopher, and becoming the odious conspirator only. Many other adepts speak their true sentiments, when they declare their belief that the publication of their proceedings can be no bar to the success of the conspiracy.

The Editors of the *Mercure*, La Harpe, Marmontel, and Champfort, had nearly been as explicit as Condorcet, when they published the following sentence, "It is the arm of the people that executes Revolutions, but it is the meditations of the sage that prepare them." These adepts, like Condorcet, represent our pretended sages as directing by silent and tortuous means, the minds of the people toward that Revolution which was to shiver the scepter of Louis XVI. and whose grand object was to break the pretended *yoke of the Priesthood* in order *to break that* of the pretended *Tyrants*, of Tyrants such as Louis XVI., the most humane and just of Kings, and whose fondest pursuit was the happiness of his subjects. Before Condorcet and our Sophisters of the *Mercure* many other adepts had shewn this concert and union, and had claimed the honour of this Revolution menacing every throne, as the glorious achievements of their school. Let us hearken to a man illustrious in the annals of Philosophism, and whom as such we may suppose well informed as to their plots.

Mr. de La Métherie is not one of the common class of adepts; on the contrary, he was one of

La Harpe and Marmontel.

La Métherie.

those who had the art of insinuating Atheism with all the seduction of natural science. So early as on the 1st of January 1790, this adept, who was deservedly looked upon as one of the most learned of the Sect, begins his observations and memoirs with these remarkable words: "At length the happy day is come when Philosophy triumphs over all its enemies. They are obliged to own, that it is the light which Philosophy has spread, more especially of late years, that has produced *the great events which will distinguish the end of this century.*" What are these great events which the learned Atheist claims in the name of Philosophy? They are those of a Revolution which discovers man *breaking the shackles of slavery,* and shaking off the yoke with which *audacious Despots* had burthened them. It is the people recovering their *inalienable right,* of making alone the laws, of deposing Princes, of changing or continuing them according to their will and pleasure, and of viewing their Sovereigns in no other light than as men who cannot infringe these popular laws *without being guilty of treason to the people.* Lest the principles on which these pretended rights were founded should be forgotten, he repeats them with enthusiastic eloquence; lest the glory of such lessons and their consequences should be attributed to any but the masters of his school, lest, in short, the intention and concert of its authors should not be sufficiently evident, he tells us, and that at the very moment when the unfortunate Lews XVI. is the sport of that legislative and Sovereign populace, "It is these truths repeated thousands and thousands of times by the Philosophers of humanity, that have operated those precious effects, so long expected;" he carefully adds, that if France is the first to burst the fetters of Despotism, it is beause the Philosophers had prepared them for such noble efforts *by a multitude of excellent writings.* And that we might be acquainted to what extent these successes prepared by Philosophy are to be carried by the concert of these lessons repeated *thousands and thousands of times,* the adept La Métherie continues, "The same lights are propagating throughout other nations, and soon they will cry out like the French, *we are determined to be free*—Let the brilliant success *which Philosophy has just gained* be a new spur to their courage—*Let us be persuaded that our labours will not be fruitless.*"

The foundation of this hope (and never let the historian lose sight of this obervation, since the Philosophers incessantly repeat it) rests on the prospect of an approaching Revolution in religious matters. It is because sects equally inimical to Royalty and Christianity are daily increasing in numbers and strength, particularly in *North America* and *Germany.* It is because the new tenets *are silently propagated,* and that all these sects unite their efforts with those of Philosophism.

He delineates the extent of their hopes, by declaring that Philosophy, after having conquered Liberty in America and France, will carry its conquests on the one side into Poland, on the other into Spain and Italy, and even into Turkey; nay, more, that it will penetrate into the most distant regions; and that Egypt, Syria, and India itself, shall be tributary to it.[7]

Were it necessary to seek further proof that this Revolution had been the work of the combined efforts, of the wishes and labors of our modern Sophisters, La Métherie will tell us, that he had clearly announced it to all Sovereigns when he said,

> Princes, do not deceive yourselves—TELL *raises the standard of Liberty, and he is followed by his fellow citizens.* The whole power of Philip II. could not prevail against Holland; and a chest of tea liberates America from the yoke of the English. In all energetic nations Liberty raises itself on the ruins of Despotism; but Joseph II. and Louis XVI. were far from thinking this warning regarded them. May Kings, Aristocrats, and Theocrats profit by this example!

Should they continue deaf to his voice, the same sage will shrug his shoulders, and, pitying, say, "These privileged persons are bad calculators of the course of the human mind and of the influence of Philosophy; and let them remember that their fall in France was accelerated by the neglect of such calculations."[8]

---

7   *Observations on Experimental Philosophy and Natural History,* January 1790. Preliminary Discourse.

8   Idem, January 1791, page 150.

Another Philosopher not less vain than La Méthérie, extolling and revealing the plans, intentions, and plots of the sect, with nearly as much perspicuity as Condorcet, is also acknowledged by it for one of its profoundest adepts. This is Gudin, who, adding his reveries to those of Jean-Jacques, makes the glory of his masters consist not only in the principles and the wish of the revolution, but in all they had done to bring it about, and which enabled them *to announce it as infallible.*

Gudin.

This adept Gudin goes much further; for he tells us, that it was not the intention of the Philosophers to operate this Revolution by the arm of the people, but by means of the King and his Ministers; that they had forewarned them that it was in vain for them to pretend to stop it. According to him,

> these same Philosophers who, under the ancient order of things, had told the King, his Council, and his Ministers, *that these changes would take place in spite of them, if they would not adopt them,* say at this present day to those who oppose the constitution, that it would be impossible to return to the old form of government, whichever might be the party that carried the day, it being too imperfect and too much discredited even by the enemies of the new constitution.[9]

These men therefore, whom we see to-day, under the name of Philosophers, so numerous and

---

9   *Supplement to the Social Contract,* chap. 2, Part III.

such zealous partizans of that Revolution which dethrones Kings; which invests the Sovereignty in the hands of the people, and executes systems the most directly opposite to the authority of Monarchs; these men, before they attempted to accomplish their plans by the arm of the people, had already revolutionized the public opinion to that degree, and were so certain of their success, that they boldly threatened both Kings and their Ministers, if they would not adopt their Revolutionary ideas, with the completion of that long wished for Revolution, in spite of all opposition.

It would be endless to quote the multitude of proofs which attest, that Philosophism only waited for the success of its plots, to glory in having contrived them. The historian will find those proofs in the numerous discourses pronounced by the adepts, either at the legislative club called National Assembly, or at the regulating club called the Jacobins; scarcely will he hear the name of Philosophers pronounced in these revolutionary dens, without the grateful acknowledgment of their being the authors of the Revolution.

I could adduce proofs of a different nature.— The adepts, for example, who many years before the Revolution entrusted with their secret those whom they wished to gain over to their party. I could name that Counsellor, that Sophister Bergier, whom Voltaire mentions as the most zealous adept.[10] I am acquainted with the person to whom

Bergier.

---

10   *Gen. Correspondence.*

this secret was entrusted five years before the Revolution, in the Park of Saint-Cloud, to whom Bergier without the least hesitation said, that the time was not distant when Philosophy would triumph over Kings and the Priesthood. That as to Kings, their Empire was at an end, and that the downfall of the grandees and nobility was equally certain. That the plans had been too well laid, and things were too far advanced, to leave room for any doubt of success. But the man who has since entrusted me with these secrets, though he gave them to me in writing, will not consent to have his name mentioned. He, like many others, at that time believed the dogmatic assertions of the Sophister, whom he knew to be one of the most profligate of the Sect, to be those of folly. And at present, like many others, not conceiving how much it imports to history that facts of this kind should be authenticated by witnesses of known veracity, he sacrifices that grand object to the delicacy of not betraying what appears to have been but a confidential communication.

Bound by such scrupulosities, I am obliged to pass over many such anecdotes, that would show the Sophisters entrusting the secrets of their plots, and foretelling as clearly as Bergier did the downfall of Kings and the triumph of Philosophy. I will consent even to suppress the name of a French nobleman who, resident in Normandy, received the following letter:

Alfonse Le Roi.

133

Monsieur le Comte, do not deceive yourself. This is not a sudden storm. The Revolution is made and consummated. It has been preparing for these last fifty years, and that by some of the greatest geniuses in Europe. It has its abettors in every cabinet. There will be no other Aristocracy but that of the mind, and you certainly will have a greater claim to that than any body else.

—This letter was written, a few days after the taking of the Bastille, by Alfonse Leroy, a physician. It needs no comment.

Testimony of the repenting Le Roi.

It is now time to call my reader's attention to that other Leroy whom we have mentioned in the first part of our Memoirs. He is not the vain Sophister glorying in his plots, not a Condorcet, a La Métherie, a Gudin, or an Alfonse, who exultingly behold the triumph of Philosphy in the crimes perpetrated and in the plots framed against the Altar and the Throne. No, this is the shame-faced and repenting adept, whom sorrow and remorse oblige to reveal a secret bursting from him in the agony of grief. But both the repentant and the proud adept perfectly agree in their evidence. For it would be a strange error to believe, that the declaration of Leroy and the object of his remorse were confined to the Antichristian Conspiracy. At the period when he made his declaration neither the constitution nor the oath of apostasy had been decreed. It had not as yet been proposed to plunder and profane the temples, and to abolish the public worship. No blow had been given to the symbol of Christianity. All was prepared and daily starting into existence; but as yet the assembly had only trespassed against the political authority and the rights of their Sovereign. It was at the sight of these first crimes that Leroy is reproached with the miserable effects of his school; and it was to this reproach he answered, *To whom do you say so? I know it but too well, and I shall die of grief and remorse.* When he disclosed all the heinousness of the plot framed by his secret academy at the Hôtel d'Holbach, when he declares that it was there that the Conspiracy, whose dire effects they then beheld, had been formed and carried on; the plots which he detests are those that he sees attacking the Throne. If he declares those at the same time which had been formed against the Altar, it is because they had been the forerunners of the above, because it was necessary to show that the hatred which the people had conceived for their King, arose from that which had been instilled into them against their God. Thus while the declaration of this unhappy adept authenticates the conspiracy of the Sophisters against Religion, it equally demonstrates that contrived against the Throne.

It would be in vain to object that this unhappy man loved his King; he calls all present to witness that he is attached to the person of Louis XVI.; how could he then join in a conspiracy against him? But it is in vain, all is consistent, all is combined in this mind racked with remorse. This unhappy Secretary of the Conspiring Academy might have loved the person of the Monarch, but detested Monarchy, detested it at least as it existed, and in the light in which his masters had taught him to consider it, that is to say, as irreconcilable with their principles of Equality, Liberty, and Sovereignty of the people. We shall see hereafter, that opinions differed very much in this secret academy. Some wished to have a King, or at least to preserve the appearance of one in the new projected order of things; others, and they were to carry the day, objected to the very name or any appearance of Royalty, and both parties were unanimous in their attacks against Royalty as then existing. The one wished for a Revolution partly combined of Montesquieu's system, partly of Jean-Jacques's. The other wished to establish it on the consequences which Jean-Jacques had deduced from Montesquieu's principles. But both were leagued in Rebellion, and both conspired to bring about a Revolution. The repenting adept wanted a half Revolution, nor did he believe that the people, when put in motion, would proceed to those excesses which he detested. He flattered himself that the Conspiring Philosophers who stirred up the populace would be able to direct its motions; that they would inspire this populace with a proper respect for the person and even for the dignity of a Prince whom he loved and respected as a Frenchman and a Courtier, while as a Sophister he dethroned him. This is all that his remorse and his protestations of attachment for the person of Louis XVI. can indicate. He wished to make him a King subservient to the views and systems of the Sophisters, and he reduced the unfortunate Monarch to be the object of the licentious outrages of the populace; such are the real causes of his grief and remorse.

But the more this remnant of affection for his King appears in his declaration, the more it corroborates his avowal. It is not without cause that a man accuses himself of having pierced the bosom of the person he loves, or of having been concerned in a conspiracy against a Monarch whose Throne he with regret beholds menaced with ruin. People do not accuse themselves of crimes which they detest. Let us weigh the declaration of the repenting adept. What has Condorcet, proud and vainly exulting in the Conspiracy of Philosophism against the Throne, told us, which the unhappy Leroy sinking under shame and remorse has not confirmed?

The haughty adept tells us, that of the disciples of Voltaire and Montesquieu, that is to say, of all the principal authors of that impiety and sophisticated polity of the age, a School or Sect was formed, uniting and combining their labors and their writings to effectuate the successive overthrow of the Religion of Christ and of the Thrones of Kings. The repentant adept shows us these same disciples of Voltaire, Montesquieu, and Jean-Jacques, uniting and coalescing under the fictitious name of Œconomists at the Hôtel d'Holbach; and he says it was there that the adepts dedicated their labors and

Their testimonies compared.

their lucubrations to the perversion of the public opinion on the sacred subjects of Religion and the Rights of the Throne. "Most of those works (his declaration says) which have appeared for a long time past against *Religion, Morality, and Government,* were ours, or those of Authors devoted to us. They were composed by the members or by the orders of the society."[11]—The unhappy Leroy not only says against religion and morality, but also against *Government*; and had he not said it, the one would be the natural consequence of the other; for the greatest part of the writings issued from this club of the Baron d'Holbach unite both objects. Soon we shall see them equally aiming at the overthrow of the Throne and of the Altar. They were the same Sophisters who had combined in one and the same plot the destruction of both.

The adept Condorcet complacently dwells on the art with which the coalesced Sophisters directed their attacks now at the Clergy then at Kings; covering truth with a veil which spared the eye that was too weak, artfully caressing religious opinions, to strike at them more surely, stirring up with still greater art Princes against the Priesthood, and the People against their Princes, fully resolved to overturn both the Altar of the Priest and the Throne of the Prince. Are not these the same stratagems which the repenting adept describes when he says,

---

11   See Part the 1st of these *Memoirs*, p. 343 [p. 321. —Ed.].

before these impious and seditious books were sent to the press, they were delivered in at our office. There we revised and corrected them, added to or curtailed them according as *circumstances* required. When our Philosophy was too glaring for the times, or for the object of the work, we brought it to a lower tint; and when we thought that we might be more daring than the Author, we spoke more openly.[12]

As to its object, its means, and its authors, we see the account of this double conspiracy perfectly coinciding, whether given by the haughty Condorcet or the repenting Leroy. Both demonstrate this school conspiring against their God and against their King, flattering themselves with success against Monarchy, and generating that Revolution which was to overturn their Thrones, but not till that period when the faith of nations, long before disordered, weakened, and at length misled by the snares of the Sophisters, threatened but a slight resistance to their attacks either against the Altar or the Throne.

The enthusiastic pride of Condorcet, and the shame and remorse of the penitent Leroy, certainly had never concerted this consistency in their depositions. The one, hardened in impiety and rebellion, preserves his secret till that period when he thinks he may violate it without endangering the success of his wicked pursuits. He enjoys at length, he glories in this success, and represents

---

12   See Part the 1st of these *Memoirs*, page 325 [p. 305. —Ed.].

his accomplices as men to be revered as the benefactors of mankind. The other, as it were to extenuate his crime, the very instant his eyes are open to
the heinousness of his past conduct, names those
who have seduced him, discloses the place where
they conspired, but to curse it; and throws all the
weight of his crimes on his perfidious masters, on
Voltaire, d'Alembert, Diderot, and their accomplices. He beholds these men who have seduced
him in no other light than as monsters of rebellion.
When such opposite passions, such different interests and sentiments agree in their depositions on
the same conspiracy, on the same means, and on
the same conspirators, truth can require no further
proofs; it is evidence, it is demonstration itself.

First steps of the Conspir-acy com-pared.
Such then is the first problem of that Revolution
so fatal to Monarchy. Voltaire forwards it with all
his might in conspiring against his God, in spreading his doctrine of modern liberty, and in artfully
attacking with his sarcastic wit and satire the pretended despots of his own country and of Europe.
Montesquieu traced in his systems the first steps
toward that disorganizing liberty. Jean-Jacques
adopts Montesquieu's principles and enlarges on
their consequences. From the Equality of the *legislative* people, he deduces the Equality and Liberty
of the *sovereign* people; from the people essentially free and exercising the right of deposing their
Kings at pleasure, he teaches the people to govern without them. The disciples of Voltaire, Montesquieu, and Jean-Jacques, united and coalesced

in their secret academy, league also in their oaths; and of those oaths that of crushing Christ and of annihilating Kings form but one. Had the proofs of these plots been supported neither by the boasting of the haughty Sophister exulting in success, nor by the declaration of the penitent adept ready to expire at the sight of such successes, still what we have to unfold of this mazy coalition, would equally demonstrate both its existence and its object from the publicity of the means employed by the Sect.

CHAPTER V.

Fourth Step of the Conspiracy against Kings.

Inundation of Antimonarchical Books.

Fresh Proofs of the Conspiracy.

he very fact of the Conspiracy against Monarchy having been carried on by the same men and in the same secret academy where the Antichristian Conspiracy had been debated and conducted with such unrelenting fury, will induce the reader to suppose that many of the artifices employed against the Altar were equally directed against the Throne. The most fatal attack on Christianity, and on which the Sophisters had bestowed their chief attention, was that which they made with the greatest success to imbue the minds of the people with the spirit of insurrection and revolt. Nothing proves this with more certainty than

The authors identically the same in both conspiracies.

the care with which they combined their attacks against the Throne with those against the Altar, in that inundation of Antichristian writings which we have seen flowing like a torrent through every class of society. This second inundation of Antimonarchical writings, by which the Sophisters were in hopes of perverting that sentiment of confidence and respect, which the people had for their Sovereign, into hatred and contempt, was only a continuation of those means which they had employed against their God. These writings are issued from the same manufactory, composed by the same adepts, recommended and reviewed by the same chiefs, spread with the same profusion, hawked about from the town to the village by the same agents of Holbach's Club, sent free of cost to the country school-masters, that all classes of people from the highest to the most indigent might imbibe the venom of their Sophistry. As it is certain that these writings were the grand means of the Sophisters in their conspiracy against Christ, so it is equally certain, that these same productions, monstrous digests of the principles of impiety and of those of rebellion, are irrefragable proofs that these same Sophisters had combined the most impious of plots against their God with the most odious machinations against all Kings.

Why their attacks on the Throne are manifested so late.

One only difference is to be observed, that the first productions of the Secret Society were not so strongly tainted with the blast of rebellion. The grand attack against Monarchy was reserved until the sect should have reason to expect that their principles of impiety had prepared the multitude for their declamations against Royalty, as they had gradually swoln in those against the pretended superstitions of Christianity. Most of those violent declamations against Sovereigns are posterior not only to Montesquieu's and Rousseau's systems, but even to the year 1761, when we beheld Voltaire reproaching the Sophisters with seeing every thing topsy-turvy, because in some of their writings they trenched upon the Royal Prerogative.

The Philosophers of the Encyclopedia had only alluded very faintly, in their first edition of that incoherent compilation, to the principles of that Equality and Liberty which have been since so much extolled by the enemies of Royalty, though it was a cause of reproach to d'Alembert, that even in his preliminary discourse, *he sees but a barbarous right in the inequality of stations*; and though the Royalist or even the Subject of every state, of every Government, might have objected to the insertion in the Encyclopedia of that proposition which the Jacobins have since so often repeated, "that the subjection in which every man is born with respect to his father or to his Prince, has never been looked upon as a tie binding unless by his own consent."[1] In short, though the Encyclopedists were the first to enter the lists in defense of Montesquieu, yet the fear of alarming the public authorities make them

In the divers editions of the Encyclopedia.

---

1   See the *Philosophical Memoirs* of the Baron XX. chap. 2, on the Art. 'Government' of the Encyclopedia.

act with great circumspection during many years on this subject. It was necessary to wait for new editions. That of Iverdun was still too early; and it was in the edition of Geneva that these revolutionary principles first make their appearance. Lest they should escape the notice of the reader, Diderot had repeated and condensed the poison, had decked them with all the array of Sophistry in at least three different articles.[2] There neither Montesquieu, Jean-Jacques, nor all the admirers of the legislative and sovereign multitude, could have cavilled at a single link in this brilliant concatenation of Sophisms. This perhaps might have given rise to those fears which Voltaire expresses in his correspondence with d'Alembert, lest this edition should not obtain the free circulation which he wished for in France. These fears, however, were ill grounded, for it became the most common in use; but at that period, that is to say, in 1773, the Conspirators had begun the inundation of those Antimonarchical Writings from the secret academy, which the slightest examination will prove to have had no other tendency, as Leroy has since declared, than to overthrow religion, morals, and *government*, and particularly those governments where the chief power is invested in the Monarch.

Concert of the Sophisters against every government existing.

In order to show their concert on this last object as we have on the other two, let us suppress, if possible, the indignation which must naturally

---

2   See Edition of Geneva, Articles 'Droit de Gens', 'Epicuriens', 'Eclectiques'.

arise on reciting the lessons of the Sophisters. Let us say to all subjects of Monarchies, to all subjects of Aristocracies, and even of all Republicans not as yet jacobinized. 'If you tremble at the sight of revolutions which menace your government, learn at least to know the sect which prepares these revolutions by means of the principles which it artfully insinuates.'

All religions and all governments are equally doomed to destruction by the Sophisters. They wish to establish every where a new order of things both in church and state. We see them all, or nearly all, teaching us, that there scarcely exists a single state on the whole globe where the rights of the equal and sovereign people are not most intolerably infringed. If we are to believe their writings and assertions, almost literally repeated by a swarm of these Sophisters, "ignorance, fear, chance, folly, superstition, and the imprudent gratitude of nations, have every where directed the establishment as well as the reformation of governments." These have been the sole origin of all societies, and of all empires which have existed until the present day. Such is the assertion of *The Social System* which the secret academy published as a Continuation of the *Social Contract* of Jean-Jacques; such are the lessons taught in the *Essay on Prejudices*, which they gave to the public under the supposed name of Dumarsais; such again is the doctrine of the *Oriental Despotism* which they attributed to Boulanger; such in fine are the principles of the *Sys-*

tem of Nature, which Diderot, with the chosen of the elect, after having given it existence, so carefully seek to circulate.[3]

Jean-Jacques, teaching *that man is born free, and yet that he is every where in chains*, asks *how this happens*; and answers, that *he is ignorant*.[4] His disciples of the secret academy were become either more learned or more daring.

The most moderate of these Sophisters, or at least those who, under the standard of the Œconomist Du Quesnay, wished to appear so, did not give the people a more flattering account of the origin or of the present state of their governments. "It must be owned," they tell us by the insipid pen of Dupont,

> that the generality of nations still remain victims of an infinitude of crimes and calamities, which could not have happened if a well-conducted study on the law of nature, on moral justice, and on real and true politics, had enlightened the majority of intellects. Here prohibitions are extended even to thought; there nations, misled by the ferocious love of conquest, sacrifice the stock of which they stand most in need for the cultivation of their lands, to these plans of usurpation. Men are torn from their half-inhabited deserts, and the scattered riches which had been sparingly sown are seized for the purpose of shedding the blood of neighbouring states,

---

3   See these works, particularly the *Social System*, chap. 2 and 3, vol. II.

4   Chap. I, book I. *Social Contract*.

and of multiplying elsewhere other deserts. On one side . . . . on the other . . . . Elsewhere . . . . Elsewhere . . . .

This fable picture is terminated by twenty or thirty lines of dots, leaving to the imagination of the reader to fill them up, or to tell us, as the gentle author will, *"Such is still the state of the world; such has always been the state of our Europe, and nearly of the whole globe."*[5]

The reader will remark, that the men who broach such doctrines on Governments, and wish to instil them into the people, take care to insert them in those works which are peculiarly devoted to the instruction of country farmers. He will also remark how exactly they follow the steps of their master Jean-Jacques. This latter, refusing to except England from the general sentence, that man was every where in chains, did not hesitate at saying,

Particularly against the English government.

> The people of England deceive themselves when they fancy they are free: they are so, in fact, only during the interval between a dissolution of one Parliament and the election of another; for, as soon as a new one is elected, *they are again in chains and lose all their virtue as a people.* And thus, by the use they make of their few moments of liberty, they deserve to lose it.[6]

---

5   *Éphémerides du citoyen*, vol. VII. Operations de L'Europe.

6   *Social Contract*, chap. 15, book III.

Reflecting adepts would have questioned Jean-Jacques to know how his equal and sovereign people could enjoy a greater degree of Liberty than the English, and how it came to pass that they were not as much enslaved every where else as they were in their assemblies, since it was only in these assemblies that the people *could exercise their sovereignty*; and in these assemblies even their sovereignty was null, their acts were illegitimte and void unless they *had been convoked by the proper Magistrate*; since on all other occasions the sole duty of this sovereign people was to obey?[7] But our passive adepts preferred viewing the English Government in the light of one that was to be cried down with the rest.

> Nations even that flatter themselves with being the best governed, such as England, for example, *have no further pleasure* but that of perpetually struggling against the Sovereign Power, and of rendering their natural imposts inadequate to the public expenditure.—Of seeing both their present and future revenues, the fortunes and mansions of their posterity, in short of half their island, sold and alienated by their representatives, &c.—England at this price, too dear by three fourths, forms a Republic, in which, luckily for her, *a couple of excellent laws* are to be found; but as to her constitution, notwithstanding all that Montesquieu has said to the contrary, it does not appear much to be envied.[8]

---

7   Chap. 12 and 13, book III.

8   Dupont on the Republic of Geneva, chap. IV.

Our respect for that nation forbids us to continue our citations from this declamatory work.— What we have already quoted will suffice to show how much the Sophisters wished by means of these scurrilous harangues to persuade all nations, that, since the sovereignty of the people was so strangely violated even in England, and if it was necessary for her to overthrow her constitution to re-establish the people in their rights, how much greater must be the necessity of a Revolution for all other nations, being their sole hope of breaking their chains.

This was only an indirect attack of the Sophisters against Kings, under whose Government most nations live. Nor must the reader expect to see Philosophism circumscribing its effects to render every throne odious, within the narrow sphere of commenting on the seditious parts of Montesquieu, Jean-Jacques, or Voltaire.

Hatred of the Sophisters against all Kings.

Montesquieu had represented prejudice as the prime mover of Monarchies. He had declared that it was very difficult for *a people to be virtuous* under that form of Government. Helvétius, sallying forth from his secret academy, and carrying these principles to greater lengths, exclaims, "The true Monarchy is no more than a constitution invented *to corrupt the morals of nations and to enslave them*; witness the Romans when they gave a King or a Despot to the Spartans and Britons."[9]

Helvétius and many others.

Jean-Jacques had taught nations, that if the *authority of Kings* came from God, it was by the same

---

9   *Of Man*, note to sect. 9, vol. II.

channel through which *sickness* and other public scourges came.[10]—Reynal follows him to inform us, that *"these kings are wild beasts who devour nations."*[11] A third Sophister presents himself who tells us, all *"your Kings are the first executioners of their subjects; and force and stupidity were the founders of their thrones."*[12]—Another tells us, "Kings are like Saturn in the heathen Mythology, who devours his own children," others again say, "the Monarchical form of Government, placing such great force in the hands of one man, must by its very nature tempt him to abuse his power; and by that means, placing himself above the laws, he will exercise *Tyranny and Despotism, which are the two greatest calamities that can befall a state."*[13] The most moderate of their declamations on Royalty supposes too great a distance between the Sovereign and the Subject for it ever to be looked upon as a wise Government;[14] and that if a King be absolutely necessary, we never should forget, that he only ought to be *the first Commissioner of the Nation.*[15]

But this necessity grieved the Sophisters to such a degree, that, to make their countrymen triumph

---

10   *Émile*, vol. IV. and Social Contract.

11   *Philosophical and Political History* &c. Book 19, vol. IV.

12   *System of Reason.*

13   See *Essay on Prejudice, the Oriental Despotism, and Social System*, chap. 2 and 3.

14   *Ibid.*

15   Helvétius, *On Man.*

over it, they incessantly repeat that France is under the yoke of *Despotism, whose peculiar property is to debase the mind and degrade the soul*; that their country even, governed by Kings, can find no remedy for its *misfortunes* but in falling a prey to a foreign enemy; that as long as they are swayed by the scepter of Kings, "they are *invincibly* and by the very *form of government brought down to brutal degradation*; and that it is in vain to diffuse light on *the French*, as it will only show them the misfortunes of Despotism without enabling them to withdraw from its oppression."

What they say to their countrymen they proclaim to all the nations of the earth. They have consecrated whole volumes to persuade them *that it is a pusillanimous fear alone that has created and still maintains Kings on their thrones.*[16] They proclaim to the English, the Spaniards, the Prussians, the Austrians, indiscriminately with the French, *that the people are as much slaves in Europe as they are in America; that the only advantage they enjoy over the Negroes is, that they may leave one chain to take another.* They proclaim that the *inequality of power* in any state whatever, and particularly the reunion of the supreme power in their chiefs, is *the height of folly*; that the spirit of Liberty and of Independence which cannot bear with a superior, much less with Kings and Sovereigns, *is the instinct of nature enlightened by reason.* They brandish that *parallel sword* which was to glide

Raynal.

---

16   See the *Oriental Despotism* in particular.

along the heads of Kings, and mow off those which *rose above the horizontal plane.*[17]

If nations, wise in experience, and despising the declamations of a seditious Philosophism, sought an asylum under the protection of a King, or if to crush anarchy they had extended the authority of the Monarch, it was then that one might behold the adepts exclaiming in their rage,

> at this humiliating sight (of a nation of the North, of Sweden, re-establishing the rights of its Monarch), who is there that does not ask himself, *what then is man?* What is that profound and original sense of dignity with which he is supposed to be endowed? Is he then born for independence or for slavery? What, then, is that silly flock, called a nation. Mean populace! silly flock! What, content to groan when you ought to roar? Cowardly, stupid populace! since this perpetual oppression gives you no energy— since you are millions, and, nevertheless, suffer a dozen of children (called Kings) armed with little sticks (called scepters) to lead you as they please; obey, but submit without importuning us with your complaints, and learn to be unhappy, if you don't know how to be free.[18]

Had every nation murdered its Sovereign at the time when Philosophism broached such doctrine, what would they have done more than practise

---

17 See *Philosophical and Political History*, by Raynal, &c. vol. Ill and IV *passim.*

18 *Ibid.*

the lessons of the Sophisters? When we see that it was the very leaders of the Sect who held such language, an Helvétius or a Boulanger, a Diderot or a Raynal; when we know that it was those very productions in which such sentiments were advanced that endeared them to the Sect, what can we suppose was the meaning of this concert, of this union of the most celebrated adepts? What could be their plans? Where did they aim their blows, if not at the Throne as well as the Altar? Was it not against them that their rage was constantly let loose? What other Revolution did they meditate, if not that which buries the altar and the throne beneath the ruins of the state?

I know what is incumbent on History to add with respect to some of these Sophisters, to Raynal, for example. I know that when this adept beheld the Revolution, he shuddered at the sight of its excesses, that he even shed tears; and that when he appeared at the bar of the new Legislators, he dared reproach them with having o'erstepped the limits which Philosophy had prescribed. But this apparition of Raynal at the bar, or rather this comic scene which had been vainly prepared by the humbled and jealous Revolutionists, in opposition to the Revolutionists triumphant in their successes, only furnishes us with a new proof of the plots of the Sophisters.—For it was in their name that Raynal dares address the new Legislators, saying, "That is not what we wished for; you have broken through the Revolutionary line which we had traced."[19] What can such language mean, and are we not authorized to answer the man who holds it, These rebels do not follow the line which you and your sages had traced for the Revolution! There was then a Revolution which you and your sages had meditated and planned. Are the plans of Revolutions against Kings carried on without the plots

---

19 Let the reader consult the discourse he pronounced at the bar of the National Assembly, and he will find that the whole drift of his speech turns on those two lines. I know that this Sophister at his retreat near Paris wept bitterly on the excesses of the Revolution, that he threw the fault principally on the French Calvinists, and cried out, "It is those wretches, I see it clearly, it is those men for whom I have done so much, that plunge us into all these horrid scenes." These words were related to me by an Attorney-General of the Parliament of Grenoble on the very day he had heard them, and a few days before the famous 10th of August, 1792. But what do such tears prove? Without doubt Raynal and his brotherhood did not wish for all those butcheries, the infamy of which he wishes to throw upon the Calvinists. But Rabaud de Saint-Étienne, Barnave, and the other Calvinists, whether deputies, actors, or leaders, were not the only men formed by his Philosophy. The masters wished for a Revolution after their fashion, but the disciples consummate it according to their own ideas. And by what right can those men who have formed the rebel, complain of the excesses, crimes, and atrocious deeds of his rebellion! Observe—We are told also, that in the end Raynal returned to his religion. He would be another great example to be added to La Harpe. If this be really the fact, if even those who have so greatly contributed to the Revolution by their impiety acknowledge that to return to that God they began by deserting, is the only means of expiating their crime, how culpable is it in those who, after having fallen a sacrifice to that Revolution, expose even in exile their impiety to public view! How unfortunate is it for them to be at once the victim of the Jacobin and the scandal of the Christian!

of rebellion? Could those Revolutions which you planned differ from those which your lessons on Equality and Liberty prognosticated! or, when you brand every nation which suffers itself to be governed by its lawful King, or which *contents itself with groaning when it ought to roar* against its Sovereign, with the appellation of *a silly flock of cowards?*—And when these nations begin to roar why should you complain? So far from having transgressed the bounds you had prescribed, our Legislative Jacobins have not yet attained the goal you had pointed out. The *parallel sword* has not yet glided over the heads of Kings; wait then till there shall not exist a single King upon earth; and even then, so far from having overshot your doctrines, Jacobinism will only have followed them to the very letter.

To such an answer, which Raynal so richly deserved, the National Assembly might have added, "Before you complain, begin by thanking us for the justice we have rendered you. One of our members,[20] friendly to Philosophers like you, has represented to us the injustice of Kings whom you had set at defiance, he has shown us in your person the sacred liberty of Philosophy oppressed by Despotism. At the very name of Philosopher, we discovered our master, the worthy rival of Voltaire, d'Alembert, Jean-Jacques, and of so many others, whose writings and concert hastened our successes. We have listened to the prayer of your friends,

---

20   The honour of Raynal's recall was attributed to Mr. Malouet.

we have restored you to Liberty under the eye of that very King, whom you taught us to revile; go and peacefully enjoy the advantages of friendship, and of the decrees of the national assembly, while it will continue to run the course which you have marked out."

Thus even the vain protestations of humiliated Philosophism, reduced to blush at the excesses naturally attendant on its doctrines, every thing in short concurs to demonstrate the existence of their Conspiracies.

But partial attacks of the adepts are not sufficient; the reader must behold them encouraging each other, pressing the execution of their plots, and the insurrection of the people against their Sovereigns. Let him hear the same Raynal convoking the adepts, and calling out to them,

> Sages of the earth, *Philosophers of* ALL NATIONS, make those mercenary slaves blush who are always ready to exterminate their fellow-citizens at the command of their masters. Make nature and humanity rise in their souls against such a perversion of the social laws. Learn that *liberty is the gift of God*, but *authority the invention of man*. Bare to the light *those mysteries which encompass the universe with chains and darkness*; and may the people, learning how much their credulity has been imposed upon, avenge the glory of the human species.[21]

---

21   *Ibid.*, vol. I.

The art and solicitude with which the Sophisters seek to preclude Kings from the succour they might one day have drawn from the fidelity of their troops, is worthy of attention. We see in these discourses by what means the French army first imbibed those principles which have been so often and so successfully employed by the revolutionists to restrain and damp their courage and their activity. We see how they succeeded in representing as rebels so many of their brethren, against whom humanity, nature, and the social laws, forbad them to turn their arms, though it were to defend the life and authority of their lawful Sovereign. We see these Sophisters, bearing down all opposition, and preparing a free course for all the fury of that horde of rebels or of pretended patriots, that they might brandish, without fear, the hatchet and the pike. The reader may observe them disposing the armies meanly to betray their Sovereigns under the pretence of fraternizing with rebels and assassins.

To these villanous precautions, which destroyed in the rebels the fear of the Royal forces, let us add the pains they took to rob Kings of what support religion and Heaven itself might have given them, that affectation of extinguishing all remorse in rebellion, and of pointing out the God who protects Kings as an object of detestation. How could it be possible for us to mistake the double tendency of doctrines at once dictated by the phrenzy of Rebellion and of Impiety!

Diderot's
doctrines
on Kings.

It is only in a numerous, fixed, and civilized state of society, that, wants daily multiplying, and interests differing, Governments have been obliged to have recourse to laws, public forms of worship, and uniform systems of religion. It is then that the governors of the people invoke that *fear of invisible powers, to restrain them, to render them docile, and to oblige them to live in peace.* It is thus that morality and policy form a part of the religious system. *Chiefs of nations,* often superstitious themselves, little acquainted with their own interests, or versed in sound morality, and blind to the real agents, believe they secure their own authority as well as the happiness and peace of society at large, by immerging their subjects in superstition, by threatening them with their invisible phantoms (of their divinity) and by treating them like children, who are quieted by means of fables and chimeras. Under the shadow of such surprizing inventions, and of which the chiefs themselves are often dupes, transmitting them from generation to generation. Sovereigns believe themselves excused from seeking any farther instruction. They neglect the laws, they enervate themselves in luxury, and are slaves to their caprices. They confide in the gods for the government of their people. They deliver over the instruction of their subjects to priests who are to render them very devout and submissive, and teach them from their earliest youth to tremble both before the visible and invisible gods.

It is thus that nations are kept in a perpetual awe by their governors, and are only restrained by vain chimeras. When the happiness of man shall become the object of real investigation, it will be with *the gods of heaven* that the reform must begin. *No good system of government can be founded on a despotic god; he will always make tyrants of his representatives.*

Is it possible to combine their attacks in a more villanous manner against the God of Heaven and the powers of the earth? Tyrants or Kings have invented a god, and this god and his priests support alone the authority of these Kings and Tyrants. This perfidious assertion is perpetually repeated throughout the famous System of Nature, and this is the work which the secret academy disseminates with the greatest profusion. But neither Diderot nor his associates will hesitate at going to much greater lengths, notwithstanding the height to which they had carried their hatred in this famous system. If we are to believe them, all the vices and crimes of Tyrants, the oppression and misfortunes of the People, all originate in the attributes of the justice of the God of the Gospel. That God of *vengeance*, so terrible to the wicked; that God, the remunerator, the consolation, and the hope of the just man, is in the eyes of the Sophister *no more than a chimerical and capricious being, solely useful to Kings and Priests.* It is because Priests are perpetually stunning both Kings and People with this God of *vengeance* and *remuneration* that Priests are wicked. Kings despotic and tyrannic, in short the people oppressed. It is on that account, we see that *Princes even the most abjectly super-*

stitious are no more than robbers; too proud to be humane, too great to be just; and who are inventing for their own use a particular code of perfidy, violence, and treachery. It is on this account, that nations, degraded by superstition, will suffer children, or Kings *made giddy with flattery, to govern them with an iron rod.* With this God of vengeance and remuneration, *these children, or foolish kings transformed into gods, are masters of the law. It lies in their breast to decide what is just or unjust.* With this God *their licentiousness has no bounds, because they are certain of impunity.—Accustomed to no other fear but that of God, they act as if they had nothing to fear.* This God of vengeance and remuneration is the cause *why history swarms with wicked and vicious potentates.*[22]

In transcribing these short extracts, we have abridged prolix chapters tending to infuse that hatred for God and kings into the minds of the people, which animated the leading adepts. Nobody could better express to what degree he was inflamed by it than Diderot himself. We have seen Voltaire, in a moment of phrenzy, wishing to see the last Jesuit strangled with the entrails of the last Jansenist. The same frantic rage had inspired Diderot with the same idea on Priests and Kings; and it was well known in Paris, that in his fits of rage he would exclaim, Ah! *when shall I see the last King strangled with the bowels of the last Priest!*[23]

---

22   *Ibid.* vol. II. chap. 8.

23   It is with regret that I recollect having been credibly informed,

The reader may be surprized at hearing that the *System of Nature* was not the most virulent production which the Club of Holbach had published to incite the people to rebellion and to persuade them to consider their Kings and Princes in no other light than as monsters to be crushed. The adept or adepts who had composed the *Social System* availed themselves of the impression Diderot's work had made. They are more reserved on Atheism, only to be more virulent against Kings. The object of this work is to persuade the people that they are the victims of a long state of warfare, which ended by throwing them under the yoke of Kings. But they were not to abandon all hope of breaking their chains, and even of loading their Kings with them, though they had been hitherto unsuccessful. There the imagination is worked upon, and the meanest subject is taught to say to his Sovereign,

Inflammatory doctrines of other adepts.

> We have proved the weakest, we have submitted to force; *but should we ever become the strongest, we would wrest that usurped power from you* whenever you exercised it for our unhappiness. It is only by your attention to our prosperity that you can make us forget the infamous titles by which you reign over us. *If we are not strong enough to shake off the yoke we*

---

that in the north of Ireland the disaffected part of the inhabitants frequently gave as a toast, May the guts of the last Bishop serve as a rope to strangle the last King. If this be true, the reader will not be at a loss to know whence they imbibed their principles.—Tr.

will only bear it with horror. You shall find an enemy in each of your slaves, and every instant you shall tremble on the thrones which you have unlawfully usurped.[24]

Such menaces will certainly be looked upon as the last stage of their conspiring fury. Nevertheless they found a higher tone; and, to teach nations to shudder at the very name of Monarchy, they roar like monsters.

Many years before the French Revolution their productions had teemed with every thing that a Pétion, a Condorcet, or a Marat could have invented in their frantic rage against Sovereigns to excite the populace to bring the head of the unfortunate Louis XVI. to the scaffold; since many years after having told us, *that truth and not politeness should be the chief object of man*, to practise this doctrine they address Kings, saying, *"Ye tigers, deified by other tigers, you expect to pass to immortality? Yes, answer they, but as objects of execration."*[25]

With the same excess of phrensy, commenting on the axiom,

Some lucky soldier was the first of Kings,

full of his Voltaire, like the Pythoness inspired by the devil, from the summit of his fiery tripod the same adept, addressing himself to all nations, tells them,

---

24 *Social System*, chap. I. vol. II.
25 *Ibid.* note.

Thousands of executioners crowned with laurel and wreaths of flowers, returning from their expeditions, carry about in triumph an *idol* which they call *King*, Emperor, Sovereign. They crown this idol and prostrate themselves before it, and then, at the sound of instruments, and of repeated, senseless and barbarous acclamations, they declare it in future to be the Sovereign Director of all the bloody scenes which are to take place in the realm, and to be the *first execution-er of the nation.*

Then, swelling his chest, foaming at the mouth, and with haggard eyes he makes the air resound with the following frightful declamation:

To the pretended masters of the earth, scourges of mankind, illustrious tyrants of your equals, *Kings, Princes, Monarchs, Chiefs, Sovereigns*, all you, in fine, who, raising yourselves on the throne, *and above your equals, have lost all ideas of equality*, equity, *sociability* and truth; in whom sociability and goodness, the beginnings of the most common virtues, have not even shown themselves, I cite you all at the tribunal of reason. If this miserable globe, silently moving through the etherial space, drags away with it millions of unhappy beings fixed to its surface, and fettered with the bonds of opinion; if this globe, I say, has been a prey to you, and if you still continue to devour this sad inheritance, it is not to the wisdom of your predecessors, nor to the virtues of the first inhabitants, that you are indebted for it; but *to stupidity, to fear, to barbarity, to perfidy, to superstition.*

Such are your titles. I am not the person who
pronounces against you; it is the oracle of ages,
it is the annals of history which depose against
you. Open them, they will assuredly furnish
you with better information, and the numerous
monuments of our miseries and of our errors
will be proofs which neither political pride nor
fanaticism can controvert.

Descend from your thrones, and, laying aside
both sceptre and crown, go and question the
lowest of your subjects; ask him what *he really
loves, and what he hates the most*: he will undoubtedly answer, that he really *loves but his
equals, and that he hates his masters.*[26]

It is thus that, assuming every tone from that of
the epigram, pamphlet, romance, system, or trag-
ic sentence, to the declamations of enthusiasm, or
the roaring of rage, Voltaire's and Montesquieu's
school, so well described by Condorcet, had succeeded in inundating all France and all Europe
with works naturally tending to efface from the
earth the very memory of a King.

Conse-
quences
of these
doctrines
and their
concert.

To place in their true light the intention and
the concert of the Sophisters, the Historian must
never lose sight of the den from whence these productions were issued, and of the art with which
and the men by whom they were spread from the
palace to the cottage: By the Secret Society of the
Hôtel d'Holbach, in Paris; by the numerous editions in the provincial towns; by the hawkers in
the country; by d'Alembert's office of instruction,

---

26 *Social System*, page 7 and 8.

and tutors, in wealthy families; and by the country school-masters in the villages, and among the workmen and day-labourers.[27] In their various attacks, let him remark the uniformity of their principles, of their sentiments, and of their hatred; and let him particularly remember, that the same authors who declaim most virulently against Kings, had already distinguished themselves by their hatred against religion. Should he hesitate at declaring the Sophisters of impiety to be also the Sophisters of rebellion; should the very evidence of the conspiracy lead him to doubt of its reality; in that case let us not refuse to solve even the doubts of the historian, and may the very objections be turned into fresh demonstrations!

I feel that it may be objected to me, that my proofs differ in their nature from those which I had chiefly drawn from the very correspondence of the Conspirators. In answer, it may be remarked, that if any cause of surprize existed, it would not be, that the letters of the Conspirators made public should contain nothing respecting the conspiracy against Kings; but it would be, on the contrary, that they had furnished us with so much evidence. We may be surprized at the assurance of the editors of those letters, who show us Voltaire conjuring d'Alembert not to betray his secret on Kings, who show us Voltaire panting after Republics; Voltaire bewailing the departure of those adepts who were expounding the new catechism of Republican Liberty in

New proofs drawn from the objections.

---

27   *See* vol. I, chap. XVI.

Paris itself; Voltaire praised by d'Alembert for the art he displays in combating Kings or pretended Despots, and in preparing Revolutions and their boisterous scenes; Voltaire, in fine, regretting that they were still too distant for him to flatter himself with living to see them. It is this same correspondence which points out d'Alembert furious at his hands being tied, and at not being able to deal the same blows on the pretended Despots as Voltaire did, but seconding him at least with his wishes in this rebellious warfare. When all these letters were made public by Condorcet and the other editors in 1785, Louis XVI. was still on the throne, and the Revolution at some distance. They had reason to fear the discovery of their plots; and it is easy to see, that many of the letters had been suppressed. Most certainly Condorcet, and the other adepts, must have had even then a strange confidence in their success, not to have suppressed many more. Besides, had these letters been entirely silent as to the Conspiracy against Kings, could even that silence invalidate the avowals of Condorcet, and of so many other adepts? The same artifices, the same calumnies, the same wishes against the Throne being combined with those against the Altar, in the productions of the Sect, could that silence weaken the evidence of the common plot for the destruction of both?

But if these plots were so visible, it will be said, are not the Magistrates to be blamed for their negligence and silence? How was it possible that these

Conspiracy denounced by the magistrates.

168

Conspirators could have escaped the severity of the laws? Here it would be sufficient to recall the favorite maxim of the Conspirators, *Strike, but hide your hand!* It would suffice, were we merely to repeat Condorcet's words when, after having exposed in the clearest terms the double conspiracy, the labors, and the concert of the Philosophers against the Altar and the Throne, he adds, that "the *Chiefs* of the Philosophers *always had the art of escaping vengeance, though they exposed themselves to hatred; and of escaping persecution, though sufficiently conspicuous to suffer no diminution of their glory,*"[28] But this silence of the Magistracy is a false imputation. The Conspirators may have concealed themselves from the tribunals, but the Conspiracy was not on that account less evident to the sight of the Magistracy; and juridical denunciations will give new force to our demonstrations. If such proofs are necessary for the Historian, let us transcribe the words of a most celebrated magistrate; let us hearken to Mr. Séguier, Attorney-General of the Parliament of Paris, denouncing on the 18th of August 1770 this very Conspiracy of the Philosophers.

"Since the extirpation of heresies which have disturbed the peace of the church," said the eloquent Magistrate,

> we have seen a system rising out of darkness, far more dangerous in its consequences than those

---

28   Above, page 120.

ancient errors, always crushed as fast as they appeared. *An impious and daring sect has raised its head in the midst of us, and it has decorated its false wisdom with the name of Philosophy.* Under this authoritative title its disciples pretend to all knowledge. Its sectaries have taken upon themselves to be the instructors of mankind. *Liberty in thinking* is their cry, and this cry has resounded from the northern to the southern pole. *With one hand they have sought to shake the Throne, and with the other to overturn the Altar.* Their object is to abolish all belief, and to instill new ideas into the mind of man on *civil and religious institutions*; and this revolution may be said to have taken place; the proselytes of the sect have multiplied, and their maxims are spread far and wide. *Kingdoms have felt their ancient basis totter*, and nations, surprized to find their principles annihilated, have asked each other, by what strange fatality they became so different from themselves.

Those who by their talents should have enlightened their contemporaries, have become the leaders of these unbelievers; they have hoisted the banner of revolt, and have thought to add to their celebrity by this spirit of independence; numberless obscure scribblers, unable to attain to celebrity by their abilities, have had the same presumption. In fine, religion can number nearly as many declared enemies, as literature can boast of pretended Philosophers. *And Government should tremble* at tolerating in its bosom such an inflammatory Sect of unbelievers, whose sole object appears to be to *stir up the people to rebellion, under pretence of enlightening them.*[29]

---

29   *S*uit of 18 August, 1770.

The formal denunciation of the double Conspiracy of the Sophisters was grounded on the peculiar attention which they paid to the propagation of their impious and regicide principles in their daily productions, and more particularly in those which this great lawyer presented to the Court as most deserving of animadversion.

Foremost among those productions stood a work of Voltaire's, the honorary president of Holbach's club. It was one of the most impious of all, and bore the title of "*God and Men.*" The second, *Christianity Unveiled*, had been written by Damilaville, a zealous adept of that club. The third, the pretended *Critical Examination*, was published by this same club under the name of Fréret, as the repenting Secretary *Leroy* declared. The fourth was the famous *System of Nature* written by Diderot, and two others of this secret academy.—So true it is, that most of that pestilential blight both of Impiety and Rebellion which has overspread the greatest part of Europe, proceeded from that den of Conspirators.[30]

"From these different productions," continued the Magistrate,

> a system of the most flagitious doctrine may be collected, which invincibly proves, that their proposed object is not to destroy the Christian

---

30 There were also some few books translated from the English: But such only as are cast aside with abhorrence in England for their impiety; that, however, was the greatest of all recommendations with Voltaire and the club.

Religion only—Impiety has not limited its plan of innovation solely to its dominion over the minds of men. *Its restless and enterprizing genius, averse to all dependence, aspires at the overthrow of every political institution, and its wishes will only then be fulfilled when it shall have thrown the Legislative and Executive Powers into the hands of the People, when it shall have destroyed the necesssary inequality of ranks and stations, when it shall have reviled the Majesty of Kings, and have rendered the authority precarious and dependent on the caprice of a blind multitude; when, in fine, by these astonishing changes, it shall have immersed the whole world in the horrors of Anarchy with all its concomitant evils.*

To these denunciations of the public Magistrate may be added those of the general assemblies of the Clergy, those of a great many Bishops in their pastoral letters, those, in short, of the Sorbonne and of every religious orator or author, who never ceased refuting the Sophisters of the day, whether in their theses, their writings, or from the pulpit. It would be vain to say, that these denunciations were only made by people seeking to strengthen their own cause by confounding it with that of Kings. But are we not to hearken to an adversary even, when he speaks for us as well as for himself, and when he produces proofs? It would be imprudence in the extreme not to hearken, and even second him, when he comes and says, 'You are leagued with my greatest enemies, but they are equally yours; I forewarn you of their hostile intentions; and if they have conspired against me, it is only to ascertain the success of the plots they have formed against you.'[31] It would have been easy to discriminate, whether the Clergy denouncing these conspiracies were actuated by self-interest or the love of truth; a slight examination of the proofs adduced in testimony of their denunciations would have sufficed. These proofs were all drawn from the productions of the Sect, from productions replete with sarcastic declamations and calumny against Sovereigns, with invitations to the people to rebellion, sowing in the same page the seeds of Anarchy with those of Impiety. And these were evidently the two-fold productions of the same men, of the same academy of authors, of the same conspirators. Were not the Clergy then authorized to point out these same Sophisters as brandishing the torch, on one side to spread the blaze throughout the temple, on the other to kindle the flames which were to reduce the royal crown and sceptre to ashes?[32] Might they not be said to have conspired more desperately against the Throne than against the Altar; and might not the latter Conspiracy have been merely a preparatory step to the completion of the former? So far then from excluding the destruction of the Throne

---

31   See the acts of the Assemblies of the Clergy, 1770. The pastoral letters of Mr. de Beaumont, archbishop of Paris. The sermons of Père Neuville, the works of the Abbé Bergier and of many others.

32   The burning of the crown and sceptre, with the other attrib-

from their wishes, and confining them to the overthrow of religion, say that to overturn Government
was their chief object: examine and compare their
doctrines, behold their concert, their constancy,
their assurance, and then candidly pronounce.

But the evidence of the Clergy shall, if it be required, be thrown aside as suspicious, though it is
now too late to attaint it with falsehood. Will the
testimony of a man who certainly had every reason
to spare the Sect also be thrown aside? I have heard
it asked, How it was possible, since the Sophisters
were said to have conspired against the Throne,
that Frederick II., the Royal Sophister, could have
been deceived by and could have leagued during so long a time with the sworn enemies of his
Throne, in short with the Sophisters of Rebellion?
But such an objection will only serve to throw new
light on the Conspiracy. Let the Royal Sophister be
the accuser, let him cover his Sophistical Masters
with ridicule. The inveteracy of his hatred against
religion, his protection of the irreligious Encyclopedists, all his conduct in short, will corroborate
his testimony when he paints these Sophisters as
empty sages conspiring equally against the Altar
and the Throne. And the time came when Frederick II. perceived that his dear Philosophers, by
initiating him into their mysteries of Impiety, had
let him into but half their secret; that by employ-

Testimo-
ny of the
King of
Prussia.

---

utes of sovereignty, has been one of the favourite ceremonies
of the Revolutionary agents. In France the crown and sceptre,
at Venice and Genoa the chair and golden book were burnt.

ing his power to crush Christ, they had planned the destruction of his throne and the extirpation of Monarchy. Frederick was not the repenting adept, like the unhappy Leroy, for his soul was too deeply immersed in impiety; but he was certainly ashamed of having been so strangely duped. Indignation and revenge succeed his admiration, and he blushes at having been so intimate with men who had made him their tool to undermine that power which he was most jealous of preserving.

He became the public accuser of those very Encyclopedists who owed the greatest part of their success to his protection. He warned Kings, that the grand object of those Sophisters was to deliver them over to the multitude, and to teach nations *that subjects may exercise the right of deposing their Sovereign when they are displeased with him*.[33] He gives notice to the Kings of France, that their Conspiracy is more particularly aimed at them.

The denunciation is clearly and formally expressed in the following terms:

> *The Encyclopedists reform all Governments. France* (according to their plans) *is to form a great Republic, and a Mathematician is to be its Legislator.*—Mathematicians will govern it, and work all the operations *of the new Republic* by fluxions.—This Republic is to live in perpetual peace, and support itself without an army.

---

33 See *Refutation of the System of Nature*, by the King of Prussia.

This ironic and sarcastic style was by no means in Frederick's natural disposition. The repute of the pretended wisdom of the Sophisters had given weight to the adepts, and contributed to the seduction of the people; and contempt was the most powerful weapon that could be employed against them. It is on this account that he represents these pretended sages as puffed up with their own merits and their ridiculous pride. But whatever may be his style, it is to guard Kings and Nations against their plots that he writes,

> The Encyclopedists (says he) are a set of pretended Philosophers who have lately started into existence. They look upon themselves as superior to every school which antiquity has produced. *To the effrontery of the Cynic* they add the impudence of uttering every paradox their brain can invent. They are a set of *presumptuous* men, who never will own themselves to be in the wrong. According to their principles, the sage can never be mistaken, he is the only enlightened person: It is from him that the light emanates which is to dissipate the dreary darkness into which the silly and blind multitude have been deluded. And God knows how they enlighten them. At one time it is by unfolding the *origin of Prejudices*; at another, it is by a book *on the Mind*, or a *System of Nature*; in short, there is no end to them. A set of *puppies*, whether from fashion or an air they assume, call themselves their disciples. They affect to copy them, and take upon themselves to be the Deputy Governors of Mankind!

CHAPTER V

While painting in such colours the pretensions
and ridiculous pride of both Masters and Schol-
ars, Frederick declares that the *madhouse* would
be their most proper habitation, *where they might
legislate over their crazy equals*; or else, to show
the ignorance of their systems, and what innumer-
able disasters they would engender, he wishes

> that some province which deserved a *severe
> punishment* should be delivered over to them.
> Then they would learn, says he, by experience,
> after having thrown every thing topsy-turvy,
> that they were a set of ignorant fellows; they
> would learn that to criticize is easy, but that the
> art of criticism is difficult; and above all, that no
> one is so apt to *talk nonsense as he that med-
> dles with what he does not understand.*[34]

Frederick, in support of regal authority, would
sometimes lay aside his epigrammatic style, and
think it incumbent on him to condescend to the
refutation of the gross calumnies which his Sophistical Masters had invented against the Throne.
It is thus that we see him refuting the *System of
Nature* and the *Essay on Prejudice*, which latter
the secret academy had published under the name
of Dumarsais. There he principally devotes himself to exposing the cunning of the Sophisters; he
shows with what wicked art the Conspirators, calumniating the Sovereigns and the Pontiffs, only
seek to instigate the hatred of all nations against

34 See *Refutation of the System of Nature*, by the King of Prussia.

them. Among others we may distinguish the author of the *System of Nature*, who in an especial manner has undertaken to disparage all Sovereigns. *"I can venture to assert,"* he says,

> that *the Clergy have never spoken to Princes all that nonsense* which the author pretends. If ever they may have represented Kings as the images of the Deity, it was doubtless only in an hyperbolical sense, to guard them by the comparison against any abuse of their authority, and to warn them to be just and beneficent, that they may imitate the general attributes given to the Deity by all nations. The author has dreamed, that treaties have been made between the Sovereign and the Ecclesiastic, in which Princes had agreed to honour and sanction the power of the Clergy provided the latter preached submission to the people. I will venture to affirm, that this is a shallow invention, and that nothing could be more ridiculous or void of foundation, than the supposition of such a fact.[35]

Though Frederick expresses himself thus on the Ecclesiastics, still the reader is not to suppose him more favourable to their cause. On the contrary, his Antichristian prejudices blind him to such a degree, that he does not so much blame the Sophisters for attacking Religion, as for having done it unskilfully; he even points out the weapons with which he wishes it had been assailed. But the more inveterate his hatred against Christianity,

---

35   See *Refutation of the System of Nature*, by the King of Prussia.

the more demonstrative are the proofs he alledges against those from whom he had imbibed it, and of their plots against the Throne. He pardons their attacks upon the Altar, he even supports their advances, but he defends the Throne. At length however he discovered and was convinced, that from the Conspiracy against the Altar the Sophisters passed to that against the Throne. It is this latter Conspiracy which he wishes to lay open; and it is with these latter plots that he charges the whole school in the person of Diderot, when he says,

> The true sentiments of the Author, on Governments, are only to be discovered toward the end of his work. It is there that he lays down as a principle that subjects ought to enjoy *the right of deposing their Sovereigns* when displeased with them. And it is *to effectuate this* that he is perpetually crying out against great armies, which would prove too powerful an obstacle to his designs. A person would be tempted to think, it was Fontaine's fable of the Wolf and the Shepherd that he was reading. If ever the visionary ideas of our Philosophers could be realized, it would *be necessary to new-mould every Government in Europe,* and even that would be a mere trifle. It would be necessary again, though perhaps impossible, that *subjects setting up as the judges* of their masters should be wise and equitable; that those who aspired to the crown should be free from ambition; and that neither intrigue, cabal, nor the spirit of independence, should prevail.[36]

---

36 See *Refutation of the System of Nature*, by the King of Prussia.

Nothing could have been more masterly applied in these observations than the comparison of the Wolf and the Shepherd. Frederick perfectly comprehended that the object of these declamatory repetitions of the Sect against the vain-glory of war, was not so much to instil the love of peace into the minds of the Sovereign, as to deprive him of the necessary forces to repress that rebellious spirit which Philosophism sought to infuse into the people. He overlooked all those common truths on the miseries of war, which the Sophisters described, as if solely capable of describing them; but when he clearly perceived their plots, the hatred he conceived for the Sect made him dedicate his talents to counteract the Philosophists in his own States, and to render them elsewhere as contemptible as he judged them dangerous.

It was then that he composed *those Dialogues of the Dead*, between Prince Eugene, the Duke of Marlborough and the Prince of Lichtenstein, in which he particularly developes the ignorance of the *Encyclopedists*; their absurd pretension of governing the universe after their own new-fangled doctrines; and, above all, their plan for abolishing the Monarchical form of Government, and of beginning by the subversion of the throne of Bourbon to transform France into a Republic.

At that period it was in vain for Voltaire or d'Alembert to solicit his protection for any of the adepts. Frederick would answer in *a dry and laconic style*, 'Let the scribblers of the sect go and seek a refuge in Holland, *where they may follow the same trade with so many of their equals.*' His indignation and contempt was expressed in such strong terms, that d'Alembert often thought it necessary to soften the expressions in his correspondence with Voltaire.[37]

Then it was that d'Alembert perceived the *great mistake* which Philosophism had committed in reuniting the Civil and Ecclesiastical power against them. It was then that Diderot and his co-operators in *the System of Nature* were nothing more than a set of *blunderheads.* Then it was that Frederick lost his title of *Solomon of the North,* and d'Alembert depicts him as a *peevish man,* or as a sick person whom the Philosophers might accost as Chatillon does Nérestan:

> My Lord, if thus it is, your favour's vain.

"Besides, he says, Mr. Delisle (the adept who was recommended and so ill received) might not have been happy in the place we wished to procure for him (to attend on the King of Prussia). *You know as well as I do what a master he would have had to do with.*[38]" As to Voltaire, who was equally in disgrace, he consoles himself by writing to d'Alembert, "What can we do, my dear friend, we must take Kings as they are, and God too.[39]

---

37 From d'Alembert, 27 Dec. 1777, vol. 69, let. 188, p. 309.

38 *Ibid.*

39 To d'Alembert, 4 Jan. 1778, vol. 69, let. 189, p. 311.

It is worthy of remark, that neither d'Alembert nor Voltaire seek to deceive Frederick as to the double Conspiracy which he attributed to their school. Silence, it is to be supposed, was judged the most prudent; and it really was so for men sensible that Frederick might bring further proofs, which would only expose their plots in a clearer light, and that before they could exult in their completion.

However numerous the proofs may be that we have already adduced of the Conspiracy against the Throne, whatever evidence may result from the wishes and the secret correspondence of Voltaire and d'Alembert, whatever may be the combination of the Systems adopted by the Sect, on one side throwing the authority of the laws into the hands of the people to constitute the Monarch the Slave of the multitude; on the other erasing the very name of King from the governments of the earth; however incontestable the object of those writings, all, or nearly all, issued from the secret academy of the Sophisters, may be,[40] all breathing

---

40   After such a variety of proofs, and the declaration of the adept
      Leroy respecting the hiding-place of the Sophisters at the
      Hôtel d'Holbach, it would be useless for us to seek any fur-
      ther testimonies. Nevertheless, we think it incumbent on us
      to say, that since the publication of the first volume we have
      met with several people, who without being acquainted with
      all the particulars that we have given, knew the chief object
      of that meeting to have been the contriving and forwarding
      of the double conspiracy. I met with an English Gentleman in
      particular, who heard the academician Dusaux positively as-
      sert, that the major part of those books which have operated
      so great a change in the minds of the people with respect to

hatred to Kings and annihilation to the Throne as well as to the Altar; whatever may be the force which the declarations of the penitent adepts, or of the accomplices exulting in their successes, may add to our demonstrations; however authentic the evidence of the public tribunals may be, denouncing to the whole universe the Conspiracy of the Sophisters against Monarchy: In short, however aggravating the indignation and denunciations of the royal adept against his former masters of impiety (reduced as he is to tear off their mask, to preserve his own throne) may be for the conspiring Sophisters, still these are only the beginning of the proofs which the Historian may hereafter collect from our Memoirs. We still have many gradations of the conspiracy to investigate, and each step will add new force to our demonstrations.

Monarchy and Religion had been composed in that club of the Hôtel d'Holbach. And certainly the testimony of Mr. Dusaux, a man so intimately connected with the Sophistical Authors of the Revolution, is as much to be depended upon at least as that of the repentant or exulting adepts of the Sect.

CHAPTER VI.

Fifth Step of the Conspiracy against Kings.

The Democratic Essay at Geneva.

t the very time when Frederick II. was denouncing this impious Sect (which he had heretofore protected with so much tenderness) as inimical to all authorities, he was far from being acquainted with the real depth of their plans. It is chiefly to Voltaire that we see him complain of the temerity of those philosophers against whom he was obliged to defend his Throne;[1] and that at a time when Voltaire and the other Encyclopedian adepts, more particularly the Œconomists, were

---

1   From Frederick, 7 July, 1770, vol. 65, let. 173, p. 409, and Correspondence of Voltaire and d'Alembert, 1770.

Govern-
ment of
Geneva
before the
Revolu-
tion of
1770.

making the first essay that ever was made of the systems of the Sect.

Geneva, that town where none but a *few beggarly fellows* believed in Christianity,[2] had been chosen for this first essay. The democracy which Calvin had established in that Republic was not in unison with their new rights of man. They beheld the people subdivided into different classes. The first class was that of citizens or burgesses, and comprehended the descendants of the ancient Genevese, or those received into this class, and it was from among them alone, that the counsellors and other officers of the Republic were chosen. They particularly had their vote in the general council. Three other classes had been formed of those who were more recently annexed to the Republic, or who had never been incorporated into the class of citizens. These were the natives, the mere inhabitants of the town, and the subjects. All these could, under the protection of the Republic, with very few exceptions, follow their divers trades and professions, acquire and cultivate lands, &c. but were excluded from the councils and principal dignities of the Republic.

However odious such distinctions may have appeared to the Sophisters, nevertheless the man who appeals to sound judgment and real principles will easily agree, that a Republic, or any State enjoying Sovereignty, has a right to admit new inhabitants on certain conditions which may be

2   First Part, page 31.

just and oftentimes necessary, without establishing on that account a perfect equality between the real and the adoptive children of the State. He who asks to be admitted knows the conditions of his admission, and the exceptions he is exposed to. He was perfectly free to accept, to refuse, or to seek an asylum elsewhere; but certainly, having once accepted and admitted of these exceptions, he has no farther right to create disturbances in the Republic, on pretence that, all men being equal, the adoptive child is entitled to the same privileges as the ancient children of the State.

But such self-evident principles were not consonant with those of the Sect. Even Voltaire had laid them aside. From the perpetual repetition of his Equality and Liberty applied to religion, he had adopted the same doctrine with respect to politics. At the distance of six miles he had long since been observing the feuds which had arisen between the citizens and the magistrates, and thought that by working a political revolution there, he might add new laurels to those which he had gained by the religious revolution in which he so much gloried.

Hitherto these disputes between the magistrates and the citizens had been confined to the interpretation of certain laws, and of the constitution. The natives, and other classes who were excluded from the legislative power, were only spectators of the quarrel, when Voltaire and the other Sophisters judged this a favourable moment to change the very constitution of the Republic, and to make an

Parts acted by Voltaire and the other Sophisters.

essay of their new Systems of Equality and Liberty, of the Legislative and Sovereign people.

All Europe is acquainted with the troubles which agitated Geneva from the year 1770 till 1782. The public prints were filled with accounts of the disordered state into which the constitution of Geneva had been thrown; but the public prints have been entirely silent as to the part which the Sophisters took in it, and which it will be the particular object of our Memoirs to reveal. We shall lay open those intrigues and secret artifices, by which they hoped to establish an absolute Democracy according to the system of Jean-Jacques Rousseau.

To form a sound judgment on these occult dealings, let men be questioned who, present on the spot, were capable of observing, and who acted the part of real citizens. Such has been the plan that we have adopted, and such inquiries will attest the authenticity of the accounts which we have followed.

Most certainly the systems of Jean-Jacques, their countryman, first gave rise to the pretensions of the natives or inhabitants of Geneva to the legislative power. They were stimulated by the insinuations of Voltaire and of the other adepts who flocked to second him.

The part which Voltaire acted was, on one side to encourage the citizens in their disputes with the magistrates, whilst on the other he would insinuate to the natives and inhabitants that they had rights to assert against the citizens themselves. He would invite first one party, then the other to his table, and to each he broached the sentiments which he wished to instil into them. To the citizens he would urge, that their legislative power absolutely made the magistrates dependent on them; and he would persuade the natives or inhabitants, that living in the same Republic and subject to the same laws, the equality of nature assimilated their rights to those of citizens; that the time was come when they should cease to be slaves, or to obey laws which they had not made; that they were no longer to be victims of such odious distinctions, or subject to taxes disgraceful, inasmuch as they were levied without their having consented to them.

Such insinuations acquired new vigour from the numerous pamphlets flowing from the fertile pen of the Premier Chief. Under the name of a Genevese he published the *Republican Ideas*, which will always bear testimony of his hatred for Kings, and show how much ground Republican Liberty had gained in his heart as he advanced in years.

As to this hatred, he expresses it in the above pamphlet, by saying,

> There never yet has existed a perfect government, because men are prone to their passions—*The most tolerable, without doubt, is the Republican, because, under that form, men approach the nearest to the equality of nature.* Every father of a family should be master in his own house, but is to have no power over the house of his neighbour. Society being an aggregate of many houses, and of many lands belong-

ing to them, *it would be* a contradictory proposition to pretend that one man should have the
sole dominion over all those houses and lands;
*and it is natural, that each master should have
his vote for the general welfare of society.*[3]

This article alone was sufficient to incite the
Genevese to revolt, particularly the natives and
others who had acquired lands under the dominion of the Republic. He told them, that to deprive
them of the right of voting was to rob them of a
natural right inherent to them. But to express himself in still clearer terms, the true disciple of Montesquieu and Jean-Jacques, he repeats their fundamental tenets; he tells the Genevese, "that civil
government *is the will of* ALL, executed by *one or
many*, by virtue of *laws which* ALL *have enacted.*"[4]
With respect to finance, it is well known, that it is
the right of the citizens to regulate and determine
what is to be granted for the expences of the state.[5]

---

3   *Republican Ideas*, No. 43. Edit. of Kell.

4   *Ibid.* No. 13.

5   *Ibid.* No. 42. Many people cannot conceive that Voltaire could
    have fallen into such Democracy. Let them read his latter
    works with attention, and particularly those from which we
    have made the above extracts, and they will find that he is even
    violent against the distinction of *Noble* (he who holds land by
    knights services) and *Roturier* (who holds lands in soccage).
    He even declares the origin and real signification of these two
    words to be no other than Lord and Slave.
       Let them read his Commentary on the Spirit of Laws, and
    they will see in what a light he viewed that nobility, among
    whom he nevertheless numbered so many admirers, and to
    whom he was so much indebted for the propagation of his Phi-

It was not possible to tell all those, who lived under the Genevese dominion without having voted at the enacting of the laws, or at the imposition of the taxes, that they were bound by no tie under their present government, and that no government could exist for them until the ancient constitution was overthrown. Let the reader judge what an impression such writings must have made, profusely spread about, and distributed with that art which we have seen Voltaire describing, when he wished to infuse his venomous doctrines into the lowest classes of the people.

But means still more perfidious were made use of. The Sophisters have been seen extolling the

---

losphism. It is not hatred which makes him say in this Commentary, "I could wish that the author (Montesquieu), or any other writer possessing such abilities, had explained more clearly why the nobility are essential to the Monarchical form of government. One should rather be tempted to believe, that it was the essence of the Feudal System, as in Germany, or of Aristocracy as at Venice." (No. 111.)

To us it appears, that, whether young or old, Voltaire often confounds all his ideas. The idea of nobility, in general, represents to us the children of men distinguished by their services either civil or military, forming a body in the state whose sentiments and education, whose very interest, often fits them for those employments which are at the disposal of the Sovereign. Undoubtedly such a distinction may take place without the Feudal System of the Germans, or the Aristocracy of the Venetians. It is possible indeed to conceive a Monarchy without a body of nobility; but most certainly such a distinction greatly tends to form a body of men more attached to the Monarch, and very useful to the State in those stations for which the general education of the multitude can seldom be a suitable preparative.

generosity of their Premier; and, as a proof, they cite the multitude of Genevese artizans who taking refuge at Ferney found a new country and protection in Voltaire's little province, and partook sufficiently of his riches to continue their trades and support their families. But when we interrogate those who on the spot could observe the secret motives of such a perfidious generosity, we hear them answer, "Voltaire, it is true, has been in some sort the founder of Ferney, of a new town;" but they will add,

> how did he people it, if it was not with those factious citizens whom he had stirred up against their country, and which he reunites at Ferney and Versoi to form a focus of insurrection, which was to force the unhappy Republic, by the desertion of its natives and inhabitants, to receive the law from the Sophisters, and to substitute their systems to the ancient laws of the Republic?

Unsatisfied with all these means and intrigues, the levelling Sect had other agents who forwarded the revolution at Geneva. It had already acquired that Clavière, who was hereafter to continue his revolutionary career at Paris; it had acquired a sort of petty Sieyès in the person of Bérenger, and a true firebrand in Segère; but above all it gloried in seeing a French magistrate leaving his country, and laying aside the comely habit of the bench for the filthy round head of the Jacobin.

Mess. Servan and Bovier.

This was Mr. de Servan, that Attorney-General of Grenoble, whom Voltaire in his correspondence with d'Alembert represents as one of the *greatest proficients* in modern philosophy, and as one of those who had chiefly *forwarded its progress.*[6] It is remarkable, that this letter bears date the 5th of November 1770, the very year of the Genevese Revolution. Like a true apostle of Equality and Liberty, Mr. Servan had hurried away to Geneva to unite his efforts to those of Voltaire. But Philosophism had not confined its succours to his talents and reputation alone. An attorney of the name of Bovier, of the same parliament, powerfully aided it with his pen. He appeared with all the arms of Sophistry. Whilst the other adepts were stirring up, in their clubs and private companies, the citizen against the magistrate, and the native and inhabitant against the citizen, Bovier, to raise his constitution of Equality from the midst of discord and civil broils, pretends to assert the real rights of the ancient constitution, not to form a new one; and from antiquity alone he appears to draw all his arguments in favor of the Equality and Sovereignty of the People.

The most revolutionary among the Genevese were surprized to see a foreign Sophister informing them, that till then they had been ignorant of their own laws; that all those distinctions of citizens, inhabitants, or natives, and all the privileges of the first, were novelties which had been usurped and

---

6   To d'Alembert, 5 Nov. 1770, vol. 69, let. 46, Page 81.

introduced into the Republic so lately as the year 1707; that before that period a very short residence entitled every new comer "to the rights of citizen, and to be admitted into the general *sovereign and legislative council.* That afer one year's residence at Geneva, every man enjoyed his share of Sovereignty in the Republic; in short, that the most perfect equality had reigned among all the individuals of the State, whether of the town or country."[7]

This was nearly the same plan which the Sect followed at that time in France, always calling for the States-General in order to re-establish the pretended constitution of the Sovereign and Legislative people. Bovier was refuted in the most complete manner, but the Sophisters knew too well that a people in a state of revolution swallow every falsehood that favors their Sovereignty. They succeeded in putting them in motion, nor were they ignorant of the means of accelerating and perpetuating their vibrations.

Parts acted by the Œconomists and particularly by Dupont de Nemours.

At that time they published at Paris a periodical work under the title of *Ephémérides du Citoyen.* The Œconomists had the direction of it, and that class of adepts was perhaps the most dangerous. They, with all the appearance of moderation, with all the show of patriotic zeal, forwarded the revolution more efficaciously than the frantic rebels of Holbach's Club. The Sect had ordained that this journal should support the efforts of Voltaire,

---

7   See the memoirs of Bovier from page 15 to 29; and the refutation of the natives of Geneva.

Servan, and Bovier, until they had succeeded in their democratic essay on Geneva. It was the hypocritical and smooth-tongued Dupont de Nemours, who was entrusted with the care of giving monthly a new impetus to the Revolutionists. His periodical publications, carefully directed towards that object, were regularly sent from Paris to Geneva to second the fury of the Democratizing Zealots.

To form a proper judgment of the artful manner in which Dupont fulfilled his trust, it would be necessary to run over all the articles which the *Ephemerous Citizen* has given us under the head *of Geneva*. There we should see the humane citizen lamenting the troubles which had already shortened the lives of some natives, and had banished many others from their country; then, fired by that love of peace and humanity which consumes the philosophic breast, he insinuates exactly such remedies as may throw the whole Republic into a flame. He represents their constitution as that of the most oppressive *Aristocracy*. He assimilates the natives and inhabitants of Geneva to the *Helots* or the slaves of Greece, who, under the dominion of free citizens, have nothing but the most abject slavery to look up to in the very heart of a Republic.[8] Then for the instruction of the Genevese *Helots* he lays down what he calls principles, or rather lessons of rebellion; such, for example, as these given to a people in the most violent ferment.

---

8   *Ibid.* chap. I, and Note.

> To say that men can tacitly or formally consent for themselves or their descendants to the privation of the whole or part of their liberty, would be to say, that men have the right to stipulate against the rights of other men, to sell and cede what belongs to others, to alienate their happiness, and perhaps destroy their very lives:—and of what others? of those whose happiness and whose lives should be the most sacred to them,—of their posterity. Such a doctrine would be a libel on the dignity of human nature, and an insult to its Great Creator.[9]

This certainly was insulting both reason and society in the grossest terms; for if every man who subjects himself to the empire of civil laws does not sacrifice a part of his liberty, he is then as free to violate those laws, though living in society, as he would be were he living among the savages in the woods of America. But it was through pity and humanity that they fed this people, in open revolution, with the most frantic licentiousness. It was to spare the effusion of blood in Geneva that Dupont taught the multitude of natives, *inhabitants*, and *burgesses*, to say to the senators,

> Do you imagine the exercise of Sovereignty to be sufficient, as if the proper exercise of it were not an obligation? Do you know that when the people have once *recognized* your authority, you are imperatively and strictly obliged, under pain of the most deserved execration, to render

---

9   *Ibid.* chap. 2.

them happy, to protect their liberty, to guarantee and defend their rights of property to the utmost extent? Republicans, if you wish your fellow-citizens to exercise Sovereignty, remember that even Kings only enjoy their power on these terms.

Would you wish to be worse Sovereigns than the arbitrary Despots of Asia? And when even those who reign over nations buried in ignorance and fanaticism abuse their monstrous power to a certain excess . . . . They are called tyrants. Do you know what happens to them? Go to the gates of the seraglios of the East, *behold the people calling for the heads of the Visirs and Athemadoulets*; and sometimes striking off those of the Sultans and Sophis. Now reign arbitrarily if you dare. Yes, dare it in your town, where the people are far from being ignorant, and, brought up with you from your childhood, have had many occasions, setting aside your dignity, to know that you are no better than they.[10]

Thus we see that our moderate and humane Sophisters would not lose an occasion, any more than Raynal, or Holbach's Club, of teaching the people to roar rather than to groan, and to wade through carnage preceded by terror to the conquest of their pretended rights.

Such lessons were intermixed with those which the Œconomists pretended to give to Sovereigns on the administration of finances. "One saw them," say the memoirs of the man who followed their

---

10   *Ibid.* chap. 2.

operations with the greatest accuracy during the whole of this Revolution,—

> one saw them insinuating themselves into all affairs of the State, to seize every opportunity of infusing the doctrines of the Sect. Amidst their lessons on œconomy, that on the razing our fortifications is not to be forgotten; their pretence was the great expence and little utility of them. Geneva, they would say, cannot be considered as a state capable of defending a fortress should it be at war with any of the neighbouring States; and with respect to a surprize, it is the inhabitants of the country that are to prove its defence:[11] A most absurd proposition for a State about a league square. But that was not their object; they wished to establish the general principle, and to apply it hereafter to France, or any other State, when the opportunity should offer.

In other words, it was the means of exposing the Sovereign to all the fury of a revolted people reclaiming by force of arms that Equality and Liberty which the Sophisters were perpetually representing to them as their inherent rights. This also was the object of those perfidious lessons which they pretended to give to the magistrates, representing them as oppressors, and presupposing the existence of that hatred against them which the adepts themselves had infused into the minds of the people. With the same art they thus again addressed us, says our observer,

---

11   *Éphém. du citoyen*, 1771, vol. I.

The natural defenders of Geneva are the people of the country, the subjects of the Republic. It is possible, nay, it is easy, to attach them so much to the Republic, that they would form the most secure advanced posts possible. But it would be necessary that their country should be far otherwise than a *harsh, severe, and exacting master*, it wouild be necessary to restore them to the free exercise of the natural rights of man, and to guarantee their possession.[12]

The Sect reaped a twofold advantage from this journal. First, by spreading it through France, and preparing the multitude to hold at a future day a similar language to their Kings; secondly, to kindle anew the flame of discord at the beginning of every month among the unfortunate people of Geneva, for whom it appeared to be written. The brotherhood at Paris continued this work until Servan, and the other agents of the Sect, had seen their plots effectuate a Revolution in Geneva, and a total overthrow of the ancient laws of that Republic.

It is true, the Sophisters did not long enjoy their success, as Mr. de Vergennes, who at first

---

12 *Éphém. du citoyen*, page 176. I have sought in vain to learn what species of oppression the people of Geneva suffered under their magistrates; I have found that it was not possible for a people to be more fondly or more justly attached to their government; that the union between the magistrates and the subjects resembled that of a numerous family with its Chiefs. The Sophisters knew this too well; but they were not speaking for the Genevese alone. They pre-supposed discord, that they might create it where it did not exist, and add to it where it already began to spread.

had viewed this Revolution with indifference, soon learned its importance. Evidence at length convinced him that all that had come to pass at Geneva was nothing more than an essay which our modern Sophisters were making of their principles and systems; that neither their plans nor their plots were to be concluded by these first successes; that they were nothing more than a prelude to the revolutionary scenes with which they threatened all Europe, and which might ere long involve France itself in the common mass of ruin.

The Sophisters had the mortification to see these first fruits of their revolutionary principles blasted by a few battalions of French troops. It was reserved to Clavière, and afterwards to Robespierre, to resume their plans, and to send the apostate Soulavie to consummate them by murder and exile, in short by all the revolutionary means which Philosophism had invented in the Castle of Ferney for the future benefit of the Jacobinical den.[13]

---

13   The above Chapter, whether with respect to the general conduct of the Sophisters, or more particularly with respect to the conduct of Voltaire, Servan, or Dupont de Nemours, during the Revolution of Geneva, has been entirely formed by memoirs with which eye-witnesses have favored us, and on the writings of the Sophisters, which have been quoted with the greatest precision.

CHAPTER VII.

Aristocratic Essay in France.

I n laying before the reader the proofs of the Conspiracy formed against Monarchy we have said, that there existed a set of Philosophers who held themselves so secure of bringing about a Revolution, that they had not scrupled to advise both the King and his Ministers to make the Revolution themselves, lest Philosophy might not be sufficiently powerful to direct the motion when once imparted. Among this class of Philosophers, who wished to be styled the *Moderates*, but whom Jean-Jacques calls the *Inconsistents*, we are to distinguish Mr. de Mably, the brother of Condillac, and one of those Abbés who bore nothing of the Ecclesiastic but the dress, and who, bestowing great application on prophane sciences, was almost entirely ignorant of those necessary for an Ecclesiastic.

Without being impious like a Voltaire or a Condorcet, even though adverse to their impiety, his own tenets were extremely equivocal. At times his morality was so very disgusting, that it was necessary to suppose that his language was ambiguous, and that he had been misunderstood, lest one should be obliged to throw off all esteem for his character. At least such has been the defence I have heard him make to justify himself from the censures of the Sorbonne. He had the highest opinion of his own knowledge in politics, and during his whole life that was his favourite topic; he believed himself transcendant in that science, and he met with others who were led to the same belief. His *mediocre* talents would have been better appreciated, had he been viewed in the light of a man led away by the prejudices he had imbibed from a scanty knowledge of antiquity, and who wished to reduce every thing to the standard of his own ideas.

Mr. de Mably had also been led away by all those Systems of Liberty, of the Sovereignty and Legislative authority of the people, of the rights of self-taxation and of contributing to the public expences only in as much as they had voted the monies themselves or by their representatives.—He was persuaded that he had found these Systems of Government among the ancient Greeks and Romans, and more particularly among the ancient Gauls. He was perfectly persuaded, that without the States-General the French Monarchy could not exist; and that to re-establish the ancient and real Constitution, it was necessary to resume those States-General.[1]

Mably and his disciples, or more properly the adherents of Montesquieu, detested the feudal laws; but they did not reflect that it was to those very laws the States-General owed their former existence. When Philip le Bel and some other Princes had found themselves under the necessity of applying to those States for subsidies, the reason was, because under the feudal system the King, like the Counts of Provence, Champagne, and Thoulouse, or the Dukes of Brittany, had their fixed revenues and particular desmenes which were supposed to suffice for the exigencies of the state. And in fact wars of the longest duration could be carried on without its being necessary to augment the revenues of the Sovereign. Armies at that time were composed of the Lords and Knights serving at their own expence and defraying that of their vassals whom they led after them into the field. Neither Mably nor his disciples would reflect that at a period when France had acquired so many new Provinces, when the armies, general officers, and soldiers, waged war solely at the King's expence, it was impossible for the ancient crown lands to supply the wants of Government. They could not

---

1   See his *Rights of the Citizen.*

conceive, that in the new system of politics, it would have been the height of imprudence for the Monarch in France to be dependent (every time he found it necesssary to repel or anticipate an attack of the foreign enemy) on the great and jealous Lord, on the seditious tribune, or on the surly deputy, perhaps even in the interest of the enemy, for the necessary subsidies on so pressing an occasion. Such reflections as these never occured to the minds of our Sophisters.

At what period and why the call for the States-General.

Filled with the idea, that Revolution and the States-General were necesssary to break the chains of the French people, we are told by his strongest adherents, that Mably went still farther than merely inviting the Sovereign and his Ministers to commence the Revolution themselves:—

> He upbraided the people in his Treatise *On the Rights of Citizens*,[2] written *in the Year* 1771, with having missed the opportunity of making the Revolution; and he lays down the means of effecting it. He advised the Parliament in future to refuse to enregister any bursal edict, to declare to the King that he had no right to impose taxes on the people, who alone were vested with the fiscal power, *to ask pardon of the people* for having co-operated during so long a time in the levy of such unjust taxes, and to supplicate His Majesty to convoke the States-General. *A Revolution*, he adds, brought about by such means would be the more advantageous as it would be

---

2   Known in English as *Concerning the Rights and Duties of the Citizen.* —Ed.

founded on the love of order and of the laws and not on licentious liberty.[3]

This system of a Revolution to be accomplished, according to Montesquieu's ideas, by vesting the legislative and fiscal powers in the hands of the people, or of their representatives in the States-General, found many supporters and abettors, and particularly among the aristocracy, as the distinction of the three states was still preserved. All that class of men which impiety had enrolled under the banners of Sophistry from among the Duke de La Rochfoucault's society, viewed this as a means for the Grandees to reassume their ancient influence in the state, and to conquer from the King and Court, that power which they had gradually lost under the preceding reigns. They were ignorant that other Sophisters were already prepared to enforce their systems of Equality in those States-General, and to assert, that *the three estates being separate, of opposite interests, and jealous of each other, mutually destroyed each other's strength; and that to this distinction was to be attributed the inefficacy; and the very little good that had arisen from all the former States-General.* The Grandees did not perceive this snare which the levelling Sophisters had laid for them; the levellers had conceived the greatest expectations from the dissentions which reigned at that period between Louis XV. and the Parliaments, and believed themselves on the eve of

---

3   Gudin's *Supplement to the Social Contract*, 3d Part, chap. I.

obtaining the convocation of those States-General where they were to consummate their revolution.

These dissentions were principally owing to an opinion originating in Montesquieu's systems, which had crept into the first tribunals of the state. Such magistrates as, according to that system, believed Liberty to be entirely annulled in every state where the people or its representatives did not partake of the legislative and fiscal powers with the King, had construed their Parliaments into the representatives of the people, and pretended that the different Parliaments, though dispersed in different towns throughout the state, constituted but one and the same body, holding their powers directly from the people, whose perpetual representatives they pretended to be, whose rights they were to support against the encroachments of the crown, and exercising for them that inalienable and indefeasable right of making laws and voting subsidies; although they were resident magistrates and fixed in different towns by the King to administer justice in his name.

This was a system of Parliaments very widely different from the idea which the French Kings, who had created them without even taking the sense of the nation, had conceived of these Judiciary Courts. It was indeed extraordinary, that tribunals either ambulant or stationary, and which the King had created at their own will and pleasure, should belong to the very essence of the Constitution; that a body of Magistrates all named by the

King should pretend to be the free chosen representatives of the people, and a magistracy so much at the disposition of the Sovereigns, that they had sold the offices; could then these men pretend to assimilate themselves to representatives deputed by the people to the States-General.[4] The states themselves never viewed the Parliaments in any other light, which is easy to be seen by what the President Hénault says on the states held in 1614:

> On this occasion I must say, that as we recognize no other authority in France but that of the King, it is by his authority that laws are made. *As wills the King so wills the Law.* On that account the States-General can only remonstrate

---

4   The denomination of *Parlement* (Parliament) which had been given to the first Tribunals of the state, had greatly contributed to the illusion, which might have been easily avoided had the old term of *Plaid* (*court leet*) been preserved, which in the ancient history of France denotes sometimes those great assemblies which the King deliberated with on important questions respecting the state, at other times those ambulatory tribunals which administered justice. It was these latter only that our Kings had perpetuated under the name of Parliaments. The difference is the more evident, as those great Assemblies or States-General never meddled with the Judiciary Power, the exercise of which constituted the sole functions of the ambulant Magistracy. In those great Assemblies or National Plaids the Clergy was always admitted as the first order of the state; whereas by the very nature of its duties, it was excluded from the *Judiciary Plaids* (see the President Hainault, ann. 1137, 1319, & *passim*); how then was it possible to confound the States-General with the Judiciary Plaids or Parliaments?

and humbly supplicate. The King hearkens to
their grievances and prayers in his prudence
and his justice.—For, was he obliged to grant
all that was asked of him, says one of our most
celebrated authors, he would cease to be their
King. *It is for that reason that during the sit-
tings of the States-General the authority of the
Parliament suffers no diminution*, as exercising
no other power but that of the King, which may
be easily seen in the minutes of the last states.[5]

It was therefore a most extraordinary claim
of these Parliaments, all created by, and exercising the authority of the King only, to pretend to
be the representatives of the people in order to
resist the power of that same King; styling themselves the habitual and permanent representatives
of the States-General, who had never formed the
least idea of such representatives, and who had always looked upon them as the King's Magistrates.
But when new systems had spread disquietude in
every breast, and produced the thirst of Revolution, illusion easily banished truth. The most re-
spectable Magistrates, overpowered by the weight
of Montesquieu's authority, and spurred on by the
Sophisters, were easily persuaded that every country was enslaved, and groaned under the most
severe despotism, where the legislative and fiscal
powers were not in the hands of the people or of
their representatives. And, lest the whole code
of laws which the King had made and the Parlia-

5   *History of France*, anno 1614.

ments proclaimed, should suddenly become null and void, these Magistrates, who had enregistered and proclaimed them, constituted themselves the representatives of the people.

These claims served as a pretence for the most invincible resistance to the orders of their Sovereign. The King's council, and particularly Mr. de Maupeou, surmised a coalition aiming at nothing less than to disorder the Monarchy, to diminish the authority of the throne, to put the Sovereign under the habitual dependence of the Twelve Parliaments, and to create disturbances and disputes between the King and his Tribunals as often as any factious Magistrate, assuming the character of a tribune of the people, should oppose the pretended will of the nation to his Sovereign. Louis XV. resolved to annihilate such Parliaments, and to create new ones more limited in their powers, and which might be restrained within the bounds of their duty with greater ease.

This resolve was being put in execution, and the Sophisters rejoiced to see the disputes daily increase. Convinced that these dissentions would necessarily oblige the King to assemble the States-General, where they should be able to find means of publishing their plans and of operating, at least in part, the Revolution they so ardently wished for, they brought forward that same Malesherbes, whom we have seen so active in seconding the Sophisters of Impiety. He was at that time President of the *Cour des Aides*, the first tribunal in Paris after the Parliament. He engaged his company to make the first signal step towards opposing the States-General to the authority of the Monarch. He formed those remonstrances since so famous among the Philosophers, because, under the cloak of a few respectful expressions, he had broached all the new principles of the Sect and all their pretensions against the authority of their Sovereign.

Malesher-
bes and
the Par-
liaments
ask for the
States-
General.

In those remonstrances we see the demand for the States-General couched in the following terms:

> Until this period at least the reclamations of the Courts supplied, though imperfectly, the want of the States-General; for, notwithstanding our zeal, we cannot pretend to say, that we have been able to make amends to the nation for the great advantages which must have accrued to it, by the intercourse between its representatives and the Sovereign. *But at present the sole resource* which had been left to the people is torn from them. By whom shall their interests be asserted against the minister? The people dispersed have no common organ by which they may prefer their complaints. *Sire, interrogate then the nation itself*, since that alone remains to which your Majesty can hearken.[6]

The other parliaments who followed Malesherbes's example were ignorant of the intentions of the Sect which had prompted him to act. They abandoned themselves to the torrent, and were hurried

---

6   *Remonstrance of the cour des aides*, Feb. 28, 1771.

away by the impulse given by the Sophisters and by the public opinion, which the system of Montesquieu on the Legislative and Fiscal Powers had new-modelled.

Misled by Malesherbes's example, the Parliament of Rouen also asked for the States-General in their remonstrances of the 19th March 1771. "Sire, Since the efforts of the Magistracy are fruitless, deign to consult the Nation assembled." But the former colleagues of Montesquieu, the Parliament of Bourdeaux, thought it incumbent on them to show more than ordinary zeal for his principles, as is to be seen by the pressing style in which their remonstrances of the 25th February 1771, are couched.

If it be true (say these Magistrates), that the Parliament, become sedentary under Philip le Bel, and perpetual under Charles VI., is not the same as the Ambulant Parliament convoked during the first years of Philip le Bel's reign, under Louis IX., under Louis VIII., and under Philip Augustus; the same as the *Placita* convoked under *Charlemagne and his descendants*; the same as those ancient assemblies of the Francs of which history has preserved the memory both before and after the conquest; if the distribution of this Parliament to different districts has changed the *essence of its Constitution*, in short, Sire, though your Courts of Parliament should not have the right of examining and verifying the new laws which your Majesty may please to propose, *still the nation cannot be deprived of that right, it is a right that cannot be lost; it is inalienable. To attack that right is not only to betray the Nation but the King himself.* It would be to overthrow the constitution of the kingdom. It would be to attack the authority of the Monarch in its very principles. Will it be believed, that the verification of the new laws being made by your Courts in Parliament *does not compensate for this primitive right of the nation?* Can public order be benefited by this power being once more exercised by the nation? Should his Majesty deign to re-establish the people in their rights, he would see us no longer claiming that portion of *authority* which the Kings, your predecessors, have entrusted us with, as soon as the nation assembled shall exercise that power itself.

It is thus that the Parliaments, a prey to a faction with whose dark designs they were wholly unacquainted, were craving pardon as it were of the people for having forgotten their inherent and inalienable rights of Legislation and of Sovereignty, at least in part, in the Assembly of the States-General. They did not foresee that a day would come when they would have to ask pardon of the people for having called for those same States-General, so fatal to the King, to themselves and to the nation.

How this demand prepared the way for the Revolution.

The Revolution would have been accomplished at that time had Louis XV. shown less resolution. It was precisely at that period when the Sect, painted in such true colors a few months before by the Attorney General of the Parliament of Paris,

212

was seeking to excite the people to revolt under pretence of enlightening them; when its disquiet and daring genius, inimical to all dependence, aspired at the overthrow of every political constitution, and whose views would only be accomplished when they had succeeded in throwing the legislative and executive powers into the hands of the multitude, *when the Majesty of Kings had been reviled, and their authority had been rendered precarious and subordinate to the capricious starts of an ignorant mob.*

It was at that period

when the numbers of the proselytes were increasing and the maxims of the Sect were spreading far and wide, when kingdoms felt themselves shaken in their foundations; when nations, astonished, asked each other, whence arose the extraordinary changes which had been operated among them?

In a word, it was at that period when Mably and his disciples were conjuring a Revolution, when the Œconomists were circulating and infusing their principles into every class of the people, when the Philosophers *foresaw the Revolution, foretold it, and proposed the manner of accomjplishing it by means of a combination with the people.*[7]

From that period the convocation of the States-General must have infallibly brought about the Revolution. The Sophisters needed no longer

---

7   See Gudin, *Suppl. to the Social Contract.*

to inspire the Magistracy with their systems. The principles were admitted, though the application of them might vary. The right of verifying and examining the laws had been recognized as *a primitive and inalienable* right inherent to the people. If the parliament in the days of its illusion only held this language to their Sovereign to assert their authority against his Ministers, still the Sophisters wished for no further declarations, *to revile the Majesty of Kings, and to render their authority precarious and subordinate to the capricious starts of an ignorant mob.* From the right of examining to the right of rejecting, or to the right of insurrection, in short, to all the rights of the Revolutionary Code, there was but one step further; and the Sophisters at the head of the multitude were ready prepared to bear down every opposition to that measure. Almost every existing law was null, because it had been made by the King without consulting the people; and all laws might be set aside, because the people had a right to examine them anew and hence proscribe them, if such was their will and pleasure.

Of those who seconded the Revolution.

Such a one, nevertheless, was to be a moderate Revolution in the language of the Sophisters. It was not only those Magistrates who, wresting from the Sovereign his rights and transferring them to the people, and hoping by that means to enjoy the whole power in their assemblies, were the abettors of this Revolution; but also that numerous class of the Aristocracy, whom we shall see hereafter carrying to the States-General all those systems of the legislative people; of a people preserving all the hierarchy of birth in their legislative assemblies; of a people adopting Montesquieu's principles only in as far as they applied to, and threw the power into the hands of the Aristocracy; in fine, this revolution was forwarded and supported by all that class of Sophisters who, contented with having asserted the principles of the *Legislative and Sovereign people*, were pleased to continue the name of King to the first minister of that people.

Louis XV. was perfectly aware that he was on the eve of losing the most precious rights of his crown. Naturally humane, and an enemy to all acts of authority, he was nevertheless determined to transmit whole and unimpaired to his successor the power which he had received on ascending the throne. He wished to die as he had lived, a King: He dissolved the Parliaments, refused to convoke the States-General, and never permitted them even to be mentioned during the remainder of his reign. But he knew that in repressing the Magistrates he had not crushed the monster of Revolution. He more than once expressed his fears for the young Prince heir to his throne. He was even so much convinced that the Sophisters would make the most violent efforts against his successors, that he would say with a tone of disquietude, *I should like to know how Berri will get over all this*; meaning his grandson, afterwards Louis XVI.,

It is averted by Louis XV.

who bore the name of Berri[8] during the life-time of his father, who died Dauphin. Louis XV. however found means to stop the Revolution which menaced France during his life-time. The conspirators perceived it necessary to defer their plans. They were content with preparing the people for its execution. In the mean time the Sect made other essays of a different nature, which shall not be lost to History.

---

8   Louis-Auguste of France, later Louis XVI, was given the title Duc de Berry at birth. The French original reads: '. . . *qui avant la mort du premier Dauphin, étoit appelé Duc de Berri.*'—Ed.

Essay of the Sophisters against Aristocracy.

he distinctions of King and Subject, of the Sovereign making and the Multitude obeying the law, were not the only points which militated against the principles of a school that recognized no other law, whether religious or political, than *Equality and Liberty*. In all civil societies there exist men elevated above the horizontal plane of the multitude, men who are to be distinguished by their rank, by their titles, or by the privileges granted to their birth, to their own services, or to those of their ancestors; men who, by the industry of their forefathers, or by their own, have acquired riches and abundance, of which their fel-

Philosophism re-kindles the hatred against the nobles and the wealthy in Germany.

low-citizens cannot partake; in fine, men who earn their bread by the sweat of their brow, while others enjoy the benefit of their labours in consideration of a salary which they pay them. If the distinctions of nobleman and commoner be not every where known, those of poor and rich are universally understood.

Whatever interest the numberless adepts in the higher classes might have had not to push too far the consequences of that Equality which they had applied to their God, there were many adepts in the lower classes who did not partake of any such restraint. Many of these latter were to be found in France, but a much greater number in Germany and Poland, and in many other parts of Europe, where the principles of our modern Sophisters had gained admittance.

As early as the year 1766, we have seen Frederick writing to Voltaire, *"That Philosophy was beginning to penetrate even into superstitious Bohemia, and into Austria, the ancient abode of superstition."* And it is to that year that we are able to trace the first seeds of a plan which was to gratify the Sophisters with a new Republic in those countries, where the distinctions of Marquis or Clown, of Noble or Burgess, of rich or poor, were to vanish from before their sight.

Conspiracy of the Austrian and the Bohemian Sophisters against the Nobility.

The whole of what we are about to relate concerning this plan, and the various essays made by Philosophism to extend its branches to Austria and Bohemia, even to Hungary and Transilvania, will be extracted from two Memorials, with which we have been favoured by persons who, being on the spot, were enabled to oberve with the greatest precision, the one the causes, the other the effects, which enabled the German Sophisters to glory in having preceded our Carmagnols and Septembrizing butchers in their Revolutionary depredations.

Scarcely had the French Philosophism penetrated to the banks of the Moldau, when those baneful principles of *Equality and Liberty* which formerly had led the Hussites and Thaborites to the enthusiastic murder of the Clergy and Nobility, to the laying in ashes the Castles and Monasteries, were seen to ferment anew. A conspiracy was formed at Prague, and it was to break out on the 16th of May. It was customary on that day for multitudes of the common people to throng into town, to celebrate the feast of St. Jean Nepomucene. At the time of this immense concourse of people from the country, some thousands of armed Conspirators were suddenly to appear; others were to make themselves masters of the bridge and gates; others again were to mix among the people; to harangue them, to announce the dawn of rising Liberty, and to exhort them to throw off the yoke of Slavery, and to take possession of those lands which they had so long watered with the sweat of their brows, and whose fruit only enriched a set of tyrannical, haughty, vain, and idle Lords.

Such language, it may easily be conceived, must have made a strong impression on men who, for the greatest part, cultivated lands which they only held at the pleasure of the Lord, in consideration of so many days work every week, employed in the culture of the Lord's lands.[1] Arms were to be distributed to this populace suddenly heated by the cry of Equality and Liberty. The Lords and the rich were to fall the first victims of their fury; the lands distributed to the murderers, and Liberty proclaimed, we should have beheld Bohemia the first Republican offspring of Philosophism.

---

1   The peasantry called Robota were not all in an equal degree of slavery. Some held their lands for three, others for four days labour per week. However just the conditions of such a servitude were in themselves, it was nevertheless difficult for the traveller accustomed to other governments not to be persuaded, that these men were very unhappy. I was of that opinion, when an unexpected sight nearly reconciled me to that mode of administration. It was an immense granary belonging to the Lord. In the middle of a large hall were vast heaps of corn; around the place as many divisions as there were families in the village, and each division contained the com belonging to one family. An overseer attended at the distributions, which were made once a week. If the stock of any particular division was exhausted, the necessary quantity was taken from the Lord's heap for the family in need, who were to replace the com so taken at the ensuing harvest. By this means the poorest peasant was certain of his sustenance. Let the reader decide, whether such a government may not be as good as others, where the poor man may often starve in the possession of perfect Liberty.

I know what might be wished for under every administration; but it is not the part of true Philosophy to overthrow existing governments in the chimerical idea of reducing, some day or other, every thing to its own plans.

Secretly however as this plot was carried on, some of the adepts ere long betrayed the secret.—Maria Theresa, the Empress Queen, found means of stifling the whole, and her council behaved with so much prudence and dexterity, that the public journals of the time scarcely mention it. Perhaps the court judged wisely, and thought it prudent to gain over the chiefs, rather than by executions to call the attention of the public to principles which have but too often stained Bohemia with the blood of its best citizens.

Notwithstanding the very small success that had attended their attempt, the Sophisters of the Danube and Moldau did not lose all hopes of effectuating their schemes of Equality. They invented a plan which drew the Empress Queen into the delusion, and still more her successor Joseph II.—The apparent object of this plan was, that proprietors whose lands were so extensive that they were unable to cultivate them, should be obliged to cede a part of such lands to the peasantry. These, in return, were to pay an annual rent to the former proprietors equal in value to the estimated revenue. Each community was to engage to punish severely every peasant who should neglect either the cultivation of the land ceded, or the payment of the settled rent.

New plans of the Austrian Sophisters.

This plan was presented to the Empress Queen with so much art, that she was persuaded it had no other view than the enriching of the state by favouring the industry and encouraging the emulation of the real cultivators.

She therefore gave orders to various agents of government to send in Memorials on the subject: and herself tried the experiment by ceding some of the crown lands on the aforementioned conditions.

The Sophisters feared the delay attendant on such deliberations; and, to hasten the general execution of their projects, they spread their propositions and plans among the peasantry. Their most ardent missionary was an intriguing priest, who ran to and fro throughout the country, preaching up this reformation of property which he thought admirable. He found it no difficult task to infuse a portion of his enthusiasm into his rustic auditors. The Nobles, viewing this plan in no other light than as a means of despoiling them of their property under the pretence of a just compensation, objected that the peasantry, become masters and proprietors of the land, would soon find means of turning the whole profit to their own use; and that Philosophism would soon invent new reasons for paying no retribution whatever to the Lords (for would it not be doubly unjust to carry any part of the produce of lands to Lords who neither cultivated nor had any *property* in them); in fine, should it ever please the peasantry to league together and refuse all payments, the Lords would have lost both their lands and money, and the Nobility, thus reduced, would be able to find no other means of subsistence than by entering into the service of their *quondam tenants.*[2]

---

2   This may serve to explain the theory of the French Emigration.

This opposition only contributed to stimulate the zeal of the levelling apostles. They had given the peasantry every hope of success, and it was easy to irritate them against their opponents. It was soon to be perceived that those vassals who had always been so mild and humble with respect to their Lords had now assumed a haughty and insolent mien. It was necessary to resort to punishments, which only added to their complaints and murmurs. The Empress Queen, still misled by the apparent justice of the plan, and the Emperor, whose Philosophism and ambition secretly enjoyed the hopes of humiliating the Nobility, were imprudent enough to receive the complaints of those whom the Lords had thought necessary to punish. This sort of connivance gave our rustic revolters reason to believe, that they had nothing to fear on the part of the government. The Sophistical Emissaries persuaded them, that they ought to obtain by force what in justice could not

Insurrection in Bohemia.

A friend of mine, who had exercised an almost boundless charity in the manor of which he was Lord, was nearly murdered in the general insurrection of 1789, by that peasantry which he had preserved from the inclemency of the foregoing winter. He was however fortunate enough to escape the hands of the assassins, and, returning to his former mansion, was received with acclamations of joy. On expostulating with his tenants on the treatment he had lately received they begged his pardon in these words, saying, "Ah Sir, we were misled; we were made to believe that if we burnt your title deeds and got rid of you, we should have nothing to pay, and should remain proprietors of the lands we hold; but we ask pardon," &c. He thus escaped the agents, but was afterwards pursued by the revolutionary leaders called Deputies, and is at present involved in the general decree of death pronounced against the Emigrants. —Tr.

be refused them. Such insinuations naturally produced violence, and in 1773, the insurrection of the peasantry against the Nobility was almost universal throughout Bohemia.

The rustics already began to burn and pillage[3] the castles; the nobility and the rich proprietors were menaced with a general massacre. The Empress Queen came to a tardy sense of the fault she had committed; but then at least she lost no time to crush the growing evil. An army of 28,000 men received orders to march and to quell the rioters. The Sophisters had not the time necessary to organize their Revolutionary bands, and the revolters were soon defeated.

Those parts of Prussia and Silesia which border on Bohemia had felt the commotion, and it was then that Frederick first divined the intentions of the Sophisters. He had not courted them so far as to disband his army. He was even more resolute than the Empress Queen in eradicating the spirit of revolt. He immediately hung up the mutineers; and our levelling Philosophists were still obliged quietly to behold those disgusting distinctions of Lords and peasants, of Nobles and rich. But they were only pacified for the moment, and never lost sight of their plans. The death of the Empress Queen gave them an occasion of making still more perfidious essays for the destruction of the Nobility.

Joseph II.'s prevention against the Nobles and plan for humbling them.

Initiated in the Sophisticated mysteries, Joseph II. had found means of combining the ideas

---

3   The fate of France 1789.

of Equality and Liberty with those of the Despot, and, under pretence of reigning like a Philosopher, levelled every thing around him, that he and his systems might tower alone above the ruined plane. With his pretended Liberty of conscience, he would have been the greatest persecutor of his age, had not the French Revolution followed him so closely. With his pretended Equality, he only sought to vilify and plunder the Nobility, and to fling their fortunes into the hands of their vassals, in order to overthrow the laws of the Empire, and those of property as well as those of religion, that he might not meet with a greater opposition from the Nobility than he would from their vassals.—With all his pretensions to genius, the most awful lessons were necessary to persuade him that the real tendency of this Philosophism of Equality and of religious and political Liberty, was the destruction of the throne as well as of the altar.

Such was the Philosophy of that Prince: whatever may have been his intentions, his innovating genius was unfortunate enough to furnish the pretext for a most cruel insurrection against the Nobility of a large portion of his dominions. The celerity with which he was accustomed to make himself obeyed, may cast cruel doubts on the dilatory manner in which he went to the succour of the unhappy victims.

All that I am about to relate concerning this memorable event, the atrocious memory of which the court of Vienna vainly attempted to stifle, shall be extracted from a relation written by Mr. J. Petty, an English gentleman whom I knew to be one of those who had escaped from the massacre, and is now living at Betchworth near Dorking, in the county of Surrey. It was to his memorial I alluded when I spoke of one more particularly instructive as to effects. The other, from which I have extracted the greater part of what has been already seen in this Chapter, has a greater application to causes, and shows the connection between those facts and the progress of Philosophism and Jacobinism in the Austrian dominions. On considering these two memorials collectively, we see that it was at Vienna where the Sophisters, under the cloak of Humanity and Liberty, were inventing every means either for the destruction of the Nobility, or to oblige the Lords to renounce their ancient rights over their vassals and villains, and that the orders given by Joseph II for the mode of defence of the frontiers of Transilvania furnished the means or the occasion for executing their plans. These orders were such, that they were calculated either to rob the Hungarian Lords of their vassals, or to throw them into open rebellion against their masters.

Antecedent to this new plan adotped by the Emperor, the chain of troops destined for the guard of the Turkish frontiers was composed of peasants or villains, who were exempted from a part of their ordinary labours in consideration of this military duty; but were not on that account exempt from dependence on their masters. In the spring of the year 1781, Joseph II sent the Major General Geny to Hermannstadt, with orders to augment the number of these guards, and to put them on the same footing as the rest of the Imperial troops; that is to say, in a state of perfect independence on their former Lords. The proposed indemnifications did not, however, prevent numerous reclamations being made. What seemed to justify this opposition, and what was easy to be foreseen (which perhaps might have been the real object of the Sophisters), was, that the peasantry flocked in crouds to be enrolled, and by that means enfranchize themselves from all submission and from any services or duties to their Lords.—I must own with truth, and in unison with Mr. Petty, that the fate of the peasantry or villains was much aggravated by the harshness of some of their masters.

In the mean time, until an answer to the reclamations of the Nobility and proprietors could be obtained from Vienna, the commander in chief at Hermannstadt thought it incumbent on him to declare, that these new enrollments should be considered as operating no change in the political situation of the peasantry, until further orders and instructions should be received from the Emperor. But those orders did not arrive, and the commander in chief had made his declaration too late.— Those villains who had enrolled themselves not only looked upon their enfranchizement as complete, but committed such excesses against their

Insurrection occasioned in Transilvania by this new plan.

former masters, that the Magistrates were obliged to apply to the commander in chief for the revocation of all the enrollments, as the only method of restoring order. But the revocation proved useless; it was well known that the Emperor had returned no answer. The peasantry, in lieu of peaceably submitting to their injured Lords, persisted in looking upon themselves as independent soldiers, when on a sudden there appeared a Valachian peasant of the name of Hoija who gathered a multitude of them around him. He, decorated with a large star and bearing a patent written in golden letters, declared himself sent by the Emperor to enroll them all. He offered to put himself at their head and to restore them to their liberty. The peasantry flocked to their new general. The Lords and Proprietors sent daily information to the government and to the commander in chief at Hermannstadt of what was passing; of the secret committees which were held in different parts, and of the insurrection which was on the eve of bursting forth. Reproaches for their apprehensions and timidity were the only answers they received.

Massacre of the Nobility in Transilvania.

The day marked out b the Conspirators was approaching, and on the 3d November 1784 Hoija appeared at the head of four thousand men. He formed different detachments and sent them to burn the castles and murder the Lords and proprietors. These forerunners of the Jacobin Galley Slaves of Marseilles executed his orders with that sanguinary fury which they had imbibed against the Nobility from the doctrines of Equality, and the rebels soon counted 12,000 men following their levelling standards. In a very short space of time fifty Noblemen were murdered. Carnage and desolation now spread from county to county; the houses of the Nobility were every where burnt and ransacked, and mere assassination could no longer satiate their sanguinary fury. The unhappy Noblemen who fell into their hands were put to the most excruciating tortures. Some were impaled alive, their hands and feet cut off, and roasted at a slow fire, for such is the humanity of levellers!!—But we will not attempt to comment on the relation we have before us; to extract is a task sufficiently distressing.

> Among the castles which were reduced to ashes the most remarkable were those of the Counts d'Esterhazy and Tekeli; and of the Noblemen who were murdered the most distinguished were the two Counts and Brothers Rebiezi. The eldest was spitted and roasted; many others of the same family, men, women and children, were cruelly massacred. The unfortunate Lady Bradisador, with whom I had spent a few days (says Mr. Petty) also fell a melancholy victim.—These barbarians seized her, cut off her hands and feet, and then left her to linger in that state till she expired. But let us turn from such horrid subjects: They recall to my mind persons forever dear to me, who fell a most wanton sacrifice to cruelty, on which I have not the courage to dilate.

The connection between the ancient and modern insurrections against the Nobility.

We also would gladly have withheld such bloody recitals from our readers; but, when compared to our Septembrizing Jacobins, they become marking features in history. And how much more striking would these lessons be, was it here the place to enumerate the many similar attacks against the nobility with which our Memoirs on Ancient Jacobinism are replete. We should there see that same Philosophism of Equality and Liberty forming the same plots and perpetrating the same atrocities against that part of society distinguished by its titles, rank, or riches; and the Aristocracy may learn from their own history the danger of encouraging sophisticated levellers, who never fawn on them but in hopes of tearing to pieces and devouring the whole of that class which is distinguished by riches and honors.

In making a comparison between the Jacobins of the present day and their forefathers, I should not conceal those horrid sights of noblemen roasting, of women mutilated, of whole families masssacred, or of the palpitating members of fathers, mothers and children in Transilvania.—Nor should I pass over those cannibals of the *Place Dauphine* burning at a slow fire (on the 3d of September 1792) the Countess of *Perignan* and her daughters, Madame *de Chevres*, and so many other victims, offering the flesh of those whom they had already butchered as food to those who were next to be sacrificed. Such horrid deeds are far from being novelties in the annals of the Sect.[4] Nor was it reserved to the Carmagnols of Paris or of Transilvania to show the example of such cruelties. These statements I know will make my reader shudder with horror, but it is a salutary tremor. At length perhaps they will cease to hearken to those Sophistical Apostles of an Equality and Liberty less chimerical than atrocious, and whose systems assimilate man to the ferocious beasts of the forest. The error is too fatal; let us therefore guard against the delusions of pride by the remembrance of deeds humiliating to nature itself. We have witnessed the sanguinary consequences of these vain systems of Equality and Liberty in our own times; let us venture to examine for a moment what course they took in the days of our ancestors.

---

4   In our *History of the Clergy during the French Revolution*, we mentioned these atrocious facts at the Place Dauphine, which some of our readers called in question, because they had not witnessed them, though in Paris at the time; but let it be recollected, it was a time when terror would scarcely permit them to raise their heads from their hiding places. Let them consult the writings of Mr. Girtanner, a Swiss physician, who was an eye witness to what he relates. They will learn that the work from which I had made the extract was only a translation from his work, nor did I know at that time that the *Baron de Pélissier Vien* was the translator, as I have since learned from himself. I have also seen Mr. Cambden, chaplain to one of the Irish regiments: He had printed the same account at Liège, and declared to me that he had only published it on the testimony of twenty different witnesses, who all assured him that Mr. Girtanner and myself had been so far from exaggerating the fact, that we had stopped far short of the horrors of that sanguinary scene.

In 1358 France had its Jacobins, and their system was *Equality and Liberty*. Froissard, one of the most esteemed French Historians, paints their conduct as follows:

> In the month of May 1358 France was stricken with a strange desolation. Some country people, without a chief, and at first not one hundred in number, assembled in the Beauvoisis, declaring that the nobility were a dishonor to the nation, and that it would be a meritorious act to destroy them all. Their companions answered, 'It is true, and evil fall upon the man who shall not do his utmost to destroy the nobility.'

They then gathered together, having no other arms than sticks tipped with iron, and knives, and immediately proceeded to the neighbouring mansion of a nobleman. After having murdered him, his wife and children, not sparing the infant babes, they set fire to his house. They then proceeded to another castle, where seizing on the Chevalier, they offered violence to his wife and daughter, and afterwards murdered them in his presence, with the rest of his children; they then butchered him, and levelled his castle with the ground.—They treated several other country houses and castles in the same manner. Their numbers increased to six thousand, and they were joined every where as they went by their equals; the others fled through terror, carrying their wives and children with them to the distance of ten or twenty leagues, leaving their houses and valuables at the mercy of the robbers. These wicked wretches, without chiefs, buffetted, burnt, and massacred every nobleman they met with, and offered the most unheard of violences to the wives and daughters of their victims. He who committed the greatest excesses and horrors (deeds that neither can nor ought to be described) was the most exalted among them, and looked upon as the most distinguished leader. I could not dare recite the treatment which women met with from them. Among other horrors which they committed, they seized a nobleman, murdered him, spitted him, and roasted him in the presence of his wife and children.[5] They forced this unhappy woman to eat of the flesh of her husband, and then made her undergo a most shocking death.

---

5   When the unfortunate Chevallier Dillon was murdered by his own soldiers at Lisle, after having made him languish from nine in the morning till seven at night with a broken thigh from a pistol ball which one of the cuirassiers under his command had fired at him in the field. As he entered the gates of Lisle he received three more shots, which put an end to his existence, and his body was dragged to the *Grande Place, where it was roasted, and pieces of his flesh sold for two-pence and three-pence to the standers-by.* On the 11th of August, I was eyewitness to the burning of the bodies of many of the Swiss in large bonfires, made of the wood-work of the guard-houses and out-houses of the Thuilleries, while men covered with blood and smoke were beating down with long poles the flesh which bloated up from the heat. Large piles of burnt bones lay by the fires, which had been kindled soon after the attack upon the palace the day before, which proved that such had been their amusement during the preceding night. —Tr.

"These wicked wretches burnt and destroyed above sixty castles in the Beauvoisin and in the neighborhood of Corbie, Amiens, and Montdidier. They destroyed above a hundred in the county of Valois, and the bishopricks of Laon, Noyon, and Soissons."[6]

It is worthy of remark, that when these wretches were asked what induced them to commit such horrors, they answered, 'That they did not know. 'Such was the precise answer which our first incendiaries gave when asked why they burned the castles; such also would have been the answer of our Transilvanian Carmagnoles. Whence did that clown who became their chief procure his star and his patents written in golden letters? Who had forged them, if not the same Sect that in 1789 forged the pretended orders of Louis XVI. sent to the peasantry in Dauphine to burn the castles and chase the nobles? The pretext was every where the same, and the like evils flowed from the same, though *hidden, source.*

Besides, there is a most terrible cloud impending over this insurrection of the peasantry in Transilvania against the nobility. In the commencement the government of Hermannstadt refused to send succours on pretence that their alarms were groundless, when it was impossible to deny the horrors committed by the insurgents. Soldiers were sent, but without orders to act. At first appearance one would have thought they were in an understand-

---

6   Froissard's Chronicle, Ed. of Lyons 1559, chap. 182.

ing with the banditti, who continued their devastations without fearing to be repressed by the soldiery. The troops, having no orders, were reduced to be tranquil spectators of the castles in flames (the incendiaries even marching before them), and heard the unhappy victims calling for succour in the agonies of death, but in vain; they had not the power to act. At length such of the nobles as had escaped the general massacre, being joined by those of the neighbouring counties, formed themselves into a body, marched against the insurgents, and defeated them in various encounters; and Horja, with his followers who were still numerous, was obliged to retire into the mountains. He there gathered fresh forces, and renewed his devastating and sanguinary course. Then at least it was impossible not to give the troops orders to act. But the cloud becomes still more impenetrable. When the insurgents pillaged Abrud-Banga the *Caisse d'Escompte* belonging to the Royal Chamber fell into their hands; but they would not touch it because it belonged to the Emperor: And soon after a detachment of a Lieutenant and only twenty-four men came to escort the chest to Zalatna. On their march a numerous party of Hotja's followers might have seized it again, when one of the insurgents advancing proposed a parly between their Chief and the Lieutenant. The Chief advanced, saying, "We are not to be considered as rebels. We love and adore the Emperor in whose service we are. Our sole object is to throw off the tyrannical yoke of the Nobility, which we can bear no longer. Go and tell the Officers of the Chamber of Zalatna, that they have nothing to fear from us."

Notwithstanding the fidelity with which they adhered to their promise, it was necessary to order the troops to act; and in various encounters many prisoners were made from the insurgents. I could wish that it had fallen to my task to praise the generosity of the nobility on this occasion. But my Historian accuses them of having cruelly revenged themselves on a multitude of unhappy persons, who had only joined the revolters through compulsion. A cruel Magistrate condemned them all indiscriminately, and in such numbers, that an Austrian Major threatened to make him responsible to the Emperor for all the innocent blood which he had spilt.

This harsh treatment of the prisoners stimulated Hoija and his followers to new cruelties against the nobility. He intrenched himself again in the mountains, and they in vain offered him a general amnesty. He was beginning to renew his depredations the following year, when he was taken by a stratagem. The insurgents, disconcerted, craved peace, and laid down their arms.

Such was the conclusion of a conspiracy, which was no more than an essay made in those distant provinces by the Sophisters of Equality and Liberty of what they were contriving elsewhere, to level every head which towered above the vulgar. The apparent cause, and which might have greatly contributed in reality, was the excessive abuse of their rights and the oppression over their vassals exercised by the nobility of Transilvania. The tone of moderation and veracity with which the relation we have followed is written, leaves no room to doubt of these oppressions; and in that point of view this terrible insurrection would be foreign to the object of our memoirs. But the insurrection of the negroes may also be attributed to the harshness of the treatment they underwent; yet it is nevertheless universally known, that all the atrocious crimes and barbarities committed by the insurgent slaves against their masters at Saint-Domingue, Martinique, and Guadaloupe, are to be traced to the plots combined by the levelling Sophisters in Paris.

It is precisely in a similar light that the insurrection in Transilvania is represented in a narrative which we received from a person who was more in the way of observing the progress of Philosophism in Vienna and the other Austrian dominions. He was acquainted with their plots, he refuted the pretences, and foresaw the fatal consequences; he even more than once declared them to the Austrian government; but he was not more hearkened to than many others whose words have been but too fatally verified by the horrid Revolution.

In the memoirs of this accurate observer on the insurrection of Transilvania, I see him combine the efforts of our modern Sophisters with those of a Sect long since lurking in the Occult Lodges of Free-masonry.

At the epoch we are now describing such indeed was the union between the Sophisters and the Craft, and such was the mutual succour which they lent to each other, that it was impossible to develop the progress of the one without seeking the origin of the other, without exposing their common hatreds and common systems, and the combinations of their mutual plots into one and the same conspiracy against Christ and his altars, against Kings and their thrones. Our object therefore in the remaining chapters will be, to reveal the mysteries of Free-masonry, to explain the means and succours it afforded to the modern Sophisters in the French Revolution, and to show how fatal their union has already been, and how much it threatens the social orders of the whole world.

CHAPTER IX.

Of the General Secret, or Lesser Mysteries, of Free-masonry.

I n treating of Free-masonry truth and justice rigorously compel us to begin with an exception that exculpates the greater part of those brethren who have been initiated, and who would have conceived a just horror for this association, had they been able to foresee that it could ever make them contract obligations which militated against the duties of the religious man and of the true citizen.

England in particular is full of those upright men, who, excellent Citizens, and of all stations, are proud of being Masons, and who may be distinguished from the others by ties which only ap-

Distinctions and expectations to be made against the Freemasons.

Of English Masons.

pear to unite them more closely in the bonds of charity and fraternal affection. It is not the fear of offending a nation in which I have found an asylum that has suggested this exception. Gratitude on the contrary would silence every vain terror, and I should be seen exclaiming in the very streets of London that England was lost, that it could not escape the French Revolution, if its Free-mason Lodges were similar to those of which I am about to treat. I would say more, that Christianity and all government would have long been at an end in England, if it could be even supposed that her Masons were initiated into the last mysteries of the Sect. Long since have their Lodgees been sufficiently numerous to execute such a design, had the English Masons adopted either the means or the plans and plots of the Occult Lodges.

This argument alone might suffice to except the English Masons in general from what I have to say of the Sect. But there exist many passages in the history of Masonry which necessitate this exception. The following appears convincing.—At the time when the Illuminées of Germany, the most detestable of the Jacobin crew, were seeking to strengthen their party by that of Masonry, they affected a sovereign contempt for the English Lodges. In the letters of Philo to Spartacus we see the English adepts arriving in Germany from London dawbed all over with the ribbands and emblems of their degrees, but void of those plans and projects against the altar and the crown which tend directly to the point. When I shall have given the history of these Illuminées the reader will easily judge what immense weight such a testimony carries with it in favour of the English Lodges. It is glorious for them to see themselves despised by the most unrelenting enemies of the altar, of the throne, and of all society.[1]

For a considerable length of time a similar exception might have been made of the generality of Lodges both in France and Germany. Some of them not only published protestations, but seceded from Masonry as soon as they perceived it to be infected by those revolutionary principles which the Illuminées had infused among the brethren.[2] In short, the number of exceptions to be made for upright Masons is beyond the conception of those who are not thoroughly acquainted with the principles and proceedings of the Sect.—In fact, how is it possible to conceive, that in so numerous an association, where its members are united by bonds and oaths to which they are most religiously attached, so very few of its adepts should be acquainted with the grand object of the association itself? This enigma would have been easily understood had we published (as we hope to do) the history of ancient Jacobinism with that of the middle age, before we had digested these memoirs of modern Jacobinism. But to supply this deficiency, and to methodize our ideas on this famous associ-

Exceptions with respect to other countries.

---

1   See letter of Philo to Spartacus.

2   See the speech of a Master pronounced in a Bavarian Lodge.

ation, we will begin by treating of the secret which is common to all degrees, that is to say, of what may be called the lesser mysteries; and thence proceeding to the secret and doctrine of the Occult Lodges, we will treat of the grand mysteries of Masonry. We will also treat of its origin and of its propagation; in fine, of its coalition with the conspiring Sophisters, and of the means it afforded them of executing their plans against the altar and the throne.

The general secret discovered by the Masons themselves. Until the 12th of August 1792, the French Jacobins had only dated the annals of their Revolution by the years of their pretended *Liberty*. On that day Louis XVI., who forty-eight hours before had been declared to have forfeited his right to the crown, was carried prisoner to the Tower of the Temple (so called because it formerly belonged to the Knights Templars). On that day the rebel assembly decreed, that to the date of *Liberty*, the date of *Equality* should be added in future in all public acts, and the decree itself was dated the fourth year of *Liberty*, the first year and first day of *Equality*.

It was on that day, for the first time, that the secret of Free-masonry was made public; that secret so dear to them, and which they preserved with all the solemnity of the most inviolable oath. At the reading of this famous decree, they exclaimed, 'We have at length succeeded, and France is no other than an immense lodge. The whole French people are Free-masons, and the whole universe will soon follow their example.

I witnessed this enthusiasm, I heard the conversations to which it gave rise. I saw Masons, till then the most reserved, who freely and openly declared, "Yes, at length the grand object of Free-masonry is accomplished. EQUALITY and LIBERTY; *all men are equal and brothers; all men are free.* That was the whole substance of our doctrine, the object of our wishes, THE WHOLE *of our* GRAND SECRET." Such was the language I heard fall from the most zealous Masons, from those whom I have seen decorated with all the insignia of the deepest Masonry, and who enjoyed the rights of *Venerable* to preside over Lodges. I have heard them express themselves in this manner before those whom Masons would call *the prophane,* without requiring the smallest secrecy either from the men or women present. They said it in a tone as if they wished all France should be acquainted with this glorious achievement of Masonry; as if it were to recognize in them its benefactors and the authors of that Revolution of *Equality and Liberty* of which it had given so grand an example to all Europe.

Such in reality was the general secret of the Free-masons. It was similar to what in the games of the ancients were called the lesser mysteries, common to all degrees; and though the word expressed the whole, it was not wholly understood by all.—Its progressive explanation, while it renders it innocent in some, renders it monstrous in others.—In the mean time, before we have accounted for this difference, let not the Mason, whatever may be his degree, inculpate us if as in Paris this famous secret ceases to continue one. Too many of the prophane were acquainted with it in that Revolutionary country, for it to remain a secret in others. Even those in England who may still wish to keep it, will vainly object that we have been misled; they will soon see whether it was possible for us to be so. Were we destitute of other evidence, we might safely assert, that those Masons did not mislead us, who were actuated by no other passion than that of the glory of the Sect when they revealed those mysteries which when secure of their execution ceased to be mysterious. Those again did not mislead us, who, formerly initiated into those mysteries, at length owned that they had been dupes: That all that Equality and Liberty which they had treated as mere play had already proved a most desperate game for their country, and might bring ruin on the whole universe. And I have met with many of these adepts since the Revolution, both in France and elsewhere, who had formerly been zealous Masons, but latterly confessing with bitterness this fatal secret, which reduces the whole science of Masonry, like the French Revolution, to these two words *Equality* and *Liberty*.

I once more conjure the upright Masons not to look upon themselves as accused of wishing to establish a similar Revolution. When I shall have verified this article of their doctrine, the essence and the basis of all their mysteries, I will show how it came to pass that so many noble and virtuous characters were initiated without even suspecting the ultimate design. But for the history of the Revolution, it is necessary that the most distant doubt should not subsist as to this fundamental secret. If this were not made clear, it would be impossible for the reader to comprehend the help which the Sophisters of Rebellion and Impiety acquired from Masonry. I shall therefore seek other proofs beside these avowals, which many others must have heard like me from the adepts, since their successes in France had made them regard secrecy in future as superfluous.

Other proofs of the secret.

Antecedent to these avowals, there was an easy method of discovering that Equality and Liberty were the grand objects of Masonry. The very name of *Free*-mason carries with it the idea of Liberty; as to *Equality* it was disguised under the term *Fraternity*, which has nearly a similar signification. But who has not heard the Mason brag of the Equality which reigned in their Lodges, where Princes and Nobles, the rich and the poor, all were *equal*, all were brothers: that distinctions of rank no longer existed when once passed the Tyler;[3] and that the sole appellation used among them was that of Brother, the only name also which gives us an idea of perfect Equality.

It is true, that it was expressly forbidden to any Mason ever to write these two words *Equality* and *Liberty* consecutively, or give the least hint that

---

3   The Officer standing at the door, with a drawn sword, to receive the sign, and admit only the real Members.

their secret resided in the union of these two grand principles; and that law was so exactly observed by their writers, that I do not remember ever to have seen it transgressed among the numerous volumes which I have read, though of the most secret sort, on the different degrees. Mirabeau himself, when he pretended to reveal the secrets of Masonry, only dared reveal them in part. The order of Free-masonry, which is spread all over the world, he says, has for its objects, Charity, *Equality of stations*, and perfect harmony.[4]—Though *this Equality of stations* seems pretty well to denote the Liberty which must exist in this Equality, still Mirabeau, who was a Mason himself, knew that the time was not yet come, when his brethren would pardon him for avowing that in these two words consisted their general secret; but this very reservedness sufficiently denotes how much both the one and the other were held precious in their mysteries. If we refer to the hymns and songs sung in chorus at their festivals, we shall generally find some verses or stanza in honour of Equality or of Liberty.[5]

---

4   *Essay on the Illuminées*, chap. 15.

5   It is for this reason, that amidst all their encomiums on benevolence, which is the chief object of their songs, we see the English always add some fines in the sense of the following:

Masons have long been free,
And may they ever be. &c.
Princes and Kings our brothers are, &c.

These lines, however, notwithstanding their tendency to

In the same way we may often remark either the one or the other to be the subject of the discourses they have pronounced, and which are sometimes printed.

Were I even deprived of these proofs, still it would be incumbent on me to declare what personal knowledge I may have acquired.

Though I have seen so many Masons who since the famous decree of *Equality* have spoken in the most open manner of this famous secret (though the oath which they had taken should have made them more reserved on it than me, who never took any oath either in their Lodges, or to the Revolution of Equality and Liberty), I should nevertheless be perfectly silent on all that I have witnessed, were I not thoroughly convinced how much it imported all nations, to be acquainted with the ultimate tendency of Masonry.

I should be sorry to see thousands of upright Masons, especially in England, take offence at the discovery of their secret; but such virtuous and upright men are not those who would prefer the vain-glory of their secret to the public welfare, or to the proper precautions to be taken against the abuses of Masonry; in a word against an abominable Sect who, under the pretence of virtue, wish to mislead the universe. I shall speak openly and without the fear of displeasing those Masons whom I esteem and revere; and shall but little trouble

---

Equality and Liberty, are not to be understood in a Jacobinal light in the mouth of an English Mason.

myself about the displeasure of others whose persons I contemn and whose plots I abhor.

During the last twenty years it was difficult, especially in Paris, to meet persons who did not belong to the society of Masonry. I was acquainted with many, and some were my intimate friends. These, with all that zeal common to young adepts, frequently pressed me to become one of their brotherhood. As I constantly refused, they undertook to enroll me notwithstanding my refusal.—The plan settled, I was invited to dinner at a friend's house and was the only prophane in the midst of a large party of Masons. Dinner over and the servants ordered to withdraw, it was proposed to form themselves into a Lodge, and to initiate me. I persisted in my refusal, and particularly refused to take the oath of keeping a secret, the very object of which was unknown to me. They dispensed with the oath, but I still refused. They became more pressing, telling me that Masonry was perfectly innocent, and that its morality was unobjectionable: In reply, I asked whether it was better than that of the Gospel. They only answered by forming themselves into a Lodge, when began all those grimaces and childish ceremonies which are described in books of Masonry, such as Jachin and Boaz. I attempted to make my escape, but in vain; the apartment was very extensive, the house in a retired situation, the servants in the secret, and all the doors locked. I am questioned, and answer most of the questions laughing. I am received *Apprentice*, and immediately after *Fellow-craft*. Having received these two degrees, I was informed that a third was to be conferred on me. On this I am conducted into a large room. There the scene changes, and takes a more serious appearance. And though they dispensed with my undergoing all the more toilsome tests, they nevertheless were not sparing in a multitude of tiresome and insignificant questions.

On finding myself obliged to go through this farce, I had taken care to say, that since they had cut off every means of retreat, I was forced to submit; but that, if I perceived any thing either against honour or conscience, they should soon find with whom they had to deal.

As yet I had only perceived a mere childish play and burlesque ceremonies, in spite of all the gravity which the brethren affected; but I had given no offence by any of my answers. At length the Venerable with the utmost gravity put the following question: "Brother, are you disposed to execute all the orders of the Grand-Master, though you were to receive contrary orders from a King, an Emperor, or any other Sovereign whatever?" My answer was "*No*."—"What *No*," replies the Venerable with surprize! "Are you only entered among us to betray our secrets! Would you hesitate between the interests of Masonry and those of the prophane?—You are not aware then that there is not one of our swords but is ready to pierce the heart of a traitor." Notwithstanding the gravity with which this question was put, and the menaces which accompanied it, I could not persuade myself that he was in earnest; but I still continued to answer in the negative, and replied, as may easily be imagined, "That it was rather extraordinary to suppose that I who had only been brought in by force could ever have come there in order to betray the secrets of Masonry. You talk of secrets, and you have told me none. If in order to be initiated I must promise to obey a man that I know not, and if the interests of Masonry can be a bar to any part of my duty, good day to you Gentlemen. It is not too late as yet. I know nothing of your mysteries, nor do I wish to know more of them."

This answer did not disconcert the Venerable in the least, and he continued to act his part perfectly well; he pressed me more earnestly, and renewed his threats. I certainly believed the whole to be a farce; but even in joke I would not promise obedience to their Grand Master, especially on the supposition that his commands could ever be contrary to those of the Sovereign. I replied once more, "Gentlemen, or Brethren, I told you before, that if there was any thing in your games either against honor or conscience, you should learn whom you had to deal with. We are now come to the point. Y ou may do what you please with me, but you shall never make me assent to such a proposition; and once more I say *No.*"

Every one kept the most profound silence except the Venerable, though they were much amused with the scene. It at length grew more serious between the Venerable and me. He would not give up the point, and renewing his question over and over again, he was in hopes, by tiring my patience, to extort a Yes. At length I found myself quite wearied out. I was blindfolded, I tore off the bandage, threw it upon the ground, and stamping with my foot, called out No, with every sign of impatience. Immediately the whole Lodge clap their hands in sign of applause, and the Venerable compliments me on my constancy. "Such are the men for us, men of resolution and courage."—"What," said I, "men of resolution! And how many do you find who resist your threats! You yourselves, gentlemen, have not you all said Yes to this question: and if you have said it, how is it possible that you can persuade me that your mysteries contain nothing against honor or conscience."

The tone I assumed had thrown the Lodge into confusion. The brethren surrounded me, telling me I had taken things too much in earnest, and in too literal a sense: that they never had pretended to engage in any thing contrary to the duties of every true Frenchman, and that in spite of all my resistance I should nevertheless be admitted. The Venerable soon restored order with a few strokes of his mallet. He then informed me that I was passed to the degree of *Master*, adding, that if the secret was not given to me, it was only because a more regular lodge, and held with the ordinary ceremonies, was necessary on such an occasion. In the mean while he gave me the signs and the pass words for the third degree, as he had done for the other two. This was sufficient to enable me to be admitted into a regular Lodge, and now we were all brethren. As for me, I had been metamorphosed into *apprentice, fellow-craft*, and master in one evening, without having ever dreamt of it in the morning.

I was too well acquainted with those who had received me, not to believe their protestation sincere, when they declared that they had never pretended to engage in any thing contrary to their duty. And in justice I am bound to declare, that, excepting the Venerable, who turned out a violent Jacobin, they all showed themselves loyal subjects at the Revolution. I promised to be present at a regular meeting, provided the oath was never mentioned to me. They promised that it never should be insisted on, and they kept their words. They only requested that I would inscribe my name on the list, that it might be sent to the Grand Lodge of the East. I refused again, and asked time to consider of it; and when I had sufficiently attended to see what these Lodges were I retired, without even consenting to inscribe my name.

On my first appearance in a regular Lodge, I was quit for a fine speech on Masonry, of which I knew but little at that time, so chiefly dwelt upon fraternity, and on the pleasure of living with brethren.

They had agreed on that day to receive an apprentice, who was to have the secret given him with all the ordinary forms, in order that I might learn it, though only a spectator. It would be useless to swell this chapter by describing the ceremonial and the trials on such occasions. In the first degrees, they appear to be nothing more than a childish play. I may refer my readers to the Key of Masonry (*la Clef des Maçons*) or to the Free-masons Catechism, and some other books of the sort, which are perfectly exact as to the ceremonial of the three degrees which I received and saw conferred upon others, excepting in some very small points of no consequence.

The grand object for me was to learn the famous secret of Masonry. The moment at length comes when the postulant is ordered to approach nearer to the Venerable. Then the brethren who had been armed with swords for the occasion drawing up in two lines held their swords elevated, leaning the points toward each other, and formed what in Masonry is called the *arch of steel*. The candidate passes under this arch to a sort of altar elevated on two steps, at the farthest end of the Lodge. The Master, seated in an arm chair, or a sort of throne, behind this altar, pronounced a long discourse on the inviolability of the secret which was to be imparted, and on the danger of breaking the oath which the candidate was going to take. He pointed to the naked swords which were always ready to pierce the breast of the traitor, and declared to him that it was impossible to escape their vengeance. The candidate then swears, "that rather than betray the secret, he consents to have his head cut off, his heart and entrails torn out, and his ashes cast before the wind." Having taken the oath, the Master said the following words to him, which the reader may easily conceive have not escaped my memory, as I had expected them with so much impatience, "My dear brother, the secret of Masonry consists in these words, EQUALITY AND LIBERTY; *all men are equal and free; all men are brethren.*" The Master did not utter another syllable, and every body embraced the new brother *equal and free.*—The Lodge broke up, and we gayly adjourned to a Masonic repast.

I was so far from suspecting any further meaning in this famous secret, that I could scarcely refrain from bursting into a fit of laughter on hearing it, and with the greatest simplicity told those who had introduced me, If that was all their secret, I had known it a long time.

And certainly there was no occasion for being a mason to learn that man is not born for slavery, but to enjoy a *true Liberty* under the empire of the laws; or if they understand *by Equality* that as we are the children of one common parent, the creatures of the same God, we are to love and help each other as brethren; such truths certainly are better taught in the Gospel than by the childish rites of Masonry. I must say, that though the Lodge was numerously attended, I did not see a single craftsman who gave any other interpretation to this famous secret. The reader will see that it was necessary to go through many other degrees before they were initiated into a very different Equality and Liberty, and even that many who rose to higher degrees were never initiated into the ultimate sense of their famous secret.

Let not people be surprized that English Masonry should be chiefly composed of good and loyal subjects, whose main object is mutually to help each other on the principles of Equality, which with them is nothing more than Fraternity. Few English craftsmen are acquainted with more than the three first degrees already mentioned; and the reader may rest assured, that with the exception of the imprudent question on obedience to the Grand Master of the Order, there is nothing which can render the secret dangerous, were it not for the Jacobin interpretation. The English good sense has banished such an explanation. I have even heard of a resolution taken by some of the chief craftsmen, of rejecting all those who might seek to introduce the revolutionary liberty among them. I have read most excellent discourses and lectures on the avoiding of abuses, in the history of their Masonry. I have there seen the Grand Master telling the Brethren that the true Equality of the craft, does not authorize the Brother when out of the Lodge to derogate from that respect and deference due to the rank which any person bears in the world, or their different political degrees and titles. I have also remarked in the secret instructions of the Grand Master many excellent lectures to conciliate the Equality and Liberty of the craft, with fidelity and submission to the laws, in short, with all the duties of a loyal subject.[6] Hence it arises, that though the English have every thing in common with the craft of other nations, as far as the degree of Master inclusive; though they have the same secret, the same word, and the same signs to know each other by, yet as they generally stop at this degree, they never are initiated into the Grand Mysteries; or we should perhaps be more correct, if we said they had rejected them. They have found means of purifying Masonry. We shall soon see how little these grand mysteries could agree with the character of a nation which has given so many proofs of its wisdom.

---

6   See the 1st part of the *History of English Masonry*.

Chapter X.

Of the Grand Mysteries or Secrets of the Occult Lodges.

W e comprehend under the designation of Occult Lodges, or the higher degrees of Masonry, all Free-masons in general who, after having past the first three degrees of *Apprentice, Fellowcraft*, and *Master*, show sufficient zeal to be admitted into the higher degrees, where the veil is rent asunder, where emblematical and allegorical figures are thrown aside, and where the twofold principle of Equality and Liberty is unequivocally explained *by war against Christ and his Altars, war against Kings and their Thrones!!!*[1] In

Object of these mysteries.

---

1   These exclamation marks don't appear in the French. —Ed.

demonstrating that such is the result of the grand mysteries of the Craft, it will not be the want, but the multiplicity of proofs that will embarrass us. These alone would fill a large volume, and we wish to comprize them in this chapter. The reader will at least dispense with the emblems, oaths, ceremonies, and trials which are peculiar to each of these higher degrees. To show their last object and to develop their doctrine is the essential point, and what we shall always have in view. We shall begin by general observations, which will enable the reader to follow these mysteries more accurately, according as they are explained.

General reasons for mistrusting these mysteries.

Notwithstanding that in the first degrees of Masonry every thing appears to partake of puerile inventions, they nevertheless contain many things which the Sect have thrown out, merely to observe the impression which they made on the young adepts, and to judge from thence to what lengths they may be led.

1st. It declares the grand object it has in view to be at one time, *the raising of temples to virtue, and the excavating of dungeons for vice*; at another, to bring the adepts *to light,* and to deliver them from the darkness with which the prophane are encompassed; and by the *prophane* are understood the remainder of the universe. This promise is contained in the first Catechism of the Craft, and none will deny it. Nevertheless, this promise alone sufficiently indicates that the Craft acknowledge a morality and teach a doctrine which brands Christ and his Gospel with error and darkness.

2dly. The Masonic and Christian æra do not coincide. *The year of Light* dates with them from the first days of the creation: This again is what no Mason will deny. But that custom clearly demonstrates that their *lights*, their *morality*, and their *religious doctrines*, are anterior to the Evangelical Revelation, or even to Moses and the Prophets; they will, in short, be whatever incredulity may please to style the Religion of Nature.

3dly. In the Masonic language, all their Lodges are but one temple representing the whole universe; the temple which extends from the *East to the West, from the South to the North*. They admit into this temple with equal indifference the Christian or the Jew, the Turk or the Idolater, in fine, without distinction of Sect or religion. All equally behold the *light*, all learn the science of virtue, of real happiness, and all may remain members of the Craft, and rise in its degrees up to that where they are taught that all religious tenets are but errors and prejudices. Though many Masons may view this re-union in no other light than that of universal charity and benevolence, which ought to extend to all mankind, whether Jew, Gentile, Idolater, or Christian, it is nevertheless much to be feared, that this re-union of error and falsehood only tends to infuse an indifference for all religious tenets into the minds of the adepts, as a preparatory step to the denial of all in the higher degrees.

4thly. It is always under the most dreadful oaths of secrecy, that the Free-masons communicate their pretended lights or their art of building temples to virtue, and dungeons for vice. When both truth and virtue had every thing to fear from the reigning tyrants, it may be conceived that they taught their lessons in private; but, so far from exacting an oath of secrecy, they condemned silence as criminal when their lessons could be made public, and commanded that what had been learned under the shadow of the night should be preached openly at noon day. Either the doctrines of the Craft are conformable to the laws of Christianity, to the peace of states, and conducive to virtue and happiness (and then what has it had to fear from Kings and Pontiffs since Christianity was established?) or, their pretended science is in opposition to the religion and the laws of the Christian world (and then we have only to say, that the evil doer seeks to hide himself).

5thly. Most certainly the Free-masons do not make a secret of what is praise-worthy in their associations. It is not that fraternal affection for their neighbour which they hide, and which they only have in common with every religious observer of the gospel. Neither do they make a secret of the sweets of that convivial Equality which accompanies their meetings and their fraternal repasts. On the contrary, they are perpetually extolling their benevolence, and nobody is ignorant of the conviviality of their regales. Their secret must therefore contain something widely different from this fraternity, and something less innocent than the mirth of the Masonic table.

Such language in general might have been held to all Masons; such reasonings might have made them suspect that the higher degrees of their association contained mysteries which it was far more interested in hiding, than their fraternity, their signs, and pass-words. That affected secrecy on the first principlees of Masonry, *Equality* and *Liberty*, the oath never to reveal that such was the basis of their doctrines, premised that there existed such an explanation of these words as the Sect was interested in hiding both from the state and church. And in reality it was to attain to this explanation of the last mysteries that so many trials, oaths, and degrees were necesssary.

To convince the reader how much these surmizes are realized in the Occult Lodges, it is necessary for us to go back to the degree of Master, and relate the allegorical story of which the successive explanations and interpretations form the profound mysteries of the higher degrees.

In this degree of Master-mason the Lodge is hung round with black. In the middle is a coffin covered with a pall: the brethren standing round it in attitudes denoting sorrow and revenge. When the new adept is admitted, the Master relates to him the following history or fable:

Allegorical
history of
Adoniram,
the foun-
dation of
all these
degrees.

Adoniram presided over the payment of the workmen who were building the temple by Solomon's orders. They were three thousand workmen. That each one might receive his due, Adoniram divided them into three classes, Apprentices, Fellow-crafts, and Masters. He entrusted each class with a word, signs, and a grip by which they might be recognized. Each class was to preserve the greatest secrecy as to these signs and words. Three of the Fellow-crafts, wishing to know the word, and by that means obtain the salary, of Master, hid themselves in the temple, and each posted himself at a different gate. At the usual time when Adoniram came to shut the gates of the temple, the first of the three met him, and demanded the *word of the masters*; Adoniram refused to give it, and received a violent blow with a stick on his head. He flies to another gate, is met, challenged, and treated in a similar manner by the second: flying to the third door he is killed by the Fellow-craft posted there, on his refusing to betray the word. His assassins buried him under a heap of rubbish, and marked the spot with a branch of Acacia.

Adoniram's absence gave great uneasiness to Solomon and the Masters. He is sought for every where: at length one of the Masters discovers the corpse, and, taking it by the finger, the finger parted from the hand; he took it by the wrist, and it parted from the arm; when the Master, in astonishment, cried out Mac Benac, which the Craft interprets by "*the flesh parts from the bones.*"

Lest Adoniram should have revealed the word, the Masters convened and agreed to change it, and to substitute the words *Mac Benac*; sacred words, that Free-masons dare not pronounce out of the Lodges, and there each only pronounces one syllable, leaving his neighbour to pronounce the other.

The history finished, the adept is informed, that the object of the degree he has just received is to recover the word lost by the death of Adoniram, and to revenge this martyr of the Masonic secrecy.[2] The generality of Masons, looking upon this history as no more than a fable, and the ceremonies as puerile, give themselves very little trouble in searching farther into these mysteries.

These sports, however, assume a more serious aspect when we arrive at the degree of Elect (*Elu*). Degree of Elect. This degree is subdivided into two parts; the first has the revenging of Adoniram for its object, the other to recover the word, or rather the sacred doctrine which it expressed, and which has been lost.

In this degree of Elect, all the brethren appear 1st Part. dressed in black, wearing a breast-piece on the left side, on which is embroidered a death's head, a bone, and a poniard, encircled by the motto of *conquer or die*. The same motto is embroidered on a ribband which they wear in saltier. Every thing breathes death and revenge. The candidate is led into the Lodge blindfolded, with bloody gloves on his hands. An adept with a poniard in his hand threatens to run him through the heart

---

2   See the degree of Master in the Works on Masonry.

for the crime with which he is accused. After various frights, he obtains his life, on condition that he will revenge the father of Masonry in the death of his assassin. He is shown to a dark cavern. He is to penetrate into it, and they call to him, Strike all that shall oppose you; enter, defend yourself, and avenge our master; at that price you shall receive the degree of Elect. A poniard in his right hand, a lamp in his left, he proceeds; a phantom opposes his passage, he hears the same voice repeat, Strike, avenge Hiram, there is his assassin. He strikes and the blood flows.—Strike off his head, the voice repeats, and the head of the corpse is lying at his feet. He seizes it by the hair,[3] and triumphantly carries it back as a proof of his victory; shows it to each of the brethren, and is judged worthy of the new degree.

I have questioned divers Masons whether this apprenticeship to ferocity and murder had never given them the idea, that the head to be cut off was that of Kings, and they candidly owned that the idea had never struck them until the Revolution had convinced them of the fact.

2d Part. It was the same with respect to the religious part of this degee, where the adept is at once Pontiff and Sacrificer with the rest of the brethren. Vested in the ornaments of the priesthood, they offer bread and wine, according to the order of Melchisedec. The secret object of this ceremony

---

3   The reader may easily conceive, that this corpse is no more than a mannikin containing bladders full of blood.

is to re-establish religious Equality, and to exhibit all men equally Priests and Pontiffs, to recall the brethren to natural religion, and to persuade them that the religion of Moses and of Christ had violated religious Equality and Liberty by the distinction of Priests and Laity. It was the Revolution again which opened the eyes of many of the adepts, who then owned that they had been dupes to this impiety, as they had been to the regicide essay in the former part.[4]

---

4   Were we less rigorous as to our proofs, we should treat in this place of the degree called the *Knight of the Sun*. But we are only acquainted with it through the medium of the *Voile levé* (*the veil raised up*) a work of the Abbé Lefranc, certainly a man of the greatest virtue and undoubted veracity, and one of those excellent Ecclesiastics who preferred falling under the butchering poniards of the Septembrizers, to betraying their religion. But this author has neglected to inform us from what sources he had drawn his documents on the Masonic Degrees. Beside, we can remark, that he was not sufficiently acquainted with the origin of Masonry, which he only traces back to Socinus: His knowledge also of the Scotch degrees appears to have been acquired from inaccurate translations, which our French authors had vitiated according to their respective purposes.

    On the other side, we know for certain, that this degree of *Knights of the Sun* is a modern creation. Its author is to be known by his Teutonic style. If we are to believe what we have been told, it owes its origin to one of those Philosophists of very high life, who was too much attached to the high rank which he enjoyed, to adopt any other Equality than that which applied to the Masonic feasts and their impiety. And nothing is to be found in this degree which militates against the throne. It is much too perspicuous for many Masons, who would have been disgusted with any thing but emblematical figures susceptible of various explanations. Nevertheless, we were acquainted with several of these *Knights of the Sun* in France. This degree was only given to such of the adepts whose impiety was unequivocal. It was rather a degree of modern Philosophism than of ancient Masonry. Under that point of view it is worthy of notice; but we only give the following account as an extract from the Abbé Lefranc's work.

When initiated into this higher degree, it was no longer possible for the adept to dissemble with himself how incompatible the Masonic code was with the slightest remnant of Christianity. Here the Master of the Lodge is styled *Adam*, while the introducer takes the name of *Veritas* (*Truth*). The following are part of the lectures which brother Veritas repeats to the new adept while recapitulating all the allegories which he has seen in the former parts of Masonry.

"Learn in the first place that the three implements with which you have been made acquainted—the Bible, the Compasses, and the Square, have a secret significtion unknown to you. By the Bible you are to understand that you are to acknowledge no other law than that of Adam, the law which the Almighty had engraved on his heart, and *that is what is called the* LAW OF NATURE.—The Compass recalls to your mind, that God is the central point of every thing, from which every thing is equally distant, and to which every thing is equally near.— By the Square we learn, that God has made every thing equal— The Cubic Stone, that *all your actions are equal with respect to the sovereign good.*—The death of Hiram, and the change of the Master's word, teach you, that it is difficult to escape the snares of ignorance, but that it is your duty to show the same courage as our Master Hiram, who suffered himself to be massacred rather than hearken to the persuasions of his assassins."

The most essential part of this discourse is the explanation which Brother *Veritas* gives of the degree of Elect. Amongst others we read the following lines:

"If you ask me what are the necesssary qualities to enable a Mason to arrive at the centre of real perfection? I shall answer, that in order to attain it, he must have crushed the head of the serpent of worldly ignorance, and have *cast off* those prej-

CHAPTER X

These mysteries are not sufficiently explained in the degree of Elect for all to comprehend them. The generality of Masons initiated in this degree give themselves little trouble to understand the real signification of them; and as long as they have

The higher degrees of Scotch Masonry.

---

udices of youth conerning the mysteries of the predominant religion of his native country. *All religious worship being only invented, in hopes of acquiring power, and to gain precedency among men; and by a flesh which covets, under the false pretence of piety, its neighbour's riches*; in fine, by Gluttony, the daughter of Hypocrisy, who, straining every nerve to restrain the carnal senses of those who possess riches, perpetually offer to them on the altar of their hearts, holocausts which voluptuousness, luxury, and perjury, have procured for them. This, my dear brother, is what you have to combat, such is the monster you have to crush under the emblem of the serpent. *It is a faithful representation of that which the ignorant vulgar adore under the name of religion.*

"It was the prophane and timid Abiram who, transformed by a *fanatical zeal into a tool of the Monkish and religious rites*, struck the first blows on the breast of our father Hiram; that is to say, who sapped the foundations of the celestial temple, which the ETERNAL had himself erected upon earth to sublime virtue.

"The first age of the world witnessed what I assert. *The most simple law of nature* rendered our first fathers the happiest of mortals. The monster Pride appears on earth, he bellows, he is heard by men and by the happy mortals of those days. He promises them happiness in another fife, and persuades them by his mellifluous words, that he *taught men to adore the Eternal Creator of all things in a more extensive and more special manner* than any person had done before on earth. *This hydra* with an hundred heads misled and misleads those men who are subject to its laws, and will continue its deceptions until the moment when the *Elect* shall appear to combat and crush it entirely." (*See the degree of Knights of the Sun*). Such doctrines need no comment.

any sentiments of religion or attachment to their Prince, they reject with indignation all interpretations which militate against either. Many of them are disgusted with the multiplicity of trials, and are content to remain in the inferior degrees, which suffice to give them the title of Masons, admit them to all the Masonic repasts, and even entitle them to the alms and benefactions which the Lodges bestow on their indigent brethren.—Those whose zeal is not cooled by this multiplicity of trials, are generally admitted from the degree of *Master*, or from that of *Elect*, to the three Scotch degrees. We shall not seek for the history and tendency of these three degrees in books which have been written to discredit the craft. The German adept who translated them into his language for the instruction of his brethren, is one of the most zealous knights for the doctrine therein contained. His whole genius is exerted in their defence, nor could we follow a more unexceptionable author. His object was to infuse light into his brethren; and we prophane beings may draw the following conclusions from his lectures.[5]

Every Mason who wishes to be admitted into the Scotch degrees, and even into all other degrees of Masonry, is first taught that until that period he has lived in slavery, and it is on that account only that he is admitted into the presence of the other brethren with a rope about his neck, praying that he may be delivered from his bonds. But

---

5   See the Scotch degrees printed at Stockholm, 1784.

when he aspires at the third Scotch degree, or at becoming a knight of St. Andrew, he must appear in a far more humiliating costume. The candidate is shut up in a dark cell, a rope with four flip knots is twisted round his neck, he is stretched upon the floor; there, by the dull light of a twinkling lamp, he is abandoned to himself to meditate on the wretched state of slavery in which he exists, and to learn properly to estimate the value of Liberty. At length one of the brethren comes and introduces him to the Lodge, leading him by the rope, holding a drawn sword in his right hand as if meant to run him through the heart, in case he made any resistance. After having undergone a long examination, and particularly after having sworn on the salvation of his soul, never to reveal the secrets with which he is entrusted, he is declared free. It would be useless to enumerate all the different oaths; it is sufficient to say, that each degree and subdivision of degree has its peculiar oath, and that they are all frightful; all call the vengeance of God and of the Brotherhood on the unhappy man who shall betray their secret. In future then we shall only treat of the doctrine of these secrets.

In the first degree of Scotch Knighthood the adept is informed, that he has been elevated to the dignity of *High Priest*. He receives a sort of benediction in the name of the immortal and invisible Jehovah, and in future it is under that title that he is to adore the Deity, *because* the signification of JEHOVAH *is far more expressive than that of* ADONAI.

In this first degree he receives the Masonic science only as descending from Solomon and Hiram, and revived by the Knights Templars.—But in the second degree he learns that it is to be traced to Adam himself, and has been handed down by Noah, Nimrod, Solomon, Hugo de Paganis, the founder of the Knights Templars, and Jaques de Molay, their last Grand Master, who each in their turns had been the favourites of *Jehovah*, and are styled the Masonic Sages. At length in the third degree it is revealed to him, that the celebrated *word* lost by the death of Hiram was this name of Jehovah. It was found, he is told, by the Knights Templars at the time when the Christians were building a Church at Jerusalem. In digging the foundations in that part on which the holy of holies of Solomon's temple formerly stood, they discovered three stones, which had formerly been parts of the foundation. The form and junction of these three stones drew the attention of the Templars; and their astonishment was extreme, when they beheld the name of Jehovah engraved on the last. This was the famous word lost by the death of Adoniram. The Knights Templars, on their return to Europe, took great care not to lose so precious a monument. They carried them into Scotland, taking particular care of that which bore the name of Jehovah. The Scotch sages on their part were not forgetful of the respect due to such precious monuments, they made them the foundation stones of their first Lodge; and as these first stones were laid on St. Andrew's day, they took the name of Knights of St. Andrew. Their successors are entrusted with the secret, and are at this day the perfect masters of Free-masonry, the High Priests of Jehovah.

If we lay aside the hermetical part of the science, or the transmutation of metals, such will be in substance the whole doctrine which is revealed to the adept initiated in the grand mysteries of the Scotch degrees.

In a sort of Cathechism, to which he answers to show that he has remembered every thing that he has seen, and all that has been explained to him in the Lodge, or, as it is then called, in Solomon's temple, the following question is asked, *Is that all you have seen?* To which he answers, *I have seen many other things, but, like the other Scotch Masters, I keep them secret in my heart.* This secret henceforth cannot be difficult to understand. It is only to view the *Scotch Master* in his new character of *High Priest of Jehovah*, or of that worship, that pretended Deism, which we have been told was successively the religion of Adam, Noah, Nimrod, Solomon, Hugo de Paganis, of the Grand Master Molay, and of the Knights Templars, and which at this day is to constitute the religion of the complete Master Mason.

These mysteries might have sufficed for the adepts. All who had obtained the Scotch degrees were declared free in future, and all were equally Priests of Jehovah. This priesthood ridded them of all the mysteries of the Gospel, and of all revealed religion. That liberty and happiness which the Sect declares to consist in the revival of Deism, sufficiently instils into the mind of the adept what he is to think of Christianity and of its divine Author. Nevertheless the grand mysteries are not exhausted. The adepts still have to discover who was the person that wrested the word, the famous name of *Jehovah*, from their predecessors; that is to say, who it was that destroyed their favourite worship of Deism. It was but too evident that the whole fable of Hiram or Adoniram and of his assassins was no more than an allegory, the explanation of which must naturally answer the questions, who is the real assassin of Adoniram? By whom was the Deistical form of worship destroyed? Who was it that wrested the famous word from the Sect? He is the person against whom the vengeance and the hatred of the Sect is directed, and it was necessary to instil the same spirit into the minds of its profound adepts. To effectuate this, we ascend to a new degree called the Knights *Rosæ Crucis*, or the Rosicrucians.

It is certainly a most atrocious blasphemy to accuse Christ of having destroyed by his religion on the doctrine of the unity of God; when on the contrary the most evident and the most attested of all facts is, that to his religion we owe the banishment of thousands and thousands of false gods, which the Idolators had made to themselves. The gospel, in declaring the unity of God, teaches us the Trinity of Persons; but this mystery like all others which we learn from revelation, humbles the Sophisters in their own minds. Fraught with ingratitude against him who has cast the idols on the dust, they have sworn an eternal hatred against the eternal Word, because he reveals a God whom in their madness they are not able to comprehend. *Christ himself* in their eyes is the destroyer of the unity of God, he is the great enemy of *Jehovah*; and to infuse the hatred of the Sect into the minds of the new adepts, constitutes the grand mystery of the new degree which they have called Rosicrucian.

As the adept was seldom initiated into this new degree before he had passed through the Scotch degrees, he is already aware, as the reader must observe, that *Jehovah* is no longer the word sought after, and here we shall see every thing related only to the author of Christianity. The ornaments of the Lodge appear to be solely intended to recal to the candidate the solemn mystery of Mount Calvary. The whole is hung in black, an altar is to be seen at the bottom, and over the altar is a transparent representation of the three crosses, the middle one bearing the ordinary inscription. The brethren in sacerdotal vestments are seated on the ground, in the most profound silence, sorrowful and afflicted, resting their heads on their arm to represent their grief. It is not the death of the son of God, who died victim of our sins, that is the cause of their affliction, the grand object of it is evident by the first answer which is made to the question with which all Lodges are generally opened.

Degree of Rosæ Crucis.

The Master asks the Senior Warden what o'clock is it? The answer varies according to the different degrees. In this it is as follows;

> It is the first hour of the day, the time when the veil of the temple was rent asunder, when darkness and consternation was spread over the earth, when the light was darkened, when *the implements of Masonry were broken*, when the flaming star disappeared, when the cubic stone was broken, *when the word was lost.*[6]

The adept who has attended to the progressive discoveries he has made in the different degrees, needs no further lessons to understand the meaning of this answer. He thereby learns that the day on which the *word* JEHOVAH was lost is precisely that on which the Son of God dying on a cross for the salvation of mankind consummated the grand mystery of our Religion, destroying the reign of every other, whether Judaic, natural, or sophistical. The more a Mason is attached to the *word*, that is, to his pretended natural Religion, the more inveterate will his hatred be against the author of Revealed Religion.

Neither is this *word*, which he has already found, any longer the object of his researches; his hatred has further views. He must seek for a new word, which shall perpetuate in his own mind and that of his brethren their blasphemous hatred for the God of Christianity; and for this they adopt the inscription of the cross.

---

6   See the degree Rosæ Crucis.

Every Christian knows the significtion of INRI, *Iesus Nazarenus Rex Iudæorum* (Jesus of Nazareth King of the Jews). The Rosicrucian is taught the following interpretation—the *Iew* of *Nazareth* led by *Raphael* into *Iudea*; an interpretation which, divesting Christ of his divinity, assimilates him to a common man, whom the Jew Raphael conducts to Jerusalem there to suffer condign punishment for his crimes. As soon as the candidate has proved that he understands the Masonic meaning of this inscription INRI, the Master exclaims. *My dear Brethren, the word is found again*, and all present applaud this luminous discovery, that—he whose death was the consummation and the grand mystery of the Christian Religion was no more than a common Jew crucified for his crimes.

It is thus that the Sect have blasphemously adopted the very word, which recals to the Christian all that love which he bears for the Son of God expiring on the cross for the salvation of mankind, as their watchword of hatred. They repeat it to each other when they meet, and INRI is to perpetuate their spite against him who loved them even unto the death of the cross.

It is not on the authority of persons strangers to the craft that we have disclosed this atrocious mystery of Occult Masonry. What I have already said respecting my initiation to the first degrees put me in the way of conversing with those whom I knew to be more advanced, and in many of these interviews it happened that, notwithstanding all their secrecy, some unguarded expressions escaped the most zealous adepts, which threw light on the subject. Others lent me their books, presuming that their obscureness and the want of the essential words, or the method of discovering them, would baffle all my attempts to understand them. I nevertheless discovered some of these words, such as *Jehovah*, by uniting several pages and only taking the bottom letter of each. This famous word discovered, I soon got knowledge of that of *Inri*. I then combined all I had seen, all that I knew of the different degrees, with what I had collected from divers conversations I had had with certain Masons, whose Philosophism was otherwise known to me. I afterwards conversed with the most candid men whom I knew to be in the same degrees. I reprobated particularly those ceremonies so evidently in derision of Religion, and which they had never beheld but as games without any object. I never met with one who denied the facts as I have stated them. They owned the different reading of the word *Inri* in the degree Rosæ Crucis, but they denied the most distant idea of the consequences which I had drawn. Some, on reflection, acknowledged them to be well founded, while others considered them vastly exaggerated.

At the time when the Revolution took place, I combined my preceding discoveries, the decrees of the National Assembly, and the secret of the first degree, and no longer doubted that Masonry was but a society formed by men who, on the first initiation of their adepts, gave them the words Equality and Liberty as their secret, leaving to well-meaning and religious Masons to interpret them according to their own principles; yet reserving to themselves to interpret (in their Occult degrees) these same words according to the full extent of the French Revolution.

One of these Brethren, who had long since been admitted to the degree Rosæ Crucis, but who was at the same time a very virtuous and religious man, was much concerned at seeing me in this opinion. He tried every means to give me a better idea of a society in which he was proud of having filled the most honorable posts. This was a topic on which we had often conversed; and he wished much to make me a convert to Masonry. He was indeed almost affronted with me for saying that he was not initiated into all the mysteries of Masonry, though a Rosicrucian, or else that this degree had its subdivisions, and that he was only partially acquainted with them. At length I convinced him of the fact, by asking the explanation of some of the Masonic *Hieroglyphics*; he owned that he had asked their meaning, but the explanation of them had been refused him; yet he had no doubt of their being as innocent emblems as the Square, the Compass, the Trowel, and many others. I knew that he had but one degree more to take, and the veil would be rent asunder. I proposed or rather marked out the means by which he might acquire that degree; and then, I told him, all illusion as to the real object of the Occult Masons would vanish. He was too eager for being initiated not to make a trial of the means I proposed; but he was convinced that it would prove ineffectual, and only furnish him with new arms to combat my unjust prejudices against Masonry. A few days after I saw him enter my room; but in such a state of agitation, that his lips could scarcely utter, "O my dear friend, my dear friend—you were in the right—Oh, how much you were in the right! . . . Where have I been? My God! Where have I been?"—I easily understood these exclamations; but the poor man could scarcely recover himself so as to continue. He threw himself into a chair as if he were exhausted, perpetually repeating, "Where have I been?—Oh how much you are in the right!"—I earnestly desired him to give me some particulars with which I was unacquainted—"Oh how much you were in the right!" he repeated again, "but that is all I can tell you."—"Oh, unhappy man," I exclaimed, "you have then taken that execrable oath, and I am the person who has exposed you to that rash deed; I sincerely ask your pardon, but I protest upon my word, that I never reflected on that execrable oath when I suggested the means by which you might convince yourself, and learn to know those detested beings who have so horribly abused your credulity. I know that it had been better for you to have been for ever ignorant of that fatal secret, than that you should learn it at the expense of so horrid an oath. I really did not reflect on it, or I should never have exposed you to it; no, I could not in conscience." It was really true, that I never had reflected on this oath. Without examining whether such wicked oaths are binding, I feared being indiscreet. But it had been sufficient for me to have shown this gentleman that I was acquainted, at least in part, with these Occult mysteries. He saw clearly by my questions, that he had taught me nothing new by an avowal which alone proves the very essence of these Occult degrees.

His fortune had been mined by the Revolution; and he declared to me, that it would from that moment be retrieved, provided he accepted of a proposal which had been made to him.—"If I chuse," said he, "to go to London, Bruxelles, Constantinople, or any other town I please, neither I, my wife, nor my children, will ever want for any thing."— "Yes," I replied, "but on condition only that you go there *to preach Equality and Liberty; in short, all the horrors of the Revolution.*"—"You are right," replied he, "*but that is all I can say*—Oh my God where have I been!—I beg you will not question me any farther."

This was sufficient for my present purpose; but I hoped in time to learn farther particulars. Nor were my hopes vain. The following is what I have gathered from various Masons who, finding me acquainted with the major part of their secrets, spoke the more openly to me, till at length, feeling how much they had been duped by this Occult Sect, they would willing have revealed all its mysteries, could they have done it without exposing themselves to danger.

Mystical Masonry.

The explanation which was given to an adept of all that he had seen before on his admission to the degree of Rosæ Crucis, depended entirely on the disposition they observed in him. If they had to do with a man who was proof against their impiety, they sought to divert him from the Church under pretence of regenerating his faith; they represented to him, that there existed an infinity of abuses in Christianity at present, with respect to Equality and Liberty of the children of God. With them the word to be recovered was, a wish for a Revolution which should revive those times when every thing was common among Christians, when the distinctions of rich, of poor, or of high and mighty Lords, were unknown. They were taught to look forward to the most happy regeneration of mankind, and almost to a new heaven and a new earth. Credulous and simple minds were caught by such magnificent promises. They looked upon the Revolution as that sacred fire which was to purify the earth; and these credulous adepts were seen to second the Revolution with the enthusiastic zeal of a holy cause. This may be called *Mystical Masonry*. Such was the craft of all those fools for whom the Occult Masons set up the Prophetess *Labrousse*, so famous in the beginning of the Revolution. Such again was the weak-minded *Varlet*, the Bishop *in partibus* of Babylon. I never could conceive where he had gathered his religious opinions, when with the greatest simplicity he complained that I had combated them. I was informed of it by a guest of his, whose reputation of great knowledge in Masonry had acquired him a seat at the Masonic repasts which the poor simple man used to give; and even at those dinners the difference was observable in the adepts, though of the same degree, each having received an explanation of the mysteries coinciding with his own disposition. Our simple Bishop viewed the whole science of the Craft in no other light than as the perfection of the Gospel; and even in his repasts he was ever mindful of the precepts of the Church, keeping abstinence on days appointed, &c. The Apostate Dom Gerles, on the contrary, was a Mason of a quite different system or explanation. He already sung those verses which in a letter since found among Robespierre's papers,[7] he delares to have addressed to truth alone:

> Ni culte, ni Prêtres, ni Roi,
> Car la nouvelle Eve, c'est toi.[8]

It was at these repasts that the Doctor La Mothe, a learned Rosicrucian, behaved with a modesty which seemed to prognosticate that one day he would equally hate both the craft of Varlet and of Dom Gerles. The latter paid his revolutionary debt to the guillotine; the other two are living,

---

7   *Procès-verbal*, No. 57.
8   Nor Worship, nor Priests, nor King, for thou art the new Eve.

and I name them because I am not afraid of being contradicted, and because these sorts of anecdotes carry strong proof with them, and explain how persons of the most pious and charitable dispositions have been misled: how a Princess, the sister of the Duke of Orléans, was so blinded as even to pant after the Revolution, which in her eyes was to be nothing less than the regeneration of the Christian world.[9]

Such explanations of the Rosicrucian degree were only for those dupes in whom they remarked a certain bias towards mysticity. The generality were abandoned to their own interpretations; but when an adept testified a great desire of acquiring new lights, and was thought able to undergo the necessary trials, he was admitted to the degree of *Kadosch,* or of the *regenerated man,* where all ambiguity ceases.

Degree of
Kadosch.

It was to this degree that the adept of whom we have before spoken was admitted. Nor was the exhausted state in which he found himself after

---

9   The art shown in this degree should prove a salutary lesson to those who, without any examination, adopt political and religious ideas, and sport them in every company that will submit to hear them. Had they only reflected on the persons who had instilled them into their minds, or on the authors of the works whence they had adopted their ideas, how many honorable but misguided persons would, on such an examination, find they were no more than the blind apostles of every religious and political iniquity, and the agents of designing men! Abuses are certainly to be reformed, and our worship ought to be pure; but reflexion can never be detrimental to him who wishes to speak on either. —Tr.

having undergone those trials to be wondered at. Adepts have told me, that no physical art is spared; that there is no machinery, spectres, terrors, &c. &c. which are not employed, to try the constancy of the candidate. We are told by Mr. Monjoie, that the Duke of Orléans was obliged to ascend, and then throw himself off a ladder. If that were all, he was most kindly treated. A deep cave, or rather a precipice, whence a narrow tower rises to the summit of the lodge, having no avenue to it but by subterraneous passages replete with horror, is the place where the candidate is abandoned to himself, tied hand and foot. In this situation he finds himself raised from the ground by machines making the most frightful noise. He slowly ascends this dark vault, sometimes for hours together, and then suddenly falls as if he were not supported by any thing. Thus mounting and falling alternately, he must carefully avoid showing any sign of fear. All this however is a very imperfect account of the terrors of which men, who had undergone these trials, speak. They declared that it was impossible for them to give an exact description of them; they lost their senses; they did not know where they were. Draughts were given to them, which, adding to their corporal strength, did not restore them to their mental faculties; but rather increased their strength only to leave them a prey to fury and terror.

Many circumstances relating to this degree made us believe at first sight that it was connected with *Illuminism*; but on examination we find it to be only a farther explanation of the Masonic allegory. Here again the candidate is transformed into an assassin. Here it is no longer the founder of Masonry, Hiram, who is to be avenged, but it is Molay the Grand Master of the Knights Templars, and the person who is to fall by the assassin's hand is *Philippe le Bel,* King of France, under whose reign the order of the Templars was destroyed.

When the adept sallies forth from the cavern with the reeking head, he cries *Nekom* (I have killed him). After this atrocious trial he is admitted to take the oath. I learned from one of the adepts, that at the time when he was about to take the oath, one of the *Knights Kadosch* held a pistol at his breast, making a sign that he would murder him if he did not pronounce it. On my asking if he believed that it was in earnest, he said that he certainly did believe so, though he could not be sure. At length the veil is rent asunder. The adept is informed, that till now he had only been partially admitted to the truth; that Equality and Liberty, which had constituted the first secret on his admission into Masonry, consisted in recognizing no superior on earth, and in viewing Kings and Pontiffs in no other light than as men on a level with their fellow men, having no other rights to sit on the throne, or to serve at the altar, but what the people had granted them, and of which they had the power of depriving them whenever they pleased. They are also informed, that Princes and Priests have too long abused the goodness and simplicity of the people; that the grand object of Masonry, in building temples to Equality and Liberty, is, to rid the earth of this double pest, by destroying every altar which credulity and superstition had erected, and every throne on which were only to be seen despots tyrannizing over slaves.

These documents concerning the degree of Kadosch are not merely taken from the works of Messrs. Monjoie and Lefranc, but from adepts themselves. Besides, it is easy to perceive how exactly this account corresponds with the avowal of the adept who was obliged to own that I was quite in the right when I told him that this was the final object of Free-masonry.

Oh how profound the combination of these mysteries! their progress is slow and tortuous; but how artfully each degree tends to the grand object.

In the first two degrees, that is to say, in those of *Apprentice* and *Fellow-craft*, the Sect begins by throwing out its *Equality* and *Liberty*. After that, it occupies the attention of its novices with puerile games of fraternity or Masonic repasts; but it already trains its adepts to the profoundest secrecy by the most frightful oaths. The different degrees compared.

In that of *Master*, it relates the allegorical history of Adoniram, who is to be avenged; and of the word, which is to be recovered.

In the degree of *Elect*, it trains the adepts to vengeance, without pointing out the person on whom it is to fall. It carries them back to the time of the Patriarchs, when, according to them, men knew no religion but that of nature, and when every body was equally Priest and Pontiff. But it had not as yet declared that all religion revealed since the time of the Patriarchs was to be thrown aside.

This last mystery is only developed in the Scotch degrees. There the brethren are declared free: The word so long sought for is, Deism; it is the worship of Jehovah, such as was known to the Philosophers of nature. The true Mason becomes the Pontiff of Jehovah; and such is the grand mystery by which he is extricated from that darkness in which the prophane are involved.

In the degree *Rosæ Crucis* he who wrested the *word*, who destroyed the worship of *Jehovah*, is Christ himself, the Author of Christianity; and it is on the Gospel and on the Son of Man that the adept is to avenge the brethren, the Pontiffs of *Jehovah*.

At length, on his reception as *Kadosch*, he learns that the assassin of Adoniram is the King, who is to be killed to avenge the Grand Master Molay, and the order of the Masons successors of the Knights Templars. The religion which is to be destroyed to recover the *word*, or the true doctrine, is the religion of Christ, founded on revelation. This word in its full extent is *Equality* and *Liberty*, to be established by the total overthrow of the Altar and the Throne.

Such are the incipient degrees, the process, and the whole System of Masonry; it is thus that the Sect by its gradual explanations of its twofold principle of *Equality* and *Liberty*, of its allegory of the founder of Masonry to be avenged, of the word to be recovered, leading the adepts from secret to secret, at length initiates them into the whole Jacobinical code of Revolution.

We are not to lose sight of the extreme care with which the adept is questioned on all that he has seen before, whenever he is initiated to a new degree, lest he should overlook the intimate connection subsisting between each; and thus in the first degrees *Equality* and *Liberty* are given to him as the secret, while the complete explanation and application of them form the mysteries of the last.[10]

The more frightful these hidden mysteries of the Lodges shall appear to the historian, the more strenuously it becomes his duty to insist on the numbers of honest Masons who never partook of these horrid mysteries. Nothing is more easy than to be duped in Masonry. Such may have been the lot of those who only seek to make acquaintances in the Lodges, or to pass their leisure hours with men apparently intimate at first sight. It is true, that this intimacy seldom extends beyond the walls of the Lodge; but the days of their meeting are often days of festivity. These repasts are certainly heightened by the temporary Equality,

---

10   I am not ignorant of the existence of several other degrees in Occult Masonry, such as those of the *Star* and of the *Druids*. The Prussians have added theirs, and the French have done as much. We though it sufficient to attach ourselves to the most common ones, as most proper to delineate the conduct and spirit of the Sect.

which adds much to the mirth of the meeting; and all cares subside for the day. What has been said of certain assemblies where decency was not respected, is most certainly the invention of calumny. The extreme order and morality of these meetings has often proved a snare to captivate those who are to be caught with outward appearances, and Cagliostro's infamous behaviour would have made many desert the Lodges. This monstrous Adonis disgusted all Strasbourg, and was betrayed by the cries of the Egyptian sisters. It was no longer the age when the mysteries of the Adamites could be approved of. He was driven from that town for having attempted to introduce them. He would in like manner have ruined the craft had he continued to confound his Lodges with those of the East. Such was not the behaviour of our modern Masonry; on the contrary it appeared, that it had neither Religion nor Government in view; and they were seldom mentioned in the generality of Lodges. It was only on the day of initiation, that the reflecting adept could surmise that it had any future object; but even on those very days the trials were rather a subject of diversion than of reflection; and, so far from meditating on the allegorical emblems, they were rather diverted from it by the Sect, until favourable dispositions had been discovered in them for their further initiation.—The Sect knew well, that a day would come when a small number of the Occult Masons would suffice to put all the inferior multitude of adepts in motion. It is thus that it may be easily explained how there have existed so many honest Masons, and how so many are still to be found who have never surmised any thing in their games but the mysteries of an innocent Equality and Liberty, no ways alluding either to Religion or the State.

In defence of English Masonry, we may add, that they allow only of the three first degrees.— Prudence and wisdom have made them reject the wish of avenging the death of Adoniram on his pretended assassin, a wish that we have seen converted in the Occult Lodges into a desire of revenging the Masons and their founder Molay, and then into a wish of avenging the Masonic Equality and Liberty by the extinction of all Kings. Nothing of this is to be found in the English Masonry; nor is that mysterious pursuit of the word which was lost by Adoniram to be traced. You are immediately informed that it is *Jehovah*. He who could wish to draw certain inferences from this, would have a long course of reasonings to run through, none of which appear to have ever been thought of by the English Masons. With them Jehovah is no more than the universal god of human nature; it is to be sure rather extraordinary that they should pretend to be the only people who have any knowledge of that God; but their conclusion is, that all mankind, and particularly the Free-masons, ought to live with and succour each other like brethren. Nothing appears in their mysteries tending towards the hatred of Christianity, or that of Kings.

Their laws and institutes with respect to Religion are comprehended in declaring,

> That a Mason will never be a stupid Atheist nor an irreligious Libertine. That though in former times every Mason was obliged to profess the religion of the state or nation he lived in, at present, leaving every one to enjoy his own private opinions, they are only bound to follow the religion in which every body agrees, a religion which consists in being good, sincere, modest, and men of honour.

Certainly such laws do not oblige the English Mason to be a Deist, but only to be an honest man, whatever may be his religion.

With regard to the civil powers, a part of their laws are expressed as follows:

> A Mason shall be a peaceable subject, and cheerfully conform to the laws of the country in which he resides. He shall not be concerned in plots or conspiracies against Government; and he shall pay proper respect to the civil Magistrate. Should a brother be implicated in rebellion against the state, he shall not be supported in his rebellion.

Such are the laws to be found in Thomas Wolson[11]

---

11   Penname under which was published *Solomon in All His Glory* in 1766, written pobably by George Smith (c. 1728 - 1785), and published originally in French under the title *Le maçon démasqué*, in 1751. —Ed.

and William Preston,[12] the one full of contempt, the other full of zeal, for English Masonry; both nevertheless agree as to the laws of the Lodges. We are not therefore to confound English Masonry with the occult Lodges, which they have prudently rejected.

We perfectly well know that many English are initiated in the occult mysteries of the Rosicrucians and Scotch degrees; but it is not their *Occult Science* which constitutes them English Masons; for the first three degrees are all that are acknowledged in England.

Having made these exceptions, we shall continue our proofs; for it is not on their degrees alone that we have founded our judgment of the occult Masons. Were we strangers to their rites and ceremonies, the reader will judge what opinions we should form on perusing the doctrines of their most celebrated writers.

---

12 William Preston (1742 - 1818), besides freemason an editor with the printer William Strahan, wrote *Illustrations of Masonry*, published in 1772, based on his extensive research into the subject. As an editor he enjoyed the respect of Edward Gibbon and David Hume. —Ed.

New Proofs of the System and Mysteries of the Occult Masons.

n order to form a proper idea of the extent of the system of the Occult Lodges of Free-masonry, let us combine in this Chapter two essential points; first, the general doctrine of the most zealous and learned Masons; secondly, their divers opinions as to their origin.

Masonic writers in general divide Free-masonry into three classes, the Hermetic, the Cabalistic (which comprehends the Martinists), and the Eclectic Masonry. Let us first take a view of the religious tenets of these different classes, and we shall find that, like our modern Sophisters, they only agree in one point, and that is in their hatred to

Division of the systems and Masonic Sects.

Christianity and Revelation; in all other points we shall find them in perfect opposition to one another with respect to their religious tenets or rather blasphemous impieties.

Hermetic Masonry.

The Hermetic Masonry, or the Scotch degrees, who work in chymistry, have adopted *Pantheism or the true Spinosism*. With them *every thing is God, and God is every thing*. That is their grand mystery, engraved in one word Jehovah on the stone brought by the Knights Templars from the Holy Land.

Let the reader refer to the preface of the zealous Knight of St. Andrew, who has given us such a circumstantial account of these degrees. He will there see our Knight reducing the result of his whole doctrine to this famous text of Hermes Trismegistus, "All is part of God; if all is part, the whole must be God. Therefore every thing that is made made itself, and will never cease to act, for this agent cannot repose. And as God has no end, so can his works have neither beginning nor end." After having recited this passage, our Pantheistical adept tells us, "Such is the summary though expressive belief of the whole Hermetic System;" in a word the whole religious system of the Scotch degrees with the discovery of which he is so much pleased.

Let not the reader suppose that he attempts to explain away the expression *all is God*. In his opinion nothing but the grossest ignorance and prejudice can disapprove of the assertion. It is in vain to object, that, making the grain of sand, the Heavens, the Earth, the animal, or man, *a part of God*, is rendering the Deity divisible; for he will answer, that it is only the grossest ignorance which hides from us, that *those millions of millions of parts are so united together and so essentially constitute a God whole, that to separate a single particle would be to annihilate the* WHOLE *itself, or the Great* JEHOVAH. But, lest the Knight of the Craft should be vain on finding himself a part of God, our Hierophant informs us, that *as the little finger is always less than the whole body; so is man, though a small particle of God, infinitely smaller than* JEHOVAH. Our adept may nevertheless rejoice, however small a particle he may be of the Deity, as the day will come when he is to be reunited to the great whole, the day when, every thing being reunited to the great Jehovah, harmony will be complete, *and true Pantheism will be established for ever.*[1]

It is to be hoped that the reader does not expect us to trouble ourselves with the refutation of so monstrous a system. The preface however is not the only part of that work which lays down this system as the tenets of these degrees; for, after the description of them, we find what are called *Solomon's Thesis*; also the *Archetype world*; and these are productions all tending to strengthen them in their impiety.[2] We shall not therefore be accused of calumniating this branch of Masonry by attrib-

---

1   Preface to the Scotch Degrees.

2   Second Part, Edition of Stockholm, 1782.

uting to it a system which makes the villain, like the just man, a constituent part of the Deity, and represents vice and virtue as the very action of the Deity; a system which promises the same destiny to the good and to the wicked, of being *re-united to the Deity*; and thus, after having ceased to be man, of being God to all eternity.

Cabalistic
Masonry.

The Cabalistic system, without being less impious, is far more humiliating for the human understanding; and that especially in an age which pretends to the high-sounding appellation of the Philosophic age, of the age of light. It was in the Prussian Lodges of the Rosicrucians that this Cabalistic system was to be found; at least before their union with the Illuminées.[3] We have authentic information, that this was adopted by certain Lodges of Rosicrucians in France a few years before the Revolution, and particuarly at Bourdeaux. To prevent, however, all possibility of being mistaken, whatever we shall say on this subject shall be grounded on the Cabalistic lectures lately printed under the title of *Telescope de Zoroastre*. They are dedicated to one of those Princes whom the author does not name, but whose zealous pursuits in these mysteries are sufficiently known by public report. With such a guide we shall not be accused of imposing on our readers.

The JEHOVAH of this Sect is no longer the *God* WHOLE; but he is at once the *God* SISAMORO, and the *God* SENAMIRA. The first is joined by the *Geni-*

---

3   Letters from Philo to Spartacus.

296

us Sallak, and the second by the *Genius* Sokak. If these famous Cabalistic words are inverted, we have *Oromasis* or the *God* GOOD, and *Arimanes* the *God* EVIL, and the Genii will become *Kallas* and *Kakos, pretty correctly Greek for* GOOD *and* BAD.[4]

Thus in attributing to Oromasis a multitude of *good* Genii or spirits like himself, and to Arimanes *evil* Genii participating of his own wickedness, we have the Jehovah of *Cabalistic Masonry*; that is to say, the *word* to be recovered in their Lodges, or the tenets to be substituted to those of Christianity.

Of these good and evil Genii, some are more perfect spirits and preside over the planets, the rising and setting of the Sun, the increase and decrease of the Moon; others, inferior to the first, but superior to the human soul, exercise their empire over the Stars and Constellations; but in both these classes, the good are the angels of life, victory and happiness, while the bad are the angels of death and calamity. All know the secrets of the past, present, and to come, and can impart this great science to the adepts. To captivate their favour, the cabalistic Mason is to study what we should call the Conjuring-book. He must be well versed in the names and signs of the planets and constellations; he must also know whether it be a good or evil Genius which presides over it, and which are the numbers that represent them. By the word Ghenelia, for example, he must understand the rising Sun, a pure, mild and active spir-

---

4   *Telescope de Zoroastre*, page 13.

it, presiding at births, and at all natural affections which are good. *Sethoporos*, on the contrary, is Saturn, the planet which may be looked upon as the head quarters of the evil Genii.

It is not our object to give a dictionary of all their Hieroglyphics, much less to describe the circles, the triangles, the table, the urns, and the magic mirrors, in a word all the science of the Cabalistic Rosicrucian. The reader has seen a sufficient specimen, to be convinced, that the whole is an incoherent system of the vilest and grossest superstition. It might be only humiliating to nature, did not the adept carry his impiety to such an extent, that he looks upon the communication with, and apparitions of the Devils, whom he invokes under the appellation of Genii, as a special favour, and on them he relies for the whole success of his enchantments. If we are to credit the masters of the art, the Cabalistic Mason will be favoured by these good and evil Genii, in proportion to the confidence he has in their power; they will appear to him, and they will explain more to him in the magic table, than the human understanding can conceive.

Nor is the adept to fear the company of the *evil Genii*. He must firmly believe, that *the worst among them*, the most hideous of those beings which the vulgar call *Devils, are never bad company for mortals*. In many cases he is to prefer the company of these evil Genii to that of the good; the latter frequently costing you your rest, fortune, and sometimes even your life; while we often have the greatest obligations to the former.[5]

From whencesoever these Genii or Devils may come, it is from them alone that the adept can learn the occult sciences, which will infuse into him the spirit of prophecy. He will be informed, that Moses, the Prophets, and the three Kings, had no other teachers, no other art, but that of Cabalistic Masonry, like him and Nostradamus.

When immersed in this delirium of folly and impiety the adept becomes dear to the Sect. He will have shown that he prefers the doctrine of *Sisamoro* and of *Senamira* to that of the Gospel; that he had rather be a madman than a Christian; and then he will have attained the grand object of the last mysteries of Cabalistic Masonry.

Those Masons who may have adopted a different course to arrive at the same end, are to take great care not to discredit the Cabal. Though they disbelieve the art themselves, let them say at least, "That there is nothing wonderful in judicial astrology but its means; that its tendency is extremely simple: That it is very possible, that at the hour of your birth a star should be in a certain position of the Heavens, and in a particular aspect, and that nature should follow a particular course, which, through a concatenation of causes, would be favourable or fatal to you." Then let them add a few Sophisms to corroborate this idea, and give themselves out for learned Philosophers, and

---

5   *Ibid.* Page 118 and 136.

the Sect will approve their conduct as tending to avenge the Cabalistic Mason, and bring his science into repute.[6]

Were I not writing for the Historian, I should fear to abuse my reader's patience with the enumeration of these absurdities of Occult Masonry. But in describing the grand causes of a Revolution *which threatens all Europe*, it is necessary at least to give a general idea of those systems of Impiety and rebellion whence it originated. We spare him the trouble of research, he will only have to verify our quotations; he will know from what sources he is to derive his proofs. Beside, one of the most dangerous arts of the Sect, is not only to hide its tenets and its variegated means of attaining its Revolutionary object, but it wishes even to conceal the very names of its different classes. That which may appear to be the farthest from Impiety or Rebellion may be the most strenuous in its attempts to revive the antique systems of the bitterest enemies to Governments and to Christianity.

---

6   See the *Continuation* of ERRORS AND OF TRUTH *by an unknown Philosopher.* Masonic Era 5784, Chap, of VICES AND ADVANTAGES. Notwithstanding the title of this book, it is far from being a *Continuation* of the work of which I am about to treat. It was only a snare laid by Holbach's club, who, seeing the immense run which Mr. de Saint-Martin's work had, adopted the tide of *Continuation* OF ERRORS AND OF TRUTH to attract the curiosity of the Public. In this pretended continuation, whole pages are copied from the works of the club, coinciding in nothing with Mr. de Saint-Martin's system, excepting in its zeal for Masonry.

CHAPTER XI

It may be matter of surprize to many, to see me
comprehend the Martinists among the latter; they
are, nevertheless, the persons whom I had in view.
As to the origin of Mr. de Saint-Martin, who has
given them his name, we are ignorant; but we defy
any body to show a greater appearance of probity, or to assume a more devout and mellifluous
mystical strain, than the hypocrisy of this spuri-
ous offspring of Curbicus the slave.[7] We have been
acquainted with men whom he had seduced, with
others that he wished to seduce, and all spoke of

---

7   *Terebinthus*, or *Budda*, a disciple of *Scythian*, a conjurer, find-
    ing that the Persian Priests opposed his designs, retired to a
    widow's house in Palestine to whom he left all his money and
    books. She bought a slave named CURBICUS, whom she after-
    wards adopted and caused to be instructed in all the scienc-
    es of Persia. After her death he quitted the name of *Curbicus*,
    to blot out the memory of his first condition, and took that of
    MANES, which in the Persian language signifies discourse. For
    an account of his doctrines many learned writers, and particu-
    larly St. Augustin, may be consulted. They are represented as
    the common sewer of all the impities of the times, and as the
    seat of empire which Satan had chosen to himself.
        Manes had the insolence to promise the King of Persia that
    he would cure his son by his prayers, and the credulous Prince,
    believing him, neglected the remedies of art, and sent away
    his physicians. The son died, and Manes was thrown into pris-
    on; but, escaping from thence, he fled into Mesopotamia; after
    various adventures however, fading into the hands of the King
    of Persia, he was flayed alive, and his carcase cast upon the
    dunghill to be devoured by wild beasts. His skin was stuffed,
    and hung up on one of the city gates.—His followers hon-
    oured him as a martyr, and, in memory of his being flayued
    with reeds, *they slept upon them*—(See the "Annals of the
    Church,"—Third Age). —Tr.

his great zeal and respect for Christ and his gospel, and for Governments. We shall seek his doctrines and his views in his own writings, in the *Apocalypse* of his adepts, in his famous book of Errors and of Truth. We have learned to our cost what labour and what pains are necessary to unravel this work of darkness; but surely the same perseverance should be shown by the disciples of truth as by the adepts of darkness.

Much patience is requisite to understand and to elucidate the code of the Martinist Mason, amidst its mysterious language of numbers and enigmas. We will spare as much as possible this trouble to our readers. Let the Hero of these doctrines appear, and he will be found to be no other than the servile copyist of the absurdities of the Heresiarch slave, and a rival of his hypocrisy. With all the tortuosities of Manes we shall behold him leading his adepts through the same paths, infusing into them the same hatred for the altars of Christianity, for the thrones of Sovereigns, and for all political establishments whatever. We will begin with his religious sytems; but though we shall compress whole volumes of impious absurdity into a few pages, still we must again appeal to the patience of the reader; for as their Martinist Masons contributed much to the Revolution, it is necessary that their sophistical reveries should be known.

We are, then, to form an idea of a *first being*; *one*; *universal*; *of himself*; *and the beginning of all principle*. At first sight, this *first being* appears to be the *God* WHOLE, or the *Jehovah* of Pantheism: and such really is the *first being* of the Martinists.[8] But this God whole comprehends a twofold God; one the principle of *good*, the other of *evil*. The former, though produced by the *first being*, *holds of itself the whole of its power, and all its worth.* It is infinitely good, and can only do good. It produces another being of its own substance, a first good like itself, but which soon becomes infinitely bad, and can do nothing but evil.[9] The *God* GOOD, though it holds all its power of itself, could neither create this *world, nor any corporeal being, without the means of the God* EVIL:[10] the one acts, the other reacts, and from their conflicts the world is framed, and bodies are formed of the *sparks*, as it were, emanating from this struggle between the *God or principle of* GOOD, *and the God or principle of* EVIL.

> Man already existed at that time, *as no origin can be anterior to man.* He is antecedent to any being in nature; he existed before the birth of the Genii; nevertheless he only came after them.[11] Man at that time existed without a body, and a much preferable state to that in which he is at present; for, inasmuch as his actual state is limited, and replete with disgust, so was his former unlimited and abounding in delights.[12]

---

8   *Of Errors and Truth*, 2d Part, page 149.

9   First Section.

10   *Ibid.* Of Temporal Causes and Concatenations.

11   *Ibid.* Of Primitive Man.

12   *Ibid.*—We think it necessary to inform our readers, that we

THE ANTIMONARCHICAL CONSPIRACY

By the ill use he made of his Liberty, he erred from the centre at which the *God* GOOD had placed him; he then acquired a body, and that was the period of his first fall. But in his fall he preserved his dignity; he is still of the same *essence* as the *God* GOOD. To convince ourselves of it,

> we have only to reflect on the nature of thought; and we shall soon perceive, that it being simple, one, and unalterable, there can be but one sort of being capable of it; as nothing can be common between beings of different natures. We shall observe, that if man has in himself an idea of a Supreme Being, of an active and intelligent cause which executes his will, he must be of the same essence as that superior Being.[13]

Therefore according to the Martinist System, *the God* GOOD, *the God* EVIL, and every *thinking being* or, in other words, God, Man, and the Devil, are of the same nature, the same essence, and the same species.

If therefore the adept does not think himself God or Devil, it is not the fault of his teachers. There is, however, a remarkable difference between man and the *God* EVIL. For the Devil, or the principle of Evil,

---

have made use of the Edinburgh edition, which is the least enigmatical. As Philosophism and Impiety gained ground, the Martinists thought they might have fewer voluntary obscurities, and they have suppressed, or given in common print, what was originally only expressed in cyphers, in which the first edition abounds.

13 *Ibid.* Of the Affinities of Thinking Beings, page 205.

separated from the *God* GOOD, can never return to him; whereas man will return to the same state he was in antecedently to time and the *sparkling* conflict. "He erred by going from four to nine, but re-establishes himself by returning from nine to four."[14]

This enigmatical jargon becomes more intelligible as the adept advances in the mysteries. He learns that the number *four* signifies *a strait line*—number *nine* the *circumference* or the *curve line*:[15] then that the sun is a *quaternary* number; that number nine represents *the moon*, and consequently *the earth, of which it is but a satellite*:[16] and hence the adept concludes, that man anterior to time was in the sun or in the centre of light. That he flew from thence by the radius, and that, passing by the moon, he remains on the earth, until the time comes when he shall be reflected back to his centre, to be incorporated with the *God* GOOD.

---

14   This was precisely the lesson Mr. de Saint-Martin was explaining to the Marquis de C. He traced his circles on the table; then, pointing to the centre, he added, "You see how every thing emanating from the centre moves in the radius to reach the circumference."—"I perceive it," says the Marquis; "but I also observe, that having reached the circumference this body emanating from the centre may proceed in a tangent or a strait line; and then I do not understand how you can demonstrate that it must necessarily be returned back to the centre." This was sufficient to disconcert the learned Doctor of the Martinists. He nevertheless continued to teach, that souls emanating from God by the number four, would return to him by the number nine.

15   *Ibid.* 2d Part, Page 106, 126.

16   *Ibid.* Page 114 and 215.

In the mean time, till he can enjoy that happiness,

> it is a most fallacious system to pretend to lead men to wisdom *by the frightful description of eternal flames in a life to come.* Such descriptions are of no avail when unfelt; therefore the blind teachers, who can only represent those torments to us in imagination, must necessarily produce but little effect upon us.[17]

The enlightened Martinist, soaring above such teachers, erases the pains of hell from his moral code; and it is worthy of remark, that this is the leading feature in the Systems of the Sophisters of the Occult Lodges, as well as of the Sophisters of the Secret Academy. We should be tempted to suppose, that they knew no means of working their salvation but by destroying the possibility of being damned; and that, by denying the existence of hell, they sought to harden themselves and all nations to crimes the most deserving of the divine vengeance.

The Martinist substitutes *"three temporal worlds.* There are but three degrees of Expiation, or three degrees of real F. M. *(Free-masonry)."* This is pretty clearly asserting, that the perfect Mason neither has sin to fear, nor penance to perform; but in every sense the reader can no longer doubt of the systematic impiety which reigns throughout these absurdities, in direct opposition to the Gospel. It was not sufficient for the Sect to

---

17   *Ibid.* First Section.

renew in their hatred the ancient blasphemies of a senseless Philosophy; but the detestation of Laws, Sovereigns, and Governments, was to mingle with their mysteries; and in this our Martinist adept only primes over the Jacobin, by the art and cunning with which he infuses his spirit of Rebellion, and broods over the downfal of the Throne.

Let not the zealous adept appear, protesting his respect for the Throne or Government; I have heard their protestations, I have heard those of their masters; but I have also heard their doctrines, and seen their transactions. It is in vain for their chief to teach them privately, or to envelop them in enigmatic language; for, had I not hereafter to unfold the iniquitous mysteries of the Illuminées, the reader would be ready to pronounce, without hesitation, that of all the conspiring Sects the Martinist Lodges are the most dangerous.

Necker, La Fayette, Mirabeau, notwithstanding their Sovereignty of the People, sought a Constitutional King;—Brissot, Sieyès, Pétion, supported the Republican system;—conventions, compacts, and oaths, were admitted by both. But the Martinist denies the legitimacy of every Empire which may have originated in violence, force, or conquest; he denies all society whose foundation rests on conventions or compacts, though freely entered into. The former are acts of tyranny, which never can be legitimated; no antiquity, no *prescription*, can render them valid, *prescription* being a mere invention of tyranny, as a palliative to injustice, in direct opposition to the laws of nature, which knows of no such invention. "The edifice formed on a voluntary association is equally imaginary as if it were on a forced association."[18] To prove these two assertions, and particularly the latter, is the main object of our hero's Sophistry. He easily decides, that it is *impossible that any social compact could have been freely entered into by all the individuals of a state.*—He asks, *whether it stands to reason that man should rely on those who had formed such a compact, or whether they ever had the power of forming it?* He examines the question, and concludes,

> that a voluntary association is neither more just nor reasonable than it is practicable, since by such an act, man must invest other men with a right (his own liberty) which he cannot dispose of himself; and since he transfers a right which he has not, *he makes a convention which is absolutely void, and which neither himself the chiefs, nor subjects can put into execution, since it can neither have been binding on the one nor the other.*[19]

Then come the innocent artifices of protestations of fidelity and submission to the reigning powers, and invitations not to trouble the order of the existing laws and governments; but stupidity itself cannot be duped by such artifices. After the

---

18   *Ibid.* Sect. 5.

19   *Ibid.* Part II. Sect. 5, Page 9.

Martinist has told us, that social compacts, though freely formed, are null, and that associations formed by force are void, what can be the submission which the civil laws, the magistrates, or the Princes can exact from their subjects?

The hero of the Martinists also shudders at the very idea of revolt or of insurrection; but then it is because the individual is exposed to acts of violence resulting from *private authority*. When the mob shall have imbibed these principles, when *private* violences are no longer to be feared, what will all these restrictions and exhortations avail for the preservation of peace and submission to the constituted authorities? Does not the Martinist try every means to persuade that same mob that there never existed a legitimate Prince, nor a lawful Government? Is he not perpetually recalling them to their *first origin*, "when the rights of one man over another were not known, because it was impossible that such rights could exist among *equal beings?*"[20]

With them, it is sufficient to observe the variations of Governments, and their succession; that some have perished, others are perishing, or will perish before the end of the world, to be convinced that they are no more than the offspring of *the caprice of man, or of their disordered imaginations.*[21]

In fine, I know that the Martinist makes profession of a true government, a real authority of man

20   *Ibid.* Part II. page 16 and 17.
21   *Ibid.* Of the Instability of Governments, p. 34 and 35.

over men, and that he pleases to call it a Monarchy. But notwithstanding all the subtleties of his mysterious language, this very profession will prove to be the most universal Conspiracy against every existing Government. He tells us, that there is a superiority to be acquired by one man over others, the superiority of learning, of means, of experience, which bring him nearer to his *original state*; and this is a superiority *of fact*, "and of necessity, because other men, having applied less and not having reaped the same advantages, will stand in need of him, from the poverty and dimness of their faculties."[22]—The reader will naturally conclude, that according to this system nobody could exercise a lawful authority over his equals, but in right of his virtues, his experience, and his means of being useful. And that is in reality the first artifice of the Sect, which immediately overthrows all idea of hereditary succession, which submits the rights of the Sovereign to the reveries of the factious and of the populace on the virtue, talents, and success of him who governs. But let us follow their windings, and unfold their mysterious writings.—"If every man," say they, "attained to the same degree of his own power, then every man would be a King."

These words evidently show, that in the sense of the Martinist, he only is not King who is not arrived at the last degree of his power, or of his strength in the *natural* state. A little further it appears, that this difference alone can constitute a

---

22   *Ibid*, p. 18.

real political authority, that such is the principle of unity, the only one by which nature allows the exercise of a legitimate authority over men, *the only light which can reunite them in a body.*[23]

The reader may believe it to be a chimerical research to seek in the history of man for a society where he alone commands whose *powers* or faculties have been the best developed in the order of nature, where he alone obeys who has not acquired this *degree of power*, but the Martinist will carry him back "to those happy days said to have had no existence but in the imagination of the poets, because, distant from them, and strangers to their sweets, we have been weak enough to believe, that because we did not enjoy them, they could not exist."[24]

Should you not immediately perceive that the only legitimate authority is that exercised of old, or in the golden age, when each father of a family was the sole king; when the son, acquiring sufficient strength and age to develope his *powers*, became king himself; should you deny these consequences, and object, that no government had ever perpetuated itself since the commencement of the world, and that consequently the rule given to discover the only legitimate government pointed out none; you are then left to your own imagination, and the adept will continue,

---

23   *Ibid.* p. 29.

24   *Ibid.*

Nevertheless, it is one of those truths which I can best affirm, nor do I pledge myself too far, when I certify to my equals, that there are governments which have *subsisted ever since man was first placed upon earth, and will subsist until the end*; and that for the same reasons which made me assert, that here below there has always been and always will be legitimate governments.[25]

What then are or can be these legitimate governments which the Martinist recognizes? What can be these governments which have subsisted from the beginning, and will subsist until the end of time? None can be surmised, but that of the Patriarchs, or of the first families governed by the sole paternal authority. In later ages can any other be found than that of isolated families, or of the Nomades, the Tartars, or the savages roaming through forests without any other chief than the father of the family? And it is there alone, that those whose age has equally developed their strength and *their power*, will find themselves all equal and each a king, that is to say, each one recognizing no other law than his own, and each acquiring at the same age all the power of a father over his children. This government may perhaps be traced in civil society; each private family abstractedly taken may be said to perpetuate this government, and it has existed and will perpetuate itself until the end of time. Now let the reader reflect on what has been

_____

25   *Ibid.* Page 35 and 36.

said on governments formed by force or free compact, on those governments which have perished, do perish, or will perish before the end of time, and which by this distinctive mark are known to be illegitimate. He will clearly perceive, that all the zeal of the Martinists for the true monarchy, for the *only legitimate* government, the *only one consistent with nature*, the only one lasting as the world, is nothing else but the wish of reducing all society, all legitimate authority, to that of a father governing his children; to overturn every throne and annihilate every law but that of the ancient patriarchs.

Such is the whole tendency of the political system of the Martinists. Many more blasphemies both religious and political might be extracted from this work; nor would it be impossible to prove, that in the sense of the Martinists, the *great adultery* of man, the true cause of all his misfortunes in this world, the real original sin of mankind, was his having divorced himself from the laws of nature, to subject himself to laws which nature condemns, to those of Emperors, of Kings, and even of Republics, in a word, to any other authority except the paternal.[26] But this matter would require us to follow all the windings of their mysterious language, a task that would be as tedious to my reader as to myself. I trust therefore that he will not be displeased with me for having spared him the labour of research, which I have endured in the task of

---

26 Part II. Sect. 5. Art. 'Adultery'.

gathering from amidst these *voluntary obscurities* some of those luminous traits which now and then escape the Sect; and the re-union of which leave no doubt as to the grand object of this Apocalypse. In reading over and studying this extraordinary code, one would be tempted to decide with Voltaire, *that there never was printed a more absurd, obscure, mad, or foolish work*; and we should be equally surprized that such a code had produced so many enthusiasts, or that we know not what Dean of Philosophy had been so much enchanted with it.[27] But it all probability this Dean had not sent the word of the enigma to Voltaire; he had not told him that this voluntary obscurity was one of the most powerful means employed by the Sect to crush the altar and the throne. The works of Voltaire himself had not the celebrity of Mr. de Saint-Martin's Apocalypse. The greater the obscurity the more it attracted the curiosity and piqued the vanity of his disciples; the adepts of the first class tutored and explained it to the young novices, and none were more eager than those of the fair sex. Their dressing-rooms were metamorphosed into secret schools, where the interpreting adept developed the mysteries of each page, and the novice in extasy applauded the mystery which was hidden from the vulgar. Little by little the novice herself became an interpreter, and founded a species of school.— This is not a mere assertion; such schools for the explanation of the code existed at Paris and in the

27   let. of Voltaire to d'Alembert, Oct. 22, 1776.

Provinces, particuarly at Avignon, the headquarters of the Martinists. I was and am acquainted with several persons who were introduced to these schools. They were the preparatory steps to initiation. There they learned the art of imposing on the simple by factitious apparitions, which ended by casting ridicule on the Sect; the art of conjuring up the dead; the art of making absent persons speak, or of seeing them at a thousand miles distance; in fine, all those arts which quacks and mountebanks of all ages have invented to delude the populace, and rob them of their money, the Martinist studied to enable them to make converts to Impiety and Rebellion.

This Sect made great progress in France and Germany; some even have reached England; and every where their grand object is to represent the French Revolution as the fire which is to purify the world.

Notwithstanding the multitude of the Martinist Masons, they are not nearly so numerous as the Eclectic Masons; and these indeed should naturally predominate in an age where the Philosophism of the Atheists and Deists only succeeds to the ancient heresies in order to absorb them all.

The appellation of Eclectic is applied to a Free-mason, as it was formerly to certain Philosophers. We are to understand by this word those of the adepts who, after having passed through the different degrees of Masonry, attach themselves to no particular system, either political or religious, into which they have been initiated, but adopt from

Eclectic Masonry.

them all whatever may best suit their political or religious views.[28] They are neither Hermetic, Cabalistic nor Martinist Masons; they are what they please, Deists, Atheists, Sceptics, an aggregate of all the errors of the Philosophism of the day. They, like the simple Sophisters of the age, have a two-fold point of union. With respect to Religion, they all admit that Equality and Liberty which denies every authority but their own reason, and rejects all revealed religion; as to governments, they admit of no Kings, unless subservient to the will of the people in right of its sovereignty. I shall be very brief on this class; it is that of the Brissots, Condorcets or Lalandes; in a word of the Sophisters of the day, whom we shall soon see combining with Masonry to operate their Revolution. Were we to expose their systems it would only be a repetition of what has been said of the Sophisters conspiring against the altar and the throne; and the multitude of these abettors of Impiety who were in our time aggregated to the Masonic Lodges would alone prove how peculiarly such plots coincided with their principles.

I know that there is another species of Eclectic Masons lately established in Germany. These not only make profession of appertaining to no particular system of Masonry, but assert also that they depend on none. According to them, all are independent, all have the right of making their own

---

28   See the *Archives of the Free-masons and Rosicrucians*, chap. 3. Edition of Berlin, 1785.

laws. It is for that reason that they have abolished the very names of Grand Lodge and of Scotch Lodge: and in this respect they may be said to have improved upon Masonic Equality and Liberty.[29] In this light the Eclectic Masons could not have been very numerous in France, as the major part of them were under the inspection of the Grand Parisian lodge called the *Grand Orient*. But our modern Sophisters had introduced into all the Lodges the true Eclectic spirit of Impiety; and sentiment was a stronger tie than a professed opinion. This sentiment, to be uniform, must agree in hating Christ and his Religion, in detesting all Sovereignty and all Legislative Power, except that of the people. The Eclectic Mason, like the Sophisters, are at liberty to substitute Deism or Atheism to Christianity, to replace Monarchy by Democracy or even by a Democratic Monarchy; but a step less towards Equality and Liberty would suffice to banish him from the Occult Lodges.

All classes therefore, every code of Masonry, Hermetic, Cabalistic or Martinists, and Eclectic, all and each forwarded the Revolution; and it little imported to the Sect which struck the blow, provided ruin ensued.[30]

I promised to add to these proofs those which more particularly result from the divers opinions of Masons on their origin. Let us here again be

29 See the *Rules of Their Association*, Frankfort, 18th May, 1783, signed Rustner and Rottberg, secretaries.
30 La Métherie's *Journal de Physique*, 1790.

only guided by the most learned and zealous of the Sect. The reader will consider whether the parents they have adopted would not suffice alone to direct their judgement on the plots of their progeny.

CHAPTER XII.

Proofs of the Origin of Free-masons Drawn from their own Systems.

et us begin by rejecting the opinions of all those demi-adepts, who in their research on Masonry, led away by the similarity of name, really believe themselves descended from the Masons who built the Tower of Babel, or who raised the pyramids of Egypt, or more particularly from those who erected Solomon's Temple, or who worked at the Tower at Strasbourg; in fine, of those who laid the foundations of so many Churches in Scotland in the tenth century. These men of mortar had never been admitted to the mysteries. If it be true that they ever constituted a part of the Brotherhood, they were soon excluded; their minds were too blunt and not sufficiently Philosophic.[1]

---

1   I make this observation, as it is very possible that the name and implements of the Craft may be borrowed from the real Masons. Many mechanical arts, in France at least, had their signs, their ceremonies, their hidden language, which constituted the secret of the profession. This language and these signs served to distinguish the workmen, and denoted the degree they had acquired, whether of Apprentice or Master; and was a method of recognizing those who on the road asked for work, or for support to enable them to continue their journey. For all men of the same profession are naturally inclined to help each other in preference to strangers.

It is very possible that in time some of the adepts initiated in the mysteries of the Sect gained admission among the mechanical Masons. These adepts may have formed others among those mechanics. Then, to form a separate society, it was only necesssary to adopt new signs, and choose different emblems from those workmen, and the Lodges were ready formed.

What may corroborate this supposition is, that there exists in France another profession, which, had it not been for one obstacle, might have undergone a similar change. This is the profession of the FENDEURS (*Hewers of Wood*). These men also form a confraternity. They have their signs, their watch-word, their secret and their convivial meetings. They call themselves *L'Ordre des* FENDEURS (*the Order of the Hewers of Wood*). They admit Gentlemen and Burgesses into their order, who are initiated into the secret, and attend their meetings and repasts in the same manner as the Free-masons do theirs. I have known men who were both Masons and *Fendeurs*, and who from their birth and stations in life had far other occupations than splitting of wood. They were as reserved with respect to the secret of the *Fendeurs* as to that of Masonry.—I knew the sentiments of these Adepts, and should not be surprised that the sole reason why they took so great an interest in the secret of the Fendeurs was from its similarity to that of Masonry, or else, that in time, our Adepts of the town were in hopes of

They were no longer wanted, when once the trowel, the compasses, the cubic stone, the truncated or entire column, became nothing more than systematic emblems; and the learned adepts blush at an origin which they consider as too ignoble.

We will subdivide into two classes the divers opinions set forth in order to ennoble their origin. In the first class, we comprehend all those who ascend back to the mysteries of the Egyptian priests, to those of Eleusis or the Greeks, or those who pretend to filiate from the Druids, or even who call themselves descendants of the Jews. In the second class, we consider those who only trace themselves from the Knights Templars, or the age of the Crusades.[2]

Various opinions of Free-Masons on their origin.

Philosophizing their Brethren of the woods. The grand obstacle to the propagation of these principles would be the difficulty and infrequency of their meetings, which are held in the midst of forests, far from the eyes of the prophane, and only in fine weather. Should the Philosophist take it into his head to convert theese repasts into those of Equality and Liberty, in a word, of the Golden Age, then Adepts would flock from all parts. Sophisticated dissertations and allegories would be introduced; but the uncouth inhabitants of the woods would no longer be able to comprehend the mysteries. Some of the signs would be changed, the emblems of the profession would be preserved, and the Sophisticated Lodges of the *Fendeurs*, established in the towns would cease to be open to the clownish mechanics from whom they had adopted their allegorical emblems. It is very possible that such may have been the case with the Mechanical Masons. This however is no more than a conjecture as to the mode of the Sect; our readers will soon see that we are not reduced to such uncertainty with regard to the origin of its secret and of its doctrine.

2   For these divers opinions let the reader consult from among

How and why the Free-Masons trace back their origin.

If we examine ever so carefully the reasons on which the learned Masons ground their filiation from the ancient Philosophers, they will be found to contain merely this assertion:

the learned and zealous Masons of Germany, the GESCHICHTE DER UNBEKANNTEN, or *the History of the Unknown*, 1780, with this Epigraph—*Gens oeterna est, in qua nemo nascitur*—ARCHIV FÜR FREYMAURER, or *the Archives of the Free-masons*, Berlin, 1784—UBER DIE ALTEN UND NEUEN MYSTERIEN, or *of Ancient and Modern Mysteries*, Berlin, 1782—DIE HEBRÄISCHE MYSTERIEN, ODER DIE ÄLTESTE RELIGIÖSE FREYMAUREREY, *the Mysteries of the Hebrews, or the most ancient religious Free-masonry*, Leipsic, 1788. Among the English Masons, he may consult THE SPIRIT OF MASONRY, *by William Hutchinson*—and among the French *Guillemain de Saint-Victor,* ON THE ORICIN OF MASONRY, &c. &c.

Let the reader remember that several of these works might have been quoted for the greatest absurdities that Masonry is guilty of. For example in the ARCHIVES OF FREE-MASONRY, several dissertations are to be found written by their Doctors on the Cabalistic art, and that even by an English Doctor, for the defence and instruction of the Rosicrucians.—I was really confounded, and almost ashamed, when among other absurdities I read, "ASTROLOGY is a science which by the situation of the stars reveals the causes of what has come to pass and foretells what is to come. This science has had its blots, but that destroys neither the foundation nor the sanctity of the art." And this is written by an English Doctor to justify the Rosicrucian Lodges, and to be preserved in their Archives. (*See these Archives in German, Part III. No.* 18, *page* 378). I have added this quotation, because I am always afraid of its being said, that I attribute incredible things to Free-masonry. I know that in one sense they are incredible, but they are so only to those who are strangers to the proofs. Were the books of Masonry in different languages to be consulted, especially those in German, they would be found to superabound in proofs.

322

that in those ancient times when men first began to desert the primitive truths, to follow a
religion and morality founded on superstition,
some sages were to be met with who segregat-
ed themselves from the general mass of ignorance and corruption. These sages, perceiving
that the grossness or the stupidity of the people
rendered them incapable of profiting by their
lessons, formed separate schools and disciples,
to whom they transmitted the whole science of
the ancient truths and of the discoveries they
had made by their profound meditations on the
nature, the religion, the polity, and the rights
of man. In these lessons some insisted on the
unity of God or true Deism, others on the unity
of the Great Being, or Pantheism. The morality deduced from these principles was pure; it
was grounded on the duties of charity, on the
rights of Liberty, and on the means of living
peaceably and happily. Lest these doctrine
should lessen in value, should be falsified or
be entirely lost, these sages commanded their
disciples to keep them secret.—They also gave
them signs and a particular language by which
they were to recognize each other. All those
who were admitted to this school and to these
mysteries were the children of Light and Liberty, while all the rest of mankind were with
respect to them but slaves and *prophane beings*; and hence their contempt for the vulgar.
This was also the reason why the disciples of
Pythagoras observed such a profound silence,
the origin of that particular and secret science
of the divers schools. Hence the mysteries of
the Egyptians and afterwards of the Greeks
and of the Druids, even the very mysteries of

the Jews themselves, or of Moses initiated in all the secrets of the Egyptians.

These divers schools and the secrets of these mysteries have not been lost; the Philosophers of Greece transmitted them to those of Rome, and the Philosophers of all nations followed the same fine of *conduct after the establishment of Christianity.* The secret was always preserved, because it was *necessary to avoid the persecutions of an intolerant Church and of its Priests.* The sages of divers nations by means of the signs which had been originally established, recognized each other, as the Free-masons do every where at this present day. The name only has been changed; and the secret has been handed down under the denomination of Free-masonry, as it was formerly under the sanction of the Magi, of the Priests of Memphis or of Eleusis, and of Platonic or Eclectic Philosophers. Such is the origin of Masonry, such are the causes which perpetuate it, and which render it the same in all parts of the world.[3]

Falsity of this origin.

This is the faithful result of what the most learned Masons have published on their origin.— It is not our object to examine how false are such ideas on the pretended doctrine of the Persian, Egyptian, Grecian, Roman or Druid sages, nor how contrary to all history. In the first place, can any thing be more absurd than to suppose, that there existed a unity of religious opinions, of morality, and of secrets among Philosophers, who have left behind them systems as variegated, and as oppo-

---

3   An Extract from the divers works cited in the Note.

site to each other, and as absurd as those of our modern sophisticated Philosophists?[4] Nor do I undertake to examine the erroneous assertion, that the mysteries of Eleusis had no other secret but the unity of God, and the purest morality.—How is it possible to suppose that those mysteries were not universally known to the people, when it is certain that all the citizens of Athens were initiated into both the lesser and the greater mysteries, according to their age?[5] Nor do I ask how it came to pass, that these same Athenians under ground were all taught their catechism on the unity of God, and how when above ground they adored such a multitude of Gods; or, again, how it happened that they condemned Socrates to death on the accusation that he did not adore all the Gods; or else, why all the Priests of the different idols only acquired by their initiation new zeal for the defence of that multitude of Gods and their altars. In fine, I will not ask how it is possible to persuade oneself that those Priests, so ardent and so zealous in their temples for the worship of Jupiter, of Mars, of Venus, and of so many other Deities, should be

---

4   Let those who wish to be convinced of the discordancy of their systems consult Cicero Questiones Academ.—*De Natura Deorum*—*De Legib.*—*De Finibus Boni et Mali.*—*De Off.* &c.—or Lactantius' *Institut. Divin.*—or the last of the Helvian Letters; where the doctrines, the systems, and the absurdities of our modern Sophisters are compared with those of the ancient sages.

5   See Mr. de Saint-Croix's work on the *Mysteries of the Ancients*.

the very persons who assembled the people during the solemnity ot the grand mysteries, to tell them that all their worship of the Gods was nothing but imposture, and that they themselves were the authors, ministers, or priests of imposture!

I know that such reflections are more than sufficient to stamp with falsehood the origin in which the learned Masons glory. But let us for a moment suppose, that these mysteries were what they have represented them to be; the very pretension of a society springing from such ancestry and glorying in perpetuating their spirit and their dogmas,—this pretension alone, I say, must class this Brotherhood among the most ancient conspirators. It would entitle us to say to the Craft, "Such then is the origin of your mysteries; such the object of your Occult Lodges! You then descend from those pretended sages, and those Philosophers, who, reduced to the lights of reason, had no farther knowledge of the true God than what their reason inspired. You are the children of Deism or Pantheism, and, replete with the spirit of your forefathers, you wish to perpetuate it! Like them you look upon every thing which the rest of mankind have learned from the lights of Revelation, as superstition and prejudice. Every Religion which adds to the worship of the Theist or detests the Pantheist, in a word Christianity and its mysteries, are with you objects of hatred and contempt! You abhor whatever the Sophists of Paganism, or the Sophists initiated in the mysteries of the idolatrous Priests, abhorred;— but those

Sophists detested Christianity, and showed themselves its most inveterate enemies. From your own avowals, then, in what light can we view your mysteries, if not as a perpetuation of that hatred and of that wish of annihilating every other Religion but the pretended Deism of the Ancients?

"You also say that you are what those Jews were, and still are, who, for all their religious tennets, only acknowledge the unity of God (provided there have existed Jews who did not believe in the Prophets and in Emmanuel the Saviour).— You have then the same sentiments toward the Christian which the Jews have. Like them, you insist on *Jehovah*, but to curse Christ and his mysteries."[6]

---

6   As for this Jewish part of the Craft, or the Free-masonry of the Jews, we recommend to our readers to peruse the treatise of a most learned and zealous Mason dedicated *Denen die es Verstehen, or to those who can understand*. He leaves no stone unturned throughout antiquity to prove the identity of the ancient mysteries of Eleusis, of the Jews, of the Druids, and of the Egyptians, with those of Free-masonry. And indeed when we reflect on the pretended history of the name of Jehovah lost by the assassination of Adoniram, it may be very probable that the Jews had had a part in Masonry, "As it is drawn from the *Chaldaic Paraphrase*, and taken from a fable invented by the Rabbins to rob Christ of his divinity and power. They supposed, that Christ being one day in the Temple of Jerusalem had seen the Holy of Holies, where the High Priest alone had a right to enter. That he there saw the name of Jehovah—That he carried it away with him—and that in virtue of this ineffable name he had wrought his miracles." (See the *Voile leve*).—The whole of this Fable is evidently directed against the tenets of the Christians on the Divinity of Christ. The importance which Masons annex to the recovering of the name of Jehovah, and

The more the Masonic works above-mentioned are read, the more conspicuous will be the justice of the reproaches we make. With some, matter is eternal; with others, the Trinity of the Christians is only an alteration of Plato's system.—Others again adopt the follies of the Martinists, or of the ancient Dualism.[7] Nothing then can be more evident. All these learned Masons who pretend to descend from the Egyptian Priests, from those of Greece, or from the Druids, only seek to establish what may appear to each to be the Religion of nature. Nor do they vary less as to its tenets than did both the ancient and modern Sophisters. They all agree in destroying faith in the minds of their adepts, by systems in direct opposition to Christianity. If they do not run into wild declamation like Voltaire, Diderot, or Raynal, it is because they wished themselves to deduce their consequences. To have expressed them too openly would have been divulging their mysteries; but one must be more than ignorant not to comprehend their meaning—How can we be blind to their intentions, when we peruse the writings of those who declare themselves to have originated in the Templars, or in those sectaries who infested all Europe under the name of Albigeois? These two sources have more analogy between them than may be supposed. Let us examine them separately,

---

particularly all their mysteries in the degree of *Rosæ Crucis*, has the same object in view.

7   See particularly the letter Aux *Illustres Inconnus*, or to the Real Free-masons, 1782.

and then judge what we have to expect from men who glory in such an origin.

As to the Templars, let us even suppose that this famous order was really innocent of all the crimes which occasioned its dissolution; what object either religious or political can the Free-masons have in perpetuating their mysteries under the name or emblems of that order? Had the Templars brought into Europe a religion, or a code of morality, that was not known? Is that their inheritance?—In that case neither your religion nor your morality can be that of Christ. Is it their fraternity, their charity, which is the object of your secrets? Did the Templars really add any thing to those Evangelic virtues? Or is it the religion of *Jehovah*, or of the Unity of God, coinciding with the mysteries of Christianity?—If so, why do you reject all *Christians who are not Masons as prophane?*

It is too late to reply, that the alarms of religion are vain and ungrounded; that religion never was the object of the Lodges. What then is that name, that worship of *Jehovah*, which the learned Masons declare to have been handed down from the Knights Templars. Whether these Knights were the authors of it, or whether they received it by tradition, or borrowed it from the ancient mysteries of Paganism and of its sages, this name I say, this worship cannot be foreign to Christianity; and is not every Christian entitled to say, 'You would not be so secret nor so ardent to revenge

Of Free-Masons attributing their origin to the Templars.

it, if it were similar to the worship established throughout the Christian world?'

Should governments partake of the same alarms, to what subterfuge will the adepts have recourse who have sworn to avenge Equality, Liberty, and every right of their association, which has been so desperately outraged in the destruction of the Templars? It will be in vain to assert the innocence real or fictitious of those too famous Knights. That vow of vengeance which has been perpetuated for nearly five centuries can hardly fall on *Philip le Bel* or *Clement V.*, or on the other Kings and Pontiffs who in the beginning of the fourteenth century contributed to the dissolution of that order? Nor will it be renewed in these days on account of the ties of blood, or through any pity for the particular individuals of the order? This vow, this oath of vengeance must be instigated by other causes—It has been perpetuated as the very object, the very doctrine of the school, as the principles and mysteries which the Masons have received from the Templars. What then can those men, those principles be, which can only be avenged by the death of Kings and Pontiffs? And what are those Lodges wherein for four hundred and fourscore years this vow, this oath of vengeance has been perpetuated?

It is evident: Nor is it necessary in this place to examine whether *Molay* and his Order were innocent or criminal, whether they were the real progenitors of the Free-masons or not; what is incontestable is sufficient; it is enough that the Masons recognize them for their ancestors; then the oath of avenging them and every allegory recalling that oath decidedly points out an association, continually threatening and conspiring against Religion and its Pontiffs, against Empires and their Governors.

But it may be asked, what lights can history throw on such an intimate connection between the mysteries of Masonry and the order of the Templars? Such a question requires much research, nor will I withhold from my reader the result of the inquiries which I have made on that subject.

The order of the Knights Templars established by Hugo de Paganis, and confirmed by Pope Eugenius III, was originally founded with all that charity which Christian zeal could inspire, for the service of those Christians who, according to the devotion of the times, went to visit the Holy Land. At first mere Hospitallers, these Knights, following the manners of the age, soon acquired great celebrity by their exploits against the Saracens. Their first repute originated in the services which were naturally to be expected from their great valor and eminent virtues: and such is the general testimony which history bears in their favour, making a wide distinction between the former and latter part of their existence. The Order soon spread through Europe, and acquired immense riches. They then began to forget their religious state, courted only the celebrity of the field, and were no longer led to it by the same spirit. It is worthy of remark,

Of the trials and depositions of the Templars.

331

that many years before their dissolution, history already reproached them not only with being lax in their former virtue, but with those very crimes which caused their destruction. In the very zenith of their glory, and at a time when it required much courage to upbraid them with their vices, we see *Matthew Paris* accusing them of converting into darkness the lights of their predecessors, of having abandoned their first vocation for plans of ambition, pleasure, and debauchery, and of unjust and tyrannical usurpation. They were already accused of holding correspondence with the Infidels, which rendered abortive all the plans of the Christian Princes; they were accused particularly of having treasonably communicated the whole of Frederick II.'s plan to the Soudan of Babylon, who, detesting such perfidy, informed the Emperor of the treachery of the Templars.[8] This testimony, to which the Historian may add many others, will serve to render less surprizing the catastrophe which befel this famous order.[9]

In the reign of *Philip le Bel*, two men who had been imprisoned for their crimes declared that they had some important discoveries to make concerning the Knights Templars. Such a declaration under circumstances so peculiar could not be thought entitled to much credit; it sufficed never-

---

8   See Matthew Paris, ann. 1229.

9   See Abbas Vispurgjensis in *Chronica*, an. 1227 & Sanut. Lib. III. Part 12, Cap. 17, &c. apud Dupuy, *Traité sur la condamnation des Templiers*.

theless to make the King determine on the dissolution of the order, and he caused all the Templars in his kingdom to be arrested on the same day. This step may be thought too precipitate: But interrogatories and a thorough examination followed; and it is on those proofs alone, and the authentic minutes of that examination, that the Historian is to found his judgment. If their avowals are perfectly free, numerous, and coincident with each other, not only in different tribunals, but in different countries, enormous as their crimes may have been, still we are forced to believe them, or reject all history, and the juridical acts of the tribunals. These juridical minutes have survived the ravages of time, and their importance has caused them to be preserved in great numbers. Let the Historian refer to the collection made by Mr. Dupuy, the King's librarian; I know no other way of forming one's judgment, and of dissipating prejudices.

It has been said, that *Philip le Bel and Clement V.* had concerted between them the dissolution of the Templars. The falsity of such an assertion is evident on the inspection of their letters. *Clement V.* at first will give no credit to the accusations against the Templars; and even when he receives incontestable proofs from *Philip le Bel*, he had still so little concerted the plan with that Prince, that every step taken by the one or the other occasions disputes on the rights of the Church or of the Throne.

It was also said, that the King wished to seize on the great riches of these Knights; but at the very commencement of his proceedings against the order, he solemnly renounced all share in their riches; and perhaps no Prince in Christendom was truer to his engagement. Not a single estate was annexed to his domain, and all history bears testimony to the fact.[10]

We next hear of a spirit of revenge which actuated this Prince; and during the whole course of this long trial, we do not hear of a single personal offence that he had to revenge on the Templars. In their defence not the most distant hint either at the revengeful spirit, or at any personal offence against the King is given; so far from it, until the period of this great catastrophe the Grand Master of the order had been a particular friend of the King's, who had made him godfather to one of his children.

In fine, the rack and torture is supposed to have forced confessions from them which otherwise they never would have made; and in the minutes we find the avowal of at least two hundred Knights all made with the greatest freedom and without any coercion. Compulsion is mentioned but in the case of one person, and he makes exactly the same avowal as twelve other Knights, his companions, freely made.[11] Many of these avowals were made in Councils where the Bishops begin by declaring that all who had confessed through fear of the tor-

---

10 Layette, Tom. III. No. 13.—Rubeus, *Hist. Ravanensis*—Bzovius ann. 1308.—Marianna, *Hist. Hispanniæ.*

11 Layette, No. 20, Interrog. made at Caen.

ture should be looked upon as innocent, and that no Knight Templar should be subjected to it.[12] The Pope, Clement V., was so far from favouring the King's prosecutions, that he began by declaring them all to be void and null. He suspended the Archbishops, Bishops, and Prelates, who had acted as inquisitors in France. The King accuses the Pope in vain of favouring the Templars; and Clement is only convinced after having been present at the interrogatories of seventy-two Knights at Poictiers in presence of many Bishops, Cardinals, and Legates. He interrogated them not like a Judge who sought for criminals, but like one who wished to find innocent men, and thus exculpate himself from the charge of having favored them. He hears them repeat the same avowals, and they are freely confirmed. He desired that these avowals should be read to them after an interval of some days, to see if they would still freely persevere in their depositions. He hears them all confirmed. *Qui perseverantes in illis, eas expresse et sponte prout recitatce fuerant approbarunt.* He wished still further to interrogate the Grand Master and the principal Superiors, *præceptores majores*, of the divers provinces of France, Normandy, Poitou, and of the Transmarine countries. He sent the most venerable persons to interrogate those of the superiors whose age or infirmities hindered them from appearing before him. He ordered the depositions of their brethren to be read to them, to know if they

---

12   See the Council of Ravenna. Rubeus, *Hist. Raven.*, Lib. VI.

acknowledged the truth of them. He required no other oath from them than to answer freely and without compulsion; and both the Grand Master and the superiors of these divers provinces depose and confess the same things, confirm them some days after, and approve of the minutes of their depositions taken down by public notaries.[13] Nothing less than such precautions could convince him of his error: it was then only that he revoked his menaces and his suspension of the French Bishops, and that he allows the King to proceed in the trials of the Templars.

Let such pretexts be forgotten, and let us only dwell on the avowals which truth alone forced from these criminal knights.

Result of their avowals.

Their depositions declare, that the Knights Templars on their reception denied Christ, trampled on the cross, and spit upon it; that Good Friday was a day which was particularly consecrated to such outrages; that they promised to prostitute themselves to each other for the most unnatural crimes; that every child begotten by a Templar was

---

13 Qui Magister & Præceptores Francis;, Terra ultra-manna, Normandix, Acquitaniae ac Pictavix, coram ipsis tribus Cardinalibus prxsentibus, quatuor tabellionibus publicis et multis aliis bonis viris, ad Sancta Dei Evangelia ab eis corporaliter tacta, prxsteto juramento quod super prxmissis omnibus, meram et plenam dicerent veritatem, coram ipsis, singulariter, libere ac sponte, absque coactione qualibet et timore, deposuerent et confessi fuerunt. (*Epist . Clementis V. Regibus Anglice, Gallice, Sicilia?, &c.*)

cast into the fire; that they bound themselves by oath to obey without exception every order coming from the Grand Master; to spare neither sacred nor prophane; to look upon every thing as lawful when the good of the order was in question; and above all, never to violate the horrible secrets of their nocturnal mysteries under pain of the most terrible chastisements.[14]

In making their depositions many of them declared they had only been forced into these horrors by imprisonment and the most cruel usage; that they wished, after the example of many of their brethren, to pass into other orders, but that they did not dare, fearing the power and vengeance of their order. That they had secretly confessed their crimes and had craved absolution. In this public declaration they testified by their tears the most ardent desire of being reconciled to the church.

Clement V., convinced at length, conceives whence the treachery proceeded, of which the Christian Princes so often complained they had been the victims in their wars against the Saracens. He permits the trials of the Templars to be continued, and a hundred and forty are heard in Paris.

The freedom of their avowals.

All repeat the same deposition, except three, who declare they have no knowledge of the crimes imputed to their order. The Pope, not content with this information taken by religious Orders and by

14   See the Vouchers brought by Dupuy, and *Extract of the Registers.*

337

French Noblemen, requires that a new trial should take place in Poitou before Cardinals and others whom he himself nominates: Again, with the same freedom and for the third time, the Grand Master and other Chiefs in presence of Clement V. repeat their depositions. Molay even requested that one of the Lay Brothers who was about his person should be heard, and this Brother confirms the declaration.

During many years these informations were continued and renewed at Paris, in Champagne, in Normandy, in Quercy, in Languedoc, in Provence. In France alone above two hundred avowals of the same nature are to be found; nor did they vary in England, where at the synod of London, held in 1311, seventy-eight English Knights are heard, and two whole months were spent in taking informations and in verifying their declarations. Fifty-four Irish were also heard, and many Scotch, in their respective countries. It was in consequence of these declarations, that the order of the Templars was abolished in those kingdoms, and that the Parliament disposed of their goods.[15] The same declarations were taken and proved in Italy, at Ravenna, at Bologna, at Pisa, and at Florence, though in all these councils the Prelates were very ready to absolve all those Knights who could succeed in their justifications.

When I hear the crimes of this order called in question, it appears to me that a sufficient atten-

---

15   Vide Valsinger in Edvardum II. et Ypodigma Neustrix apud Dupuy.—*Essai de Fred. Nicolai.*

tion has not been paid to the multiplicity of the avowals of these Knights, and of the diversity of nations which judged them. It would be one of the most extraordinary facts in history to see two hundred of these Knights accusing themselves of the greatest abominations. It would be a still greater atrocity to see so many Bishops, Noblemen, Magistrates, and Sovereigns, of different nations, sitting in judgment on the Templars, and publishing to the world, as free and uncontrolled, declarations which had only been extorted from them by the fear of torture. Such a conduct would be still more horrible than that of the Templars themselves; and would it not be equally extraordinary to see so many different nations agreeing to use the rack to extort such depositions from them? But for the honor of humanity such means were not employed in the trials of the Templars, by the Bishops and Grand Bailiffs, the King's Commissaries, the Cardinals, and Commissaries of Clement V. nor by himself in France. Such methods were not resorted to by the councils nor by the tribunals of other nations. Never was a cause of greater importance pleaded; and, from the numerous and authentic documents which are still extant, it is evident, that Judges never were more fearful of confounding the innocent with the guilty.

Let not the dissolution of another celebrated Order, though in a very different way, be objected. The Jesuits were abolished, but they were not brought to trial; not a single member of the Order has been heard in its defence, nor have any members deposed against it. I should be the first to condemn them, could proofs similar to those against the Templars, be adduced against them.

Let us for a moment suppose the Templars entirely innocent of the crimes imputed to them, what could have been the virtue and courage of an order, which could demean itself so much, as to make such declarations against itself? How can the Free-masons glory in such an ancestry, who, if their crimes were not monstrous, must themselves have been monsters of the basest cowardice.

The vulgar may be led away by the tardy protestations of Guy and Molay; but do the vulgar ever distinguish between the obstinacy of despair and that serene firmness and constancy which are the attendants on virtue? They are not aware that false honor, like truth, may have its martyrs. During three years Molay persevered in his avowal, and he repeated it at least three times; when he pretends at length to deny it, his expressions are those of rage, and he throws down the gauntlet to whoever shall pretend to assert that he had made *any deposition* against his Order; at the place of execution he declares *that all that he has said* against his Order was false, and that if he deserved death it was *for having accused his order falsely* both before the Pope and the King. Amidst these contradictions, can the Historian receive such protestations of innocence? Much less is he to attend to the popular fable of Molay having cited Philip le Bel and

Clement V to the tribunal of God within a year and a day, and that both the Pope and the King died within the year; for history not only varies as to the day, but even as to the year of Molay's execution.[16]

---

16   It has been said to have taken place in the different years 1311, 1312, and 1313. The first of these dates appears to me to be correct, because the execution of the Grand Master certainly took place while the Commissaries of the Pope were at Paris, and they only resided there from August 1309 till May 1311. It is in vain to alledge the protest of the Abbot of Saint-Germain as Lord of the Manor against the execution of two Knights Templars on his land; for, supposing this regarded the execution of Guy and Molay, we have the answer to the protest in date March 1313, whereas Clement V only died on the 20th April 1314; so that even in that case the citation must have been of no avail.

Boccacio, who is so often quoted on the death of Molay, does not so much as mention it. When people make such a display of what this author has said concerning the constancy of the Grand Master and the other Templars executed at the same time, some attention should be also paid to his commencing with saying, that "these Knights were strangely fallen off, on account of their great riches, from their pristine virtue; that they were ambitious, voluptuous, and effeminate; that so far from making war in defence of the Christians, according to their institute, they left that duty to be discharged by people whom they had hired, or by valets; and that in the days of *Jacques Molay* their virtues had degenerated into vices." All that Boccacio says afterwards on the constancy and death of the Grand Master and his companions, which so greatly excites his enthusiasm, is solely grounded on the account his father gave him, who was a merchant and at Paris at that time; his ideas on the subject, as is easily perceived, are merely those of the vulgar. I shall always return to the same point. Let us examine the authentic documents and the minutes of the proceedings. When they are to be had, and they still exist in great numbers, they are real points by which we are to be guided. Such has been the line of conduct (the only satisfactory one) held by Mr. Dupuy, in his Treatise on the Condemnation of

As a last resource in defense of the Order, the very nature and infamy of the crimes of which the Templars were accused have been alledged as a proof of their innocence. But most certainly the more infamous those crimes, the more debased must have been the members of the Order to accuse each other of them. But all these crimes, however infamous and incredible, only serve to discover the abominable Sect which introduced them among their adepts, and from whom the Templars evidently learned their frightful mysteries. That hatred of Christ, that execrable immorality, even to the atrocious infanticide, all are to be found in the tenets, they are even in the principles of that incoherent medley of *Begards, Cathares*, and of that shoal of sectaries which flocked from the East to the Western States about the beginning of the eleventh century.

I would willingly assert that it was the smaller part of the Templars who suffered themselves to be carried away by such abominations. Some even at Paris were declared innocent. In Italy a still greater number were absolved, of all those who were judged at the Councils of Mayence and Salamanca, none were condemned; and hence we may conclude, that of the nine thousand houses belonging to the Order many had not been taint-

---

the Templars. This work is written with candor; and though he has not made the most of his proofs, he abounds in authentic documents and extracts from the minutes of the trials, and furnishes far more than are necessary to satisfy our judgment.

ed, and that whole provinces were to be excepted from the general stain of infamy. But the condemnations, the juridical depositions, the method of initiating the knights, almost become general; the secrecy of their receptions, where neither Prince nor King, nor any person whatever, could be present during the last half century, are so many testimonies which corroborate the divers accusations contained in the articles sent to the Judges; that is to say, that at least two-thirds of the Order knew of the abominations practiced, without taking any steps to extirpate them. *Quod omnes, vel quasi dux partes ordinis scientes dictos errores corrigere neglexerint.*

This certainly cannot mean that two-thirds of the Knights had equally partaken of these abominations. It is evident on the contrary, that many detested them as soon as they were acquainted with them; and that others only submitted to them, though initiated, after the harshest treatment and most terrible threats. Nevertheless, this proves that the greatest part of these Knights were criminal, some through corruption, others through weakness, or connivance; and hence the dissolution of the Order became necessary.

Another reflection which strikes me as being of weight, though I do not know that any one has made it, is, that between thirty and forty thousand Knights not only survived the condemnation of the order, but also survived Philip le Bel and Clement V. The greater part of these had only been condemned to canonical penance, to so many days fasting or prayer, or to a short imprisonment.— They lived in different parts of the world, where they had nothing to fear from *their persecutors and tyrants*. Conscience, honour, and many other motives, should have induced these survivors to make their recantations after having made juridical depositions of such an abominable nature against their Order; most certainly if they had made them through fear or seduction, it was a duty incumbent on them. Nevertheless, of those thousands of Knights heard in so many different states there is not a single one that makes his retractation, not one who leaves such a declaration to be published after his death. What men are these Knights? If their depositions be true, how monstrous must that order have been by its crimes; if they be false, what monsters of calumny was it composed of? That fear may have made them swerve from truth during the reign of Philip le Bel, I will admit; but that King being dead, what becomes of such a plea?

Such nevertheless are the men whom the Masons glory in their descent from. Yes, and their descent is real. Their pretensions are no longer chimerical. Were they to deny it we should force them to recognize as their progenitors not the whole of the Order, but that part whose ancient corruption and obstinate hatred against the Altar and the Throne, when added to their thirst of revenge, must render them still more formidable to both Kings and Pontiffs.

Were we to trace the descent of the Free-masons by the Templars, we should not have the assurance of those who suppose the Grand Master
Molay, when in the Bastile, creating the four *Lodges*, that of Naples for the East, of Edinburgh for the
West, of Stockholm for the North, and of Paris for
the South.[17] Yet, following nothing but the archives
of the Free-masons themselves, and the apparent affinities which subsist between them and the
Knights Templars, we are entitled to say to them—
'Yes, the whole of your school and all your Lodges
descend from the Templars. After the extinction of
their Order, a certain number of criminal Knights,
who had escaped the general proscription, formed
a body to perpetuate their frightful mysteries. To
their pre-existing code of Impiety they added the
vow of vengeance against Kings and Pontiffs who
had destroyed their Order, and against all Religion,
which proscribed their tenets. They formed adepts

---

17 This account is to be found in an Almanac printed at Paris un-
    der the tide of *Etrennes Interessantes* (1796-97). I don't know
    from whence the writer has drawn this anecdote, nor on what
    grounds he says that the Duke of Sudermania as Grand Master
    of the Mother Lodge of the North, was accessary to the assas-
    sination of the King his brother Anckarstroem. Though this
    writer shows some knowledge of the Craft, he is so ignorant in
    other respects that it is impossible to take him for an authori-
    ty:—For example, he says, that the Jesuits were Free-masons,
    that it was they who poisoned the Emperor Henry VII., and
    that the Emperor died two hundred years before a Jesuit exist-
    ed. This fable of the Jesuits Free-masons is an artifice devised
    by the Illuminées, and we shall see them own to it, to divert the
    attention of States from their own Sect and conspiracies.

who were to perpetuate and transmit from generation to generation the same mysteries of iniquity, the same oaths, and the same hatred against the God of the Christians, Kings, and Priests.—These mysteries have descended to you, and you perpetuate their impiety, their oaths, and hatred. Such is your origin. Length of time, the manners of each age may have varied some of your signs and of your shocking systems; but the essence is the same, the wishes, oaths, hatred and plots are similar. You would not think it, but every thing betrayed your forefathers, and every thing betrays their progeny.'

Let us then compare the tenets, language, and signs. What a similarity, and how many are common to both!

In the mysteries of the Templars, the Initiator begins by opposing the God who cannot die to the God who dies on the cross for the salvation of mankind. "Swear," he says to the candidate, "that you believe in *a God the Creator of all things, who neither did nor will die;*" and then follow blasphemies against the God of Christianity. The new adept is taught to say, that Christ was but a false prophet, justly condemned in expiation of his own crimes and not of those of mankind. *Receptores dicebant illis quos recipiebant, Christum non esse verum Deum et ipsum fuisse falsum Prophetam; non fuisse passum pro redemptione humani generis, sed pro sceleribus suis.*[18] Can any one here mistake the Jehovah of the Masons, or the I*ew of*

18   2d Art. of their Avowals. See Dupuy, p. 48.

346

Nazareth led by Raphael into Iudea to suffer for his crimes?[19]

The God of the Templars, who never could die, was represented by the head of a man, before which they prostrated themselves as before their real idol. This head is to be found in the Masonic Lodges in Hungary, where Free-masonry has preserved the greatest number of its original superstitions.[20]

This head is to be found again in the *Magic Mirror* of the Cabalistic Masons. They call it the Being of Beings, and reverence it under the title of Sum (*I am*). It represents their great Jehovah, source of all beings. And we may look upon it as one of the links which compose the general chain by which the Historian may connect the History of Masonry with that of the Templars.

These same Knights in hatred of Christ celebrated the mysteries of *Jehovah* more particularly

---

19 See above, p. 284.

20 See Kleiner's Report to the Emperor Joseph II. I never saw this Report written by Kleiner, whom the Emperor Joseph II had ordered to get himself received, that he might know what he ought to depend upon with respect to the Masons and Illuminées. The Report was printed by order of the Emperor; but the Free-masons and Illuminées bought it up with such rapidity, that scarcely a copy escaped them. I am acquainted with a Nobleman who has read and even made extracts from it; and it was through his means that I learned this anecdote concerning the head being preserved in the Hungarian Lodges. It appears that some of the Templars revered it as the head of their first founder, while others worshipped it as the image of the God whom they adored.

on Good Friday, *præcipue in die Veneris Sancta*; and it is the same hatred which assembles the Rosicrucians on that day, according to their statutes, to dedicate it more particularly to their blasphemies against the God of Christianity.

Among the Templars, Equality and Liberty was masked under the name of Fraternity.

Qu'il est bon, qu'il est doux, de vivre en freres,[21]

was the favorite canticle during their mysteries. It has since been adopted by the Masons, and is the mask that conceals all their political errors.

The Templars were bound to secrecy by the most terrible oaths, subjected themselves to the vengeance of the Brethren and to death itself, if ever they revealed the mysteries of the Order. *Injungebant eis per sacramentum, tie prædicta revelarent sub pœna mortis.* The same oath subsists among the Masons, and the same threats for any one who shall violate secrecy.

The precautions lest any *profane being* should be present at their mysteries are similar. The Templars always began by sending out of their houses whoever was not initiated. Armed brethren were placed at the doors to keep off all curious people, and sentries were placed on the roofs of their houses, which they always called Temples.[22] Hence originates the *Brother Terrible, or the Tyler*, who

---

21   How pleasing, how happy it is to live like brethren.
22   *Ibid.*

stands at the doors with a drawn sword, to defend
the entrance of the Lodge against the prophane
multitude. Hence that common expression among
Masons the *Temple is covered*, to say the sentries
are placed; no prophane Being can gain admittance, not even by the roof, we may now act with
full liberty. Hence also the expression it rains, sig-
nifying the Temple is not covered, the lodge is not
guarded, and we may be seen and over-heard.

Thus every thing to the very symbols,[23] their language, the very names of *Grand Master*, of *Knight,
of Temple*, even to the columns *Jachin and Boaz*,
which decorated the Temple of Jerusalem, and
which are supposed to have been given to the care
of the Templars, all in a word betray our Free-masons to be the descendants of those proscribed
Knights. But what 'a damning proof do we find in
those trials, where the candidate is taught to strike

---

23 Without doubt there is a variety of other symbols which do
not come from the Knights Templars, such are the flaming
star, the sun, the moon, and the stars. The learned Masons in
their secret journal of Vienna attribute these to the founder
of the Rosicrucians, called Brother *Ros-Crux*. He was a Monk
of the thirteenth century, who imported both his magic and
mysteries from Egypt. He died, after having initiated some few
disciples, who for a long time formed a separate association;
they at length united with the Free-masons, and formed one
of their occult degrees. Or it would be more correct to say that
there exists now a-days in this degree nothing more than the
name and the magic art of the ancient Rosicrucians, with the
stars and other symbols borrowed from the firmament. Every
other part is confounded with, and merged in, the mysteries
and plots of Masonry.

with his poniard the pretended assassin of their Grand Master;[24] in common with the Templars it is on Philip le Bel that they wreak their vengeance; and in every other King the Sect behold this pretended assassin. Thus with all the blasphemous mysteries against Christ we see them perpetuating those mysteries of vengeance, hatred, and combination against Kings. The Masons then are correct when they claim the proscribed Knights for their forefathers. The same plans, the same means, the same horrors could not be more faithfully transmitted from father to son.

We shall conclude this chapter by a few observations which will not leave any subterfuge to those who may still entertain doubts concerning the crimes that brought dissolution on this proscribed Order. Let us suppose the whole of this Order to have been perfectly innocent of all the accusations of impiety, or of principles dangerous to governments. It is not in this state of innocence that they are recognized by the Masons as their forefathers. The profound adepts only acknowledge the Templars as their progenitors, because they are convinced that those Knights were guilty of the same impiety and of the same plots as themselves. It is in these crimes alone, and in these conspiracies, that they recognize their masters; and as infidels and conspirators it is that they invoke them.

---

24   See above, page 322.

Under what title do the Condorcets and the Sieyès, under what title does Fauchet or Mirabeau, Guillotin or Lalande, Bonneville or Volney, and so many others who are known to be at once the profoundest adepts of Masonry and the heroes of Impiety and Revolutionary Rebellion—under what title can such men challenge the Knights Templars as their progenitors, if not because they believe that they have inherited those principles of Equality and Liberty which are no other than hatred to Christ and hatred to Kings? When Condorcet, summing up the studious research of thirty years, falsifying all the facts of history, and combining all the cunning of Sophistry to extort our gratitude for those *secret associations destined to perpetuate privately and without danger among a few adepts,* what he calls *a small number of plain truths, as certain preservatives against the predominant prejudices*; when he extols the French Revolution as the triumph so long preparing and expected by these *secret societies*; when he promises to solve the question hereafter, whether the Knights Templars, whose dissolution was the summit of *barbarity and meanness, are not to be numbered among these associations.*[25] When he holds such language, under what point of view can the Knights Templars have inspired him with such deep concern? With him, these secret associations, so deserving of our gratitude, are

---

25 *Esquisse des Progres*, &c. Epoque 7.

those of the pretended sages, "indignant at seeing nations oppressed, even in the sanctuary of their consciences, *by Kings, the superstitious or political slaves of the priesthood.*" They are the associations of those generous men

> who dare examine the foundations of all power or authority, and who revealed to the people the great truths, *that their Liberty is inalienable; that no prescription can exist in behalf of tyranny; that no convention can irrevocably subject a nation to any particular family: that Magistrates, whatever may be their titles, functions, or powers, are only the officers, and not the masters of the people: that the people always preserve the right of revoking those powers emanating from them alone, whether they judge it has been abused, or consider it to be useless to continue them. In short, that the people have the right of punishing the abuse as well as of revoking the power.*[26]

Thus we see Condorcet tracing back the germ at least of all the principles of the French Revolution to these *secret associations*, which he represents as the benefactors of nations, and as preparing the triumph of the multitude against the altar and the throne. All therefore he does or promises to do in future, when he proposes the question, whether the Knights Templars are not to be numbered among those secret associations, can only originate in the hope of tracing to them principles, oaths, and

---

26   *Ibid.* Epoque 8.

means which in time would operate similar revolutions. All this zeal of Condorcet for the secret association of the Templars, is no other than the hopes of finding them guilty of that same hatred against Royalty and the Priesthood with which his own heart is inflamed.

The secret which he has half disclosed, more daring adepts have betrayed; it has escaped them amidst their declamations. In the delirium of fury, and in the cavern as it were of their regicide trials, they publicly invoke the *reeking dagger*, they exclaim to their Brethren,—"Let the interval of ages disappear and carry nations back to the persecutions of Philip le Bel— *You who are or are not Templars*—help a free people to build in three days and for ever, a Temple in honor of Truth—*May tyrants perish*, and may the earth be delivered from them!"[27]

Such then is the explanation which the profound adepts give of the mysterious names of *Philip le Bel* and of the Templars. The first recalls to their mind, that in all revolutions Kings are to be immolated, and the second, that there existed a set of men leagued in the oath of delivering the earth from its Kings. That is what they call restoring Liberty to the People, and building the Temple of Truth!—I had long feared to exaggerate the depravity and the plots of the proscribed Knights; but what crimes can history impute to them which are not compre-

---

27 Bonneville, *Esprit des Religions,* p. 156, 157, 175, &c.

hended in this terrible invocation of the adepts at the dawn of the Revolution? It is when they grow more daring, and stimulate each other to those crimes which overthrow the altar and the throne; it is at that period hat the most furious adepts, at once Masons and Jacobins, recall the name and the honor of the Templars to be avenged, and their oaths and plots to be accomplished. The Templars were then, what the Jacobin Masons are at this day; their mysteries were those of the Jacobins. It is not to us that objections are to be made on this accusation. Let the profound adepts of Masonry and Jacobinism defend their own assertions; let the offspring be persuaded that they have wronged their forefathers: and even could that be demonstrated, still it would be evident that the mysteries of the Occult Lodges consist in that hatred of the Altar and the Throne, and in those oaths of rebellion and impiety, which the adepts extol as their inheritance from the Templars.—Still it would be evident that the oath (the essence of Jacobinism) of overturning the Altar and the Throne is the last mystery of the Occult Masons, and that they only recognize the Templars as their progenitors, because they believed the mysteries of those famous though proscribed Knights contained all the principles, oaths, and wishes which operated the French Revolution.

CHAPTER XIII.

Farther Declarations of the Free-masons as to their Origin.

The real Founder of Masonry.— True and first Origin of their Mysteries and of all their Systems.

he learned adepts were not mistaken when they numbered the Knights Templars in the ancestry of Free-masons. We have seen by the comparative statement of their mysteries how much they coincided with each other; but it still remains to be shown whence the Templars had received their systems of impiety. This observation has not escaped those of the adepts who gloried so much in the impiety of their mysteries. They have extended their researches with that view, to ascertain whether there had not exited some of *those secret associations* in Europe whence they might trace their origin prior to the Templars. The

Sophister, the famous adept shall speak. The result of his researches are only announced; death cut the thread of those ideas which he had promised to develop in the extensive work he was meditating on the *progress of the human mind*, and of which his admirers have only published the general plan under the title of *Esquisse d'un tableau general sur des progrès de l'esprit humain* (*Sketch of a general Table of the Progress of the Human Mind*). But in this sketch we find more sufficient to dissipate the remaining cloud, and to rend the veil which as yet the adepts had not thought prudent entirely to withdraw. The text of this famous adept shall be laid before the reader: a very few reflections will then suffice to lead us to the fountain head whence sprung all the mysteries and systems of Free-masonry, and to develop to its full extent the true spirit with which it is actuated.

> In the South of France, says our Sophisticated and Masonic Adept, whole provinces united to adopt a Doctrine more simple, a Christianity more pure, where man, subject only to the Deity, judged according to his own lights what the Deity had pleased to reveal in the books emanating from him.
>
> Fanaticised armies, led by ambitious Chiefs, devastated these provinces. Executioners led by Legates and Priests immolated those who had escaped the fury of the soldiery; a tribunal of Monks was established, who were to condemn to the flames all that were suspected of hearkening to the dictates of reason.

They nevertheless could not hinder this spirit of Liberty and research from gaining ground. Overpowered in the state where it had dared to appear, and where more than once intolerant hypocricy had combated it with savage war, it would reproduce and spread itself in a neighbouring country. It was to be found at all times until that period when, seconded by the invention of printing, it grew in power sufficiently to deliver a great part of Europe from the yoke of the Court of Rome.

At that time there existed a class of man, who, despising all superstitions, were content secretly to despise them, or who at most took the liberty of making them, now and then, the objects of their sarcastic wit; the more stinging as they were worded in terms of the utmost respect.

As a proof of this spirit of Philosophism or Impiety at that period, Condorcet cites the Emperor Frederick II., his Chancellor Peter de Vigne, the works entitled LES TROIS IMPOSTEURS (*the three Impostors*), LES FABLIAUX and the DECAMERONE DI BOCCACCIO; it is then that he adds those words already cited in the preceding chapter, but necessary to be repeated,

We will examine whether at a time when Philosophic Proselytism would have been attended with danger, *secret associations were not formed, destined to spread and perpetuate privately and without danger, among a few adepts, a small number of simple truths as certain preservatives against the predominant prejudices.*

We will examine whether that celebrated order (the Templars), against which the Popes and Kings so barbarously conspired, are to be numbered among these associations.[1]

I will avail myself of this indication of Condorcet. Those *men of the South*, among whom he promised to seek the origin of these secret associations, are known. They are that motley crew, followers of Manes, who during many ages, spreading from the East into the West, inundated France, Germany, Italy, and Spain at the time of Frederick the II.; they are that horde of sectaries known by the names of *Albigeois, Cathares, Patarins, Bulgares, Begards, Brabanters, Navarrese, Bearnese, Coteraux, Henriciens, Leonists,* &c. &c.; in fine, sectaries who, under a hundred different and uncouth names, recall to the mind of the reader every thing that had been broached by the most direful enemies of morality, government, and the altar, and that had as yet appeared in Europe. I have studied their tenets in their divers ramifications. I have viewed that *monstrous whole* of all the *Jehovahs* which Masonry could invent. In their twofold principle is to be found the twofold God of the Martinist and Cabalistic Mason. In the diversity of their opinions is to be found the concord of Eclectic Masonry against the God of Christianity. In their principles are to be

---

1   *Esquisse d'un Tableau*, &c. Epoque 7.

seen the germ and the explanation of the most infamous mysteries of the Occult Lodges, and of their forerunners the Templars. They declare the flesh to have been created by the evil spirit, that they might have the right of prostituting it. All is in the direct line of succession, the Cathares, the Albigeois, the Knights Templars, and our Jacobins of the Occult Lodges, all proceed from the same parental stock. This is still more evident when we consider their disorganizing principles of Equality and Liberty, which declare that no submission is due *to the Spiritual or Temporal powers.*—This was the distinctive mark of the Albigeois; it was by this distinction they were pointed out to the Magistrates as the persons amenable to the laws enacted against the Sect. Let us follow them.

At that period when the multitude of the sectaries empowered them, with arms in their hands, to triumph over their opponents, we see them resorting to all the frantic rage of Jacobinized Masonry against the very name of Christian. Even before the spiritual and temporal authorities had united their efforts to subdue their savage rage, they had already exercised all the cruelties and ferocities of a Robespierre: Jacobin like, they went *beating down the churches and the religious houses, killing without mercy the widow and the fatherless, the aged parent and the infant child, making neither distinction of age nor sex; and, as the sworn enemies of Christianity, ravaged and destroyed*

every thing both in Church and State.[2]

---

2   All this would be amply proved had we published our Memoirs on Ancient Jacobinism. In the mean time our readers may consult what remain of the contemporary writers or those who lived soon after, for the opinions and actions of these sectaries. Such, for example, as Glaber, who witnessed their first appearance at Orléans 1017; Reinier, who was one of their adepts during seventeen years; and Philichdorf, Eberard, and Hermanngard, who lived with them. They may also consult St. Antoninus, Fleuri, Collier, Baronius; but above all let the Councils which condemned these Sects be attended to, and their decrees compared with history; and then will vanish many false prejudices imbibed against the means adopted both by church and state for the irradicating of those sectaries, who, truly Jacobins, aimed at the absolute destruction of all civil society, and of Christianity itself. How is it possible to doubt of the tendency of their disorganizing Equality and Liberty, when we know that the proof necessary and pointed out to the Judges for the conviction of these sectaries, consisted in showing that the accused was one of those who held that *no obedience was due to the civil or spiritual powers, and that no authority was entitled to punish any crimes.* Such is precisely the doctrine of the Council of Taragone, to know whether the famous degrees of the third and fourth Councils of Lateran are applicable to the accused—*Qui dicunt potestatibus ecclesiasticis vel scecularibus non esse obediendum et poenam corporalem non esse infligendam in aliquo casu et similia* (Concil. Tarag. anno 1242). How then can it be asserted, that the furies of these sectaries were only in reprisal of the Crusade published against them, when we see that the very first decree issued in this crusade was precisely to rid Europe of their rebellious principles, and of the cruelties which they were already exercising in the states of Thoulouse under the title of *Coteraux*, in Biscay under that of *Basques*, and in many other countries under different names, *Brabantionibus, Aragonensibus, Navariis, Bascolis, Coterellis, et Triaverdinis, qui tantam in Christianos immanitatem exercent, ut nec Ecclesiis nec Monasteriis deferant, non viduis non pupillis, non seni-*

bus et pueris nec cuilibet parcant cetati aut sexui, sed more Paganorum omnia perdant et vastent (Cone. Lateran. 1179). Such nevertheless is the first motive stated and the first decree issued of this famous crusade. What have Robespierre and the other Jacobins done more to deserve it?

It is inconceivable how much people have been mistaken both with respect to this decree and to that issued on the same subject by the fourth Œcumenical Council of Lateran, anno 1215. They were represented as the church assuming the power of deposing Sovereigns, as usurping all civil and temporal power. And such is the interpretation given to those very decrees which hindered the Jacobins of those days from executing the very plans which our contemporaries have carried into effect against the altar, the throne, and all civil society! Had I but leisure for digesting the materials I have collected, both the church and her councils would be amply avenged of such calumny. I hope hereafter to publish a particular dissertation on that subject, and to be able to show how strangely those decrees have been misconceived, from a want of knowing the history of those times and of the men against whom they were issued.—Let us suppose for an instant Philip d'Orléans, in virtue of the oath of allegiance common in the Feudal System, summoning all his vassals to follow him and unite with his Jacobins in the destruction of the throne, of the laws, of all society and of religion; will any man of sense believe the vasssals to be bound, by their oath, to carry arms under and to follow Philip's standard and thus second his Antisocial Conspiracy? Is it not evident, on the contrary, that no oath can bind subjects to support such a war, that all oaths are null, which can only be fulfilled by the destruction of the throne, the annihilation of the laws, and of the basis of all civil society; that in such a position, it is the cause of the sovereign, of the laws, and of society, that is to be defended in spite of all oaths? Well, I will pledge myself to prove that the famous decrees of the Councils of Lateran against the *Albigeois* were no more than a similar decision, that, so far from encroaching on the authority of Kings, they were issued in their defence, in defence of their persons, of their authority, of the laws, and of civil society; that

When at length the public authority had triumphed over these ferocious sectaries, they shrunk back into their dens or Occult Lodges, and reduced themselves again to secret associations. Then they had their oaths, their occult doctrines, their signs and their degrees, as the Occult Masons have their perfect masters; and their apprentices were only admitted partially to the secrets.[3]

In future we may dispense with Condorcet's researches on the secret associations of these famous

---

had it not been for those decrees both sovereignty and the empire of the laws would long since have been at an end.

I should have numerous errors to combat, and one in particular which I shall not forget. I know there are men so much biassed in favour of the Albigeois and the Vaudois, as to represent them as the ancestors of the Anglican Church, in proof of its antiquity. Such were the pretensions of the English Editor of the translation of Mosheim's *Ecclesiastical History. (See his notes on the articles Vaudois and Albigeois).* Though the cause of the Anglican Church is not my own, still I will serve it better than all those feeble writers.—I will avenge it of the shame of such an origin. I will prove, that, so far from descending from the Vaudois. they openly condemned their disorganizing principles both before and after the reign of Henry VIII, and that there never existed the least connection between it and the Albigeois. It is the exclusive privilege of the Jacobins, and Condorcet's secret associations, to descend from and glory in such progenitors.

3   *Est valde notandum quod ipse Johannes et Complices sui, non audent revelare praedictos errores credentibus suis, ne ipsi discedant ab eis—Sic tenebant Albanenses, exceptis simplicioribus quibus singula non revelabantur (Reinier de Cataris Lugduni & Albanenses.)* Such are exactly the secrets of the first and of the Occult Lodges, of the simple dupes and of the consummate adepts.

sectaries. That is not the point to be sought for in their history. We know they had their oaths, their signs, their secret language, their fraternity, their propaganda, and, above all, *secrets which a father could not reveal to his children, nor a child to a parent; secrets which a brother could not mention to a sister, nor the sister to her brother.*[4]

What is the most remarkable is the coincidence pointed out by Condorcet between the mysteries of the sectaries, those of the Templars, and those again of the secret associations of our days. We know whence the sectaries of the South sprung; we know their common father; if he is to be the progenitor of Free-masonry, the stock is not honourable. To be sure it will trace the Masonic mysteries back to the immense space of sixteen centuries, but if this origin be true the adept need not glory in it. History has spoken clearly. The true parent of the *Albigeois*, of the *Cathares, Begards, Bulgares, Coteraux, and Patarins*, of all those sects in fine mentioned by Condorcet, is the slave sold to the Palestine widow; it is the slave *Curbicus*, more generally known under the name of *Manes*. It is not we who have traced the Masonic Lodges and their mysteries to this slave; it is Condorcet; he is the person to be blamed by the adepts. We were sorry to reveal so humiliating an origin; but we only raised the veil pointed at by Condorcet. He had seen that slave, indignant at the fetters which disgraced his youth, seeking to revenge himself

---

4   Philichdorf, *contra* Waldenses, chap. 13.

on society for the baseness of his origin. He heard him preaching liberty, because he had been born in slavery; preaching equality, because born in the most degraded class of the human species. Condorcet did not dare say that the first Jacobin Mason was a slave; but he pointed out the offspring of Curbicus in the sectaries of the South, in the order of the Templars. He has shown the brethren, who have inherited from these sectaries and the Templars, to be the adepts in Masonry, and that was sufficiently saying that they all sprung from one common parent.

But let us beware of deciding on this single proof. If the mysteries of Masonry really are to be traced back to Manes, if he be the true father, the founder of the Lodges, we are first to prove it by his tenets, and then by the similarity and conformity of their secrets and symbols. We beg the reader's attention to the following comparative statement; the reesult will not be unimportant to history, and it particularly interests those who are to watch over the welfare of nations.

I. With respect to tenets, till the existence of Eclectic Masonry, that is to say, till the Impious Sophisters of the age introduced into the rites of the Lodges their impious mysteries of Deism and Atheism, no other God, no other *Jehovah* is to be found in the Masonic code but that of Manes or the universal Being, subdivided into the *God* GOOD and the *God* EVIL. It is that of the Cabalistic Masonry, and of the ancient Rosicrucians; it is that of the Martinists, who seem to have only copied Manes and his Albigeois adepts. A most extraordinary fact is, that in an age when the Gods of Superstition were to disappear before the Gods of our modern Sophisters, the God of Manes should have preserved his ascendancy in so many branches of Masonry.

II. At all times the follies of the Cabal, and of Magic founded on the distinction of this twofold God, had been received in the Masonic Lodges.—Manes also made magicians of his Elect.[5]

III. Manes in particular is the founder of that religious fraternity which the Occult Masons interpret into a total indifference for all religion.—That Heresiarch wished to gain over to his party men of every sect; he preached that they all tended to the same end, and he promised to receive them all with the same affection.[6]

IV. But above all, what we should particularly attend to, and compare both in the code of Manes and of the Occult Lodges, are the principles of disorganizing Equality and Liberty. That neither Princes nor Kings, Superiors nor Inferiors might exist, this Heresiarch taught his adepts, that all laws and all magistracy was the work of the evil principle.[7]

---

5   *Magorum quoque dogmata Manes novit, et in ipsis volutatur.* (*Centuriatores Magdeburgenses ex Augustino.*)

6   V. Baronius in Manetem.

7   *Magistrates civiles et politias damnabant ut quæ a Deo malo conditae et constituae sunt.* (*Centuriatores Magdeburgenses,*

V. Lest there should be either poor or rich, he inculcated that the whole belonged to all, and that no person had the right of appropriating to himself a field, a house, &c.[8]

Such doctrines must naturally have suffered many modifications in the Occult Lodges as well as among the disciples of Manes. He aimed at the abolition of all laws and of Christianity, at the establishment of Equality and Liberty, by means of superstition and fanaticism; our modern Sophisters were to give his systems a new direction, that of their impiety. The Altar and the Throne were equally to be victims to them; and Equality and Liberty, in opposition to Kings and to God, were the last mysteries of Manes, as they are of our modern Sophisters.

VI. The same conformity is to be found between the degrees of the adepts before they are initiated in the profound secrets. The names are changed; but Manes had his *Believers*, his *Elect*, and his *Perfects*. These latter were impeccable, that is to say, absolutely free; because no violation of any law could inculpate them.[9] These three degrees correspond with those of *Apprentice, Fellow-craft*, and *Perfect Master*. The name of Elect has been preserved in Masonry, but it constitutes the fourth degree.

Tom. II, in Manetem.)

8   *Nec domos, nec agros, nec pecuniam ullam possidendam.* (*Ibid.* Ex Epiphanio & Augustino.)

9   Hieronimus, *Prœmium Dialogorum contra Pelagium.*

VII. The same terrible and inviolable oaths bound the disciples of Manes as bind the adepts of the Occult Lodges, to keep the secrets of their degree. St. Austin had been admitted to the degree of *Believer* nine years, without being initiated into that of *Elect*—"Swear or forswear yourself, but be true to your secret," was their motto.[10]

VIII. The same number and almost identity of signs. The Masons have three which they call the *sign*, the *gripe*, and the *word*. The Manichæans also had three, that of the *word*, of the *gripe*, and of the *breast*.[11] This latter was suppressed on account of its indecency; it can be traced to the Templars; the other two are still extant in the Lodges of Masonry.

Every Mason who wishes to know whether you *have seen the light*, begins by offering his hand to know whether you are acquainted with the gripe. It was precisely by the same method that the Manichæans recognized each other, and felicitated a Brother on having seen the light.[12]

IX. If we penetrate into the interior of the Masonic Lodges, we shall find representations of the sun, of the moon, and of the stars. These are noth-

---

10   *Jura, peijura, secretum prodere noli. (Augustinus de Manichceis.)*

11   *Signa, oris, manuum et sinus. (Centuriatores Magdeburgenses ex Augustino.)*

12   *Manichaeorum alter alteri obviam factus, dexteras dant sibi ipsis signi causa, velut a tenebris servati. (Ibid. ex Epiphanio.)*

ing more than Manes's symbols of his *God* GOOD whom he brings from the sun, and of the different genii which he distributed in the stars. If the candidate is only admitted into the Lodge blindfold, it is because he is yet in the empire of darkness, whence Manes brings his *God* EVIL.

X. I do not know whether any of the Masonic adepts are sufficiently informed of their own genealogy to know the real origin of their decorations, and of the fable on which the explanations of the Occult Degrees are founded. But the following is a striking proof of their descent from Manes. In the degree of Master every thing denotes mourning and sorrow. The Lodge is hung in black, in the middle is a *Sarcophagus* resting on five steps, covered with a pall. Around it the adepts in profound silence mourn the death of a man whose ashes are supposed to lie in this tomb. This man is at first said to be Adoniram, then Molay, whose death is to be avenged by that of all tyrants. The allegory is rather inauspicious to Kings; but it is of too old a date not to be anterior to the Grand Master of the Templars.

The whole of this ceremonial is to be found in the ancient mysteries of the disciples of Manes. This was the ceremony which they called *Bema*. They also assembled round a *Sarcophagus* resting on five steps, decorated in the like manner, and rendered great honors to him whose ashes it was supposed to contain. But they were all addressed to Manes. It was his death that they celebrated;

and they kept this feast precisely at the period when the Christians celebrated the death and resurrection of Christ.[13]

The Christians frequently reproached them with it; and in our days the same reproach is made to the Rosicrucians, of renewing their funeral ceremonies precisely at the same time, that is, on the Thursday in Holy Week.[14]

XI. In the Masonic games *Mac Benac* are the two words which comprehend the secret meaning of this mystery. The literal signification of these words, we are told by the Masons, is, *the flesh parts from the bone*. This very explication remains a mystery, which only disappears when we reflect on the execution of Manes. This Heresiarch had promised by his prayers to cure the King of Persia's child, on condition that all the doctors were dismissed. The young Prince died and Manes fled; but, falling again into the hands of the King, he was flayed alive with the points of reeds.[15] Such is the clear explanation of *Mac Benac*, the flesh leaves the bones, *he was flayed alive*.[16]

---

13 *Plerumque Pascha nullum celebrant—sed Pascha suum, id est diem quo Manichaeus occisus, quinque gradibus instructo tribunali, et preciosis linteis adomato, ac in promptu posito, et objecto adorantibus, magnis honoribus prosequuntur.* (*August, contra Epist. Manich.*)

14 *See* Mr. Le Franc's *Degree of Rosicrucian.*

15 Epiph., Baronius, Fleuri, Sic.

16 Were it objected, that every thing in this degree appears grounded on the story of Adoniram and Solomon's Temple, I would answer, Yes, as to words; but as to facts nothing relating

XII. The very reeds bear testimony of the fact. People are surprized at seeing the Rosicrucians begin their ceremonies by seating themselves sorrowfully and in silence on the ground, then raising themselves up and walking each with a long reed in his hand.[17] All this is easily explained again, when we reflect that it was precisely in this posture that the Manichæans were used to put themselves, affecting to sit or lay themselves down on mats made of reeds, to perpetuate the memory of the manner in which their master was put to death.[18] And it was for this reason that they were called *Matarii*.

Were we to continue our comparative statement we should meet with many other similarities; we should find, for example, that Fraternity so much extolled by the Craft, and which would be deservedly applauded were it not confined solely to their own body. A similar reproach was made to the Manichæans, that they were always ready to succour one of their own sect, but extremely hard on the poor of other descriptions.[19]

---

to the death of Adoniram is to be found in the History of Solomon or of his Temple. All is allegorical, and entirely applicable to Manes. The *Mac Benac* is inapplicable to the Templars. Beside, the whole of this ceremony is far anterior to them. They may have shaped the fable according to their own profession; but they have preserved the leading feature, the Mac Benac, which carries us back immediately to Manes.

17 Mr. Le Franc's *Degree of Rosæ Crucis.*

18 *Centuriatores Magdeburgenses, Baronius,* &c.

19 *Quin et homini mendico, nisi Manichaeus sit, panem et aqua non porrigunt. (Augustinus de Moribus Manichceorum et*

The same zeal for the propagation of their mysteries is also observable in both. The modern adepts glory in their Lodges being spread all over the world. Such also was the propagating spirit of Manes and of his adepts. Addas, Hermas, and Thomas went by his orders to establish his mysteries, the first in Judea, the second in Egypt, and the third in the East, while he himself preached in Persia and Mesopotamia. Beside, he had twelve Apostles, though some say twenty-two; and in a very short space of time we see his doctrines, like the Free-masons, spreading all over the world.[20]

Attending only to the most striking similarities, we have seen the Occult degrees of Masonry founded on the *Bema* of the Manichæans. It was Manes whom they were to avenge on all Kings, on Kings who had condemned him to be flayed alive, and who, according to his doctrines, had only been instituted by the evil spirit; and the word to be recovered was that doctrine itself, to be established on the mins of Christianity. The Templars, taught by the adepts dispersed throughout Egypt and Palestine, substituted, at their dissolution, their Grand Master Molay for Manes, as the object of their vengeance; and the spirit of the mysteries and the allegory remained the same. It is always Kings and Christianity that are to be destroyed. Empires and the Altar to be overturned, in order to re-establish the Equality and Liberty of human nature.

---

contra Faustinum.)

20   *Centuriatores Magdeburgenses ex Epiphanio.*

The result of these researches are certainly not flattering to the Craft; it traces the origin of their Lodges and of their doctrines on Equality and Liberty to a slave flayed alive for his impostures. However humiliating such an origin may be, still such must be the result of the researches of him who seeks the source whence all their mysteries are derived. Their Occult secrets are all founded on this man who is to be avenged, and on that word or doctrine which is to be recovered in their third degree. The whole of this third degree is an evident repetition of the *Bema* of the Manichaean degree of *Elect*, the famous Mac Benac is clearly explained by the species of punishment inflicted on Manes, and every thing leads us back to the Palestine Widow's slave.[21] We may defy the Masons to find any ceremony similar to theirs of *Mac Benac* either before or since the *Bema* of the Manichæans, if it be not the *Bema* itself; it is to that therefore that we must refer back; it is there we must rest to find the source of the Masonic mysteries.

---

21   Will not this circumstance of the Widow explain a custom with the Masons, who, when they find themselves exposed to any danger, and that they have hopes of being heard by any of the brethren, in order to make themselves known and to obtain succour they hold their hands on their heads and call out, *help from the children of the widow?* If the modern Masons are ignorant of the fact, the ancient adepts were well acquainted with it; and all history asserts, that Manes was adopted by the widow to whom Budda, Scythian's disciple, fled for refuge, and that this Heresiarch inherited all the riches he had left her. *Help from the children of the widow*, therefore, naturally alludes to the children of Manes.

The silence observed on this origin by the most learned Masons proves that they were ashamed, but not that they were ignorant of it. It must at least have been difficult for them to have so often in the mysteries of the cabal commented on the *Jehovah* of Manes, subdivided like their own, into the *Good* and *Evil* principle, without knowing the grand author of this system, and who has given his name to the Sect of the twofold God; without recognizing him, otherwise so famous as a profound adept in all the mysteries of the cabal, or of magic and astrology.

It could hardly be possible for the Hero of the Martinists not to have seen that his Apocalypse was nothing but the Heresiarch's code. It cannot be supposed that Condorcet, tracing the origin of the secret associations, and bringing the Templars so near to the *Albigeois*, could have been ignorant of what all history asserts, that the *Albigeois* and all the ramifications of those sects of the South (the *Vaudois* excepted) were really no other than Manichæans; beside, that all those infamous proceedings of the Templars had long since been attributed to the children of Manes; and that all those horrors are easily explained by his doctrines.

When we see the principal adepts of Masonry, such as Lalande, Dupuis, Le Blon, De L'Aulnaye, seeking to substitute the errors of the Manichæans and of the Persians, to the mysteries of the Christian religion, it is still more difficult to believe that they had not surmised the real author of their mysteries.[22]

It may be possible that the History of the Templars and of their Grand Master, as more interesting to the adepts, may have obliterated the remembrance of so humiliating an origin.

The object of our researches has not been to humble the Masonic body, but to develop the snares of a Sect justly branded with infamy from the very first days of its existence. Our object is particularly to make men sensible at length how much it interests both religion and the state to investigate the grand object of a secret association spread throughout the universe, an association whose secret is beyond a doubt contained in those two words *Equality* and *Liberty*, confided to the adepts in the very first degrees of Masonry; of an association whose last mysteries are no more than the explanation of these words to the full extent which the Jacobinical Revolution has given to them.

The hatred which a slave had conceived for his bonds makes him invent the words *Equality* and *Liberty*. The detestation of the condition in which he was born makes him believe that the evil spirit alone could have been the Creator of those Empires which contain Masters and Servants, Kings and Subjects, Magistrates and Citizens. He declares Empires to be the work of the Evil spirit, and he binds his disciples by an oath to destroy them. He

---

22 *See* Remarks on the *General and Particular History of Religion*, by Mr. Le Franc.

374

at the same time inherits the books and all the absurdities of a Pagan Philosopher, a great Astrologer and Magician, and composes his code, a monstrous digest of these absurdities, and of the hatred he had conceived against the distinctions and laws of society. He creates mysteries, distributes his adepts into different classes or degrees and establishes his sect. Though justly punished for his impostures, he leaves them his execution as a new motive to stimulate their hatred against Kings. This Sect spreads itself from the East to the West, and by means of its mysteries perpetuates and propagates itself. It is to be met with in every age. Crushed a first time in Italy, France, and Spain, it spreads anew from the East in the eleventh century. The Knights Templars adopt its mysteries, and the dissolution of that Order lends a pretence to new-model their games. The hatred of Kings and of the God of the Christians is only stimulated by these new motives. The times and manner of the age may vary the forms or modify the opinions, but the essence remains; it is always the pretended light of Equality and Liberty to be diffused; it is the Empire of pretended Tyrants, whether religious or political, of Pontiffs, of Priests, of Kings, of Christ himself, which are to be destroyed, in order to re-establish the people in that two-fold Equality and two-fold Liberty, which proscribes the religion of Christ and the authority of Kings. The degrees and mysteries are multiplied and precautions are redoubled lest they should be betrayed; but their last oath is always hatred to the

God who died on the Cross,—hatred to the Monarch seated on the Throne.

Such is the historical sketch of Masonry, and the main point of its secrets. Let the reader compare the proofs we have adduced from the very nature of its degrees, the proofs taken from the dissertations of the most learned adepts of the most zealous Masons on their mysteries; all those, in fine, which we have drawn from their various opinions on the origin of their association; and I do not think he can entertain any doubt as to the grand object of this institution. Let him then reflect on the manner in which we were led back by Condorcet from the Masons of the day to the slave Curbicus, and how we discover in this Heresiach and his adepts the real authors of the code and mysteries of Free-masonry; and I do not apprehend that he can any longer entertain a doubt as to their first and real progenitors.

Still it remains for us to show how these same mysteries promoted the plans of the Sophisters of Impiety united with those of Rebellion, in the execution of their plots for effecting the grand Revolution. But let us not terminate this chapter without repeating our protestations in favor of the immense number of Masons who have never been initiated in the Occult Mysteries of the Sect. Let us admire the wisdom of English Masonry in rejecting all those degrees where an explanation of the mysteries begins to develop their dangerous principles. Let us admire and applaud them for having transformed this conspiring Sect of other states into an association evidently useful to their own. The more strongly we have insisted on the importance to all Empires of investigating the dangerous principles of the Occult Lodges, the better pleased and the more ready we are to do justice to those whom we have seen so generally adopting the principles of a benevolent Equality, and of a Liberty secured by subjection to the laws.

CHAPTER XIV.

Sixth Step of the Conspiracy against Kings.

Coalition of the Sophisters and of the Free-masons.

T he generality of Free-masons of the present day do the Scotch the honour of looking upon their Grand Lodge as the stock whence all the others sprang: It is there, they tell us, that the Templars convened for the preservation of their mysteries: it is thence that they suppose Masonry spread through England into France, Germany, and other states. This is not an improbable conjecture with respect to the actual form[1] and

---

1   I say with respect to the *actual form of their Lodges*, and not as to the substance of their mysteries; for there had existed Free-masons long since in England who pretended neither to descend from the Knights Templars nor the Grand Lodge in

Scodand. This is to be seen in a manuscript written two hundred and fifty years ago and still preserved in the Bodleian Library at Oxford. This manuscript is a copy of certain questions written about a hundred years before by Henry VI. in his own hand. The date then of the original is about three hundred and thirty years back, as Henry VI. departed this life in 1471. (*See Mr. Locke's Letter and this Manuscript in W. Preston's Illustrations of Masonry, book III, Sect. I.*)

There are two important remarks to be made on this manuscript. First, that the adept questioned on the origin of Masonry makes no mention of the Templars; on the contrary he says, that all the important secrets of which it is in possession were brought into Europe by Venetian merchants coming from the East. (*Corned ffyrste jfromme the este ynn Venetia — 3d answer.*) Locke suspects that in those times of monkish ignorance, the Masons might have mistaken the Venetians for the Phenicians. Mr. Locke could not have chosen a more unfavourable moment for his suspicion, as the Masons and even the Monks had by means of the crusades learned to distinguish between the *Phenicians* and *Venetians*, and particularly between *Tyr* and *Venice*—Nothing was more natural than the answer made by the Mason to Henry VI., 'That the mysteries had been brought from the East by the *Venetians*.' All Masons agree that the Templars learned them in the *East*. It is very natural that the *Venetians*, so famous in those days for their commerce in the East, should have taken these mysteries whence the Templars afterwards did, and whose history had not yet been incorporated with that of Free-masonry. But the reader will remark, that every thing leads us back to Manes, to the countries whence, it is well known, the sect and its mysteries spread into Europe.

The second observation to be made on this ancient Manuscript is, that even in England Free-masonry already comprehended all those systems of *Cabal*, of *Astrology*, and of *Divination*, sciences all founded on the twofold principle of Manes. The art of living *without fear or hope* is also to be remarked, the grand object of Manes, as well as of all impious wretches; the art of making perfection and true liberty consist in disbe-

present aspect of their mysteries; but, from whatever part they may have spread throughout Europe, it is an undoubted fact, that Lodges existed in France and in most other states in the beginning of this century.

In 1735 they were proscribed by an edict of the States of Holland; two years later they were prohibited in France by Louis XV.; and in 1738, Clement XII. published his famous Bull of excommunication against them,[2] afterwards renewed by Benedict XIV. In 1748, they were proscribed in Switzerland by the Council of Berne.

First obstacles to the propagation of Masonry.

From the very nature of their mysteries, this association could long resist the storms by which it was assailed. Men trained to the art of hiding themselves had no other precautions to take than to avoid the publicity of large assemblies. It was in the very nature of their tenets that they found the greatest obstacles to their propagation. England, it is true, disgusted with an Equality and Liberty which the civil feuds of its Lollards, Anabaptists

---

lieving a future state, which may constitute the hopes of the just man and the terror of the wicked. And this is confounded in the general terms of the Manuscript — *The art of wunderwerckynge, and of foresayinge thynges to comme* — the *skylle of becommynge gude and pafyghte wythouten the holpynges of* FERE *or* HOPE *(8th answer).* Amidst all the panegyrics bestowed on Masonry in this ancient record such are the documents contained in it. Though so much extolled by Masons, the reader will certainly not receive it as a proof of the pretended innocence of their mysteries.

2   *In eminenti apostolarus*, issued on 28 April 1738. —Ed.

and Presbyterians had taught it to appreciate, had rejected from its Masonic games all explanations tending to the overthrow of Governments; but it did not clear itself of all the adepts who still remained attached to the disorganizing principles of the ancient mysteries. It was this species of adept that preserved the greatest zeal for the propagation of its tenets; it was some of these who, wishing to attract Voltaire into their party, had made Thiriot write, that notwithstanding the title of *Equality and Liberty* given to his Letters, he did not go to the point.

Unfortunately for France and for the rest of Europe, such was the species of adepts which took the lead in the propagation of their mysteries—*at first their progress was slow and imperceptible.*—It had cost Voltaire much to adopt their disorganizing principles, and it would necessarily cost many young men much more, who, not having stifled all sentiments of religion, repressed not only that spirit of independence but even that of curiosity and the desire of knowing a secret only to be acquired by an oath which might be perjury in itself.

In France particularly it must have been difficult to inculcate mysteries, whose last secret was apostasy and rebellion, in men as yet unaccustomed to declamations against Sovereigns and the social order. Policy at first, and afterwards the progress of the Sophisters, removed every difficulty. The Free-masons, according to custom, sought to gain an ascendancy over the mind of some man

who might protect them against and avert the indignation of the Sovereign; and with the apron
they request the Prince Conti to accept the title of
Grand Master of the French Lodges. The Prince
consented to be initiated, and on that occasion the
construction was put upon the mysteries which is
artfully given whenever a candidate is received,
whose sentiments, rank, or grandeur, is known
to militate against the disorganizing principles
of Equality and Liberty. Many Princes and some
Sovereigns fell into a similar error. The Emperor
Francis I. would also be initiated; and he protected the brethren, who never revealed any secret to
him which could shock his known piety. Frederick
II. was also a Free-mason. The adepts told him all
their secrets against Christ, but guarded against
the most distant hint of applying Equality and Liberty to the rights of the throne, which he was so
jealous of maintaining.

In fine, the policy of the Craft went so far as to
gain protectors even among the Princesses by initiating them in the lesser mysteries. Maria Char-
lotte, at present Queen of Naples, believed, without
doubt, that she was only protecting most faithful
subjects; she petitioned in favour of the proscribed
brethren, who were even in danger of suffering.
A medal struck on the occasion, her health drank
with that of the Grand Master at the Masonic feasts,
appeared to be an infallible pledge of the gratitude
of the Craft: and under her auspices they spread
far and near. But when the Conspiracy burst forth

at Naples this protected brotherhood were found to be a nest of conspiring Jacobins. The plot had been contrived in their Lodges, and the protecting Queen stood foremost on the list of proscriptions.

Many Lords and Noblemen, true and accepted Masons, had joined in the conspiracy; but the Court soon discovered the occult plot, in which it had been decided that all the nobles, though Jacobin Masons, should be massacred immediately after the Royal Family by the equal and clouted-shoed brethren.

In animadverting on these facts, of which the Historians of the Revolution will have to treat hereafter, my design is to draw the attention of my reader to that policy of which so many great personages have been the miserable dupes. The Occult Masons would go in quest of them, and initiate them in all the mysteries against religion.—The initiation of these Noblemen quieted the fears and averted the attention of Government from the Lodges, seeing them frequented by men who were the natural allies of the throne. And this policy of the Occult Lodges proved one of the most successful tools for their success. The names of the most faithful servants of the crown screened the rebellious plots of their occult mysteries; and that of Conti easily quieted Louis XV. with respect to the Masons. The Police of Paris made no farther enquiries, and the Lodges were tolerated. The Sophisters and the progress of Impiety furnished them with new and more efficacious means of multiplying their Lodges.

According as Voltaire and Holbach's club succeeded in inundating Europe with their impious
writings, the Craft extended its conquests. It was
then easy for the Philosophists to make themselves
be listened to by men already disposed to the secret mysteries by their Antichristian and Antimonarchical publications, and to inspire them with
desire for a new order of things to be learned in
their Lodges. Curiosity, stimulted by impiety, daily
made new converts to the Sect. Impiety continued,
propagated, and spread wide the spirit and fashion of Masonry, and that was the great service rendered to it by the Sophisters of the age.

On their side, the Sophisters of Impiety and
Rebellion soon perceived the connection between
the mysteries of Masonry and their Philosophism.
They were desirous of being acquainted with those
mysteries whose profound adepts were their most
zealous disciples; and soon all the French Philosophists became Masons. Many years before the
Revolution, it was difficult to meet with a Sophister
who was not a Free-mason. Voltaire alone had not
been initiated. The Craft had too great obligations
to him; it was indebted to him for too many of their
adepts, not to testify their gratitude to him. Scarcely had this octogenary infidel arrived at Paris when
they prepared the most pompous *fête* for his admission to the mysteries. At eighty years of age he
was *admitted to the light*. After having taken the
oath, the secret which flattered him the most to
learn was, that the adepts, in future his brethren,

Voltaire received a Free-Mason.

had long since been his most zealous disciples. That their secret consisted in that *Equality* and *Liberty* which he had himself opposed to the Gospel of his God and to the pretended Tyrants of the Earth. The Lodge resounded with such applause, the adepts rendered him such honours, and he so perfectly felt the cause of them, that, thinking his pride gratified and his vow of hatred accomplished, he blasphemously exclaimed, *This triumph is well worth that of the Nazarene.* The sacred formula of the mysteries was so dear to him, that the ancient adept Franklin having meanly presented him with his children to bless, he only pronounced over them the words *Equality and Liberty*.[3]

If, after all the proofs we have given of the meaning attached to those words of the profound adepts, any one should doubt of their application to Christ and the throne, let him reflect on the interpretation of them given by Voltaire to the Genevese; and particularly what extent he gave them on his admission among the brethren of *Equality and Liberty*: let him be carried back to this initiation, let him behold the crowned adept, those who crown him, and those who surround him, and can any other proof be required of the object of their mysteries than the list of these attendant brethren. There on the same line he would behold Sophisters and Masons, and particularly those who by their writings have prepared the downfall of the Altar and the Throne, who by their votes have decreed

---

3   See the *Life of Voltaire*.

it, and by their crimes have consummated so iniquitous an undertaking. There he would meet the
impious brethren, such as Voltaire, Condorcet,
Lalande, Dupuis, Bonneville, Volney, and all the
other blasphemers both modern and ancient;
there again he would see the rebellious brethren,
a Fauchet, Bailly, Guillotin, La Fayette, Menou,
Chapelier, Mirabeau, and Sieyès; there in the same
Lodge he would find the adepts of Holbach's club,
and those of *Philip l'Égalité*. Whence this concord,
what object can unite so many *impious* brethren,
so many *rebellious* brethren in the same Lodge, if
not the identity of their secret mysteries? and why
this concourse of the Sophisters to the Masonic
Lodges, if not for the mutual succour they are to
afford each other?

It was not sufficient for the heroes of the Encyclopedia to unite under their standards against
Christ the infidels of the court and of every class.
Many in all classes who had remained faithful to
their God were also true to their King. Even in the
impious part of the Aristocracy many men were to
be found, whom fortune, ambition, or custom attached either to the person or to the existence of
the Monarch. There existed a public force, which
the duty or interest of its chiefs might oppose to
their machinations; and a multitude of Citizens
might have risen against the Conspirators.

But however numerous the disciples of impiety
may have been, still the multitude sided with the
altar and the throne. The Sophisters saw they had

not as yet sufficiently triumphed over the public opinion; they felt that it was necessary to acquire strength.

Having long meditated on the arts of rebellion, they soon perceived what advantages might be drawn hereafter from the Masonic Lodges. From the period of their coalition a revolution was made in the French Masonry, the adepts of which soon became the children of the Encyclopedia. The Martinists alone, with some few Cabalistic Lodges, remained true to their slave Curbicus; all others adopt the impiety of Voltaire. The real source of the mysteries was to be traced by the forms preserved; but it was at this period that all those novelties were introduced which make it more difficult to trace them. It was on this coalition that all our Duallist Masons were transformed into Atheists, Deists, or Pantheists. It was then that the degrees of the *Knights of the Sun and of the Druids* were added to the former ones; but they are nothing more than the impious degrees of modern Sophistry.

Be they however children of Manes, or the offspring of the Encyclopedia, it was always the same conspiracy which constituted the grand object of the Occult Lodges. To secure the triumph of Holbach's club, the Sophisters had only to assure themselves of the support of the pikes;[4] and by means

---

4   I hope the reader will remark here, that the swearing in of the multitude is the last step of a conspiracy, and not the first, as some (little versed in these black arts) are perpetually repeating; and that as long as the authors remain undiscovered, it

of the interior intercourse of the Masonic Lodges they hoped to effectuate it. At the head of this correspondence was a general office called the *Grand Orient*, apparently under the direction of the Grand Master, but really conducted by the most profound adepts. This was the seat of Government, the high tribunal where all the Masonic differences or suits were settled; it was also the supreme council whose orders could not be violated or disobeyed without incurring the penalties of perjury.

It was to this tribunal that the different Lodges spread throughout the country sent their deputies, who, residing there, were entrusted with the forwarding of orders, and with notifying their execution. Every Lodge had its president called the *Venerable*, whose duty consisted in forwarding the orders of the *Grand Orient*, or in preparing the brethren for the orders they were to receive. All instructions were transmitted in a secret language, in a particular cypher, or by private means. Lest any false brother or Mason, not subject to the inspection of the *Grand Orient*, should intermix with the real adepts without being discovered, there was a watch-word which changed every quarter, and was regularly sent by the *Grand Orient* to every Lodge under its inspection.

Government of the Lodges.

Every branch of this government was bound by the oaths of not revealing to the prophane the secrets of Free-masonry. Each lodge sent its con-

---

is but of little avail to discover the vulgar and often misled agents. —Tr.

tributions quarterly for the maintenance of the central office, and to cover all expences which this office judged necessary to be incurred for the general interest of the craft. Those Lodgees that were not under the inspection of the *Grand Orient*, were under a similar government of a Mother Lodge, which also had its Grand Master and kept the same sort of correspondence.

This part of their constitutions was generally known to all the brethren; but I have often repeated that with respect to the Occult Lodges they were in the dark. The day was to come when the greatest novice in the art was to show as much zeal as the most profound adept. To effectuate this, it was only necessary to fill their ordinary Lodges with hair-brained young fellows, ignorant citizens, and even thick-headed workmen, who had been previously misled by the impious doctrines of the Sophisters, and with all those who were carried away by that torrent of declamation, calumnies, &c. directed against the altar, the throne, and all the higher orders of society.

With such a species of brethren the Occult Mysteries were unnecessary, and without any further instructions the warhoop of Equality and Liberty was more than sufficient to excite their enthusiasm and direct their blows. A chief in each Lodge, or a very few adepts in direct correspondence with the central office of the Conspirators, might easily be informed of the day and hour on which it was necesssary that the minds of these underling adepts should be worked up to revolutionary fury, and to point out the objects and persons on whom they were to vent their rage. Nor was it impossible to organize those bands of *Brigands* and firebrands into Lodges, and thus distribute to each the different parts of levelling butchers and of revolutionary executioners. These Lodges, multiplied throughout the state in the towns and villages, might, under the direction of the central office or committee, turn out at the same instant all over the country, thousands and tens of thousands of adepts all enthusiastically arrayed under the banners of Equality and Liberty, armed with pikes, hatchets, and torches, carrying fire and desolation wherever their course was traced, knowing beforehand what victims were to be sacrificed, what castles and country houses to be burnt, and what heads to be carried before the triumphant levellers of Equality and Liberty; thus preserving the most exact accord in the midst of rebellion, levelling at one blow all public force, all public justice, disorganizing every thing and throwing every thing into confusion. But, in order to establish its new empire and organize its own power, it only had to transform its secret dens of conspiracy into Jacobin clubs, and its grand adepts into municipal officers. Thus at length, it gave birth to a Revolution irresistible, consummated, and irreparable even in the first hours of its existence, and before any one had though of measures to oppose it.

In thus describing what might have been done by means of that tenebrous secrecy of the Masonic government and Lodges, I have only anticipated what really was done by the Sophisters to effectuate the French Revolution. As early as the year 1776 the central Committee of the *Grand Orient* instructed the directing adepts to prepare the Brethren for insurrection, and to visit the lodges throughout France, to conjure them by the Masonic oath, and to announce that the time was at length come to accomplish it in the death of tyrants.

Deputies sent from the *Grand Orient*.

The adept who was intrusted with the visitation of the Northern provinces was an officer of infantry called Sinetty. His Revolutionary Apostleship led him to Lille. The regiment of La Sarre was at that time in garrison there. The Conspirators wished particularly to gain proselytes among and make sure of the military brethren; Sinetty was far from succeeding according to his wishes; but the method and plans he adopted are all that can be necessary for our object. To explain this matter to our readers, we will lay before them the relation made by one of the officers of La Sarre, the eye-witness, and one of the many whom Sinetty had chosen to be present at the meeting where he was to disclose the object of his Apostleship.

"We had," said this worthy officer to me,

> our Lodge. It was to us, as to most other regiments, a mere plaything. The trials to which the new candidates were subjected afforded us much amusement. The Masonic feasts made

us spend our leisure hours agreeably, and re-
freshed us from our labors. You very well understand that our *Equality* and *Liberty* was
not that of the Jacobins. The greatest part and
nearly the whole of the officers gave proofs of
this at the Revolution. We indeed little thought
of any such Revolution when an officer of infantry called Sinetty, a famous Mason, presented himself at our Lodge. He was received as a
brother. At first he did not appear particular.
A few days after he invited about twenty of us
to meet him at a tea-garden called the Bonne
Aventure, a little out of Lille. We thought he
wished to return the compliment of the feast
we had given him, and expected a common
Masonic repast, when on a sudden he holds
forth, declaring he had important secrets to
communicate from the *Grand Orient*. We lis-
ten to him; but judge of our surprize when we
heard him in the most emphatic and enthusiastic tone declare, That at length the time was
come, that the plans so ably conceived and so
long meditated by the true Masons were on the
eve of being accomplished; that the universe
would be freed from its fetters; Tyrants called
Kings would be vanquished; religious superstitions would give way to light; Equality and
Liberty would succeed to the slavery under
which the world was oppressed; and that man
would at length be *reinstated in his rights.*'

While our orator continued these declamations we stared at each other, as much as to say,
'What is this madman about?' We hearkened
to him for a whole hour, and silently; meaning afterwards to joke among ourselves. What
appeared to us the most extravagant was the

confident manner in which he asserted, that it would be vain in future for Tyrants or Kings to pretend to oppose their vast plans; that the Revolution was infallible and near; and that the altar and the throne would be overturned.[5]

He soon perceived that we were not Masons of his stamp, and left us to go and visit other Lodges. After having laughed for some time at what we conceived to be the conceits of a heated brain, we forgot the scene till the Revolution (which convinced us but too forcibly how much we had misconceived the man) recalled it to our minds.

When I had determined on publishing this fact, I knew how necessary it would be to authenticate it by the signature of him to whom we are indebted for the above account; but it may easily be conceived that he did not wish to have been looked upon as having betrayed the secrets of the Lodge. Fortunately there are now in London many who were present at that meeting; for example, Mr. de Bertrix, Mr. Le Chev[r] de Myon, all formerly officers of the regiment of La Sarre. Though I have not the honour of their acquaintance, and that they may be

---

5   Nothing perhaps can show the danger and impolicy of oaths of secrecy more than this passage: For, any rebel, provided he be bound by the same oath, may come and make propositions to you of the most dangerous tendency; and if, through weakness or depravitiy, they are hearkened to, he finds Conspirators ready made; if rejected, they are still kept secret by those who are supposed to be bound to secrecy, forgetting that in this case by the very act they become perjured to their oath of allegiance and to their God. —Tr.

a little surprized at seeing themselves named here, still I am not afraid of being contradicted by them, either as to the mission or the manner in which Sinetty fulfilled it; and especially when I add that it was their attachment to their King which misled them with respect to this designing madman. So far were they from any revolutionary ideas, so well did they know the dispositions of the French officers, and so firmly did they think the authority of the King established, that they believed this Sinetty to be a madman, and all his message from the Master Lodge to be no more than the reveries of a heated brain. Now that the Revolution has dissipated the illusion, I leave the historian and the reader to meditate on so important a fact. The consequences flow of themselves. They manifest all that the Brethren, either Sophisters or Masons, coalesced in their central committee, expected from the chosen adepts which they had sent into the provinces to prepare the insurrection. But it was reserved to Sieyès and Condorcet to establish in the very centre of Free-masonry an Apostleship much more general, whose object was to Jacobinize not the Lodges only but the whole Universe.

That Condorcet, whom we have observed so jealous of fraternizing with the *Albigeois*, *Patarins*, or *Cathares*, in short, with all the Jacobins of the middle age, had, without doubt, studied their means. What history relates of them, to inflame the indignation of the reader, is exactly what he adopted and imitated of their abominable artific- *Establishment of the Masonic propaganda.*

es; and he even surpassed them.[6] This zeal so com-

---

6   Notwithstanding I have already given various proofs of the coincidences between the modern Jacobins and those of the middle ages, 1 think it proper to lay before my reader an historical fragment very precious, though little known. It is a letter written in 1243, by one Yvon of Narbonne to Gerald Archbishop of Bourdeaux, and preserved by Matthew Paris, a contemporary author. In this letter Yvon says, that, accused of leaning towards the Errors of the *Patarins*, he thought it prudent to seek safety in flight. Arrived at Como, in Italy, he meets with some Patarins, and declares himself to be persecuted for professing their doctrines. He is received as a brother, sumptuously treated, and entrusted with information, of which he gives the following account: "For three months," says he, "I was among them, well fed, splendidly and voluptuously feasted; learning each day some new error or rather horror against faith, to all which I pretended to assent. *By dint of good treatment they obliged me to promise, that in future, whenever I was in company with Christians*, I would do my utmost to prove that the faith of Peter never saved any body. *As soon as they had wrested from me this oath*, they began to discover their secrets to me. They told me, among other things, that from several towns in Tuscany and from almost all the towns in Lombardy, they carefully sent some of their most docile disciples to Paris, who were there to apply to all the subtilties of Logic and intricate questions of Divinity, in order to prepare them for maintaining their own errors and combating the Apostolic Faith. That beside this they had a great number of merchants whom they sent to the different fairs with a view of perverting the richer laity, and in a word all those with whom they conversed or associated at table. Thus by the extent of their commerce they on one hand enrich themselves by other men's money, and on the other pervert souls."

This, beyond a doubt, is a secret society, a perfect Propaganda. When we reflect that this society was entirely composed of Manichæans, teaching that all men were free and equal, and were to obey neither *the spiritual nor temporal power*, one an hardly view them in any other light than as Jacobin Masons.

mon to the adepts did not appear active and ardent enough for him. He joined with Sieyès to found in Masonry itself a true Apostleship of Jacobinism.

The Lodge established at Paris, Rue Coq-heron, and presided over by the Duke de La Rochefoucault, was more particularly frequented by the profound Masons. After the *Grand Orient,* this was the Lodge wherein the deepest plots were contrived, where Sieyès and Condorcet, with the most zealous of the brethren, held their meetings. This was also the hotbed whence sprung the Propaganda. Of all the writers who have treated of this establishment, none were better acquainted with it than Mr. Girtanner, who lived at Paris in the midst of the Sophisters and Masons. He afterwards lived with the Jacobins, and pryed into every thing with

---

Still less can we mistake them when we observe the new adept travelling from Como to Milan, to Cremona, to Venice, and even to Vienna, always received and feasted by the Brethren, only making himself known and getting himself acknowledged by *means of certain signs which were always secretly given to him, Semper in recessu accepi ab aliis ad alios inter signa. (Math. Paris. Hist. Ang. ann. 1243).*

It is true, that this is a letter written by a penitent adept, who is sorry for having swerved from the true faith, lamenting the horrors he had been guilty of with the other brethren, and only consoling himself with the happy recollection of having reclaimed several from their errors, and craving pardon and penance for his past wickedness. But these circumstances all become new proofs of his sincerity, and only depict in stronger colours the connection between the secret associations of the children of Manes, the true Jacobins of the middle age, and the secret associations of the Occult Masons, or of our modern Jacobins.

the eye of a correct observer. A learned Foreigner and a Physician were qualities which rendered him less suspicious, and he was much in their confidence. What we are about to lay before our readers concerning the Propaganda is nearly all extracted from his Memoirs on the French Revolution.

> The Club of the Propagandists is widely different from that of the Jacobins, though both frequently unite. That of the Jacobins is the grand mover of the National Assembly; that of the Propaganda aims at nothing less than being the mover of all human nature. This latter was in existence as early as the year 1786. The Chiefs are the Duc de La Rochefoucault, Condorcet, and Sieyès.

For the honour of this unfortunate Duke, we hasten to say, that the Revolution soon reclaimed him from his errors. He had made himself Grand Master of several Lodges, and was the tool of Sieyès and Condorcet, who made use of his riches to forward their plans. When he beheld the disorganization of France succeeding to the first Constitutionalists, his zeal for the Propaganda was greatly abated. He at length abandoned it, and Condorcet and Sieyès remained the sole Chiefs.

"The grand object of the Propagandists' Club," says Girtanner,

> is to establish a philosophical order of things, paramount to all the received opinions of human nature. To be admitted into this society

it is necessary to be a stickler for the Modern Philosphy, that is to say, Dogmatic Atheism; or else be ambitious, or discontent with the present Government. The first requisite on your initiation is, a promise of the most profound secrecy. The candidate is then informed, that the number of adepts is immense, and that they are spread all over the world. That all are perpetually in quest of false brethren to make away with them, and to revenge themselves on any who should betray their secret. The candidate then promises to keep no secret from the brethren, but always to defend the people against the Government; to oppose all arbitrary orders, and to do all in his power to introduce a general toleration of religions.

This association is composed of two sorts of members, those who pay and those who do not. The first class subscribe at least three Louis a year, and the rich double the sum. The subscribers are about five thousand; all the rest engage to propagate the principles of the society, and to act according to its views. These latter may be fifty thousand.

In 1790, the general fund of the order amounted to twenty millions of livres (900,000 l.) in specie; and according to statements made, they were to be ten millions more before the end of 1791.

They have two degrees, that of candidate and that of initiated. Their whole doctrine rests on the following basis, *want and opinion are the two agents which make all men act. Cause the want, govern opinions*, and you will overturn all the existing systems, however well consolidated they may appear.

They will also add, it is impossible to deny that the oppression under which men live is most frightfully barbarous. It is incumbent on the lights of philosophy to quicken the minds of men, and to spread the alarm against oppressors. That once done, it will need only to wait the favorable moment when all minds will be disposed to embrace the new systems, which must be preached throughout all Europe at the same time. If any opponents obstruct the way, let them be gained by conviction or by want. If they persist in their opposition, treat them like Jews, and refuse them every where the rights of Citizens.

A very curious article in their code, and which should not be overlooked (as being probably suggested by the little success they obtained at the outset), is that which instructs the brethren not to try their plan until they are certain of having created want. It also says, that it would be better to defer the scheme for fifty years than fail in it through too much precipitation.

"The Propaganda found much difficulty in gaining footing in Holland; and it only succeeded at last by persuading the people there that they must be led away by the general torrent.—At present it draws large sums of money from all those provinces for the general fund."[7]

Such is the account given by Mr. Girtanner as early as the month of February 1791. A letter, dated Paris, September 1, 1792, confirms them all, saying,

---

7   See Girtanner, Vol III, in German, from page 470 to 474.

"You may rest assured, that all that I wrote to you concerning the Propaganda is perfectly exact. At most there are but a few slight errors in the figures, as in the round numbers, which must be taken as approximations. *The Propaganda is at present in full activity.* YOU WILL SOON PERCEIVE ITS EFFECTS. At the very period when Mr. Girtanner was writing this, it is easy to perceive to what extent they flattered themselves with success. The orator of the club established at Bruxelles under the name of THE FRIENDS OF THE PEOPLE had already exclaimed:

> Every where fetters are forged for the people; but Philosophy and Reason shall have their turn; and the day shall come when the Supreme and Sovereign Lord of the Ottoman Empire shall lie down to rest a Despot, and find himself on waking a simple Citizen.[8]

---

8   *Ibid.* It is worthy the attention of every Englishman, that the work on the Rights of Man, which appeared under the name of Thomas Paine, was published as early as the year 1791; that it was profusely spread all over Great Britain and Ireland (in the latter of which places it may be said to have been the forerunner of the unhappy broils we have since witnessed), and it was sold (as I am credibly informed) as low as for 3d. or 4d. to the Irish Peasantry. We should swell this note to a volume were we to enumerate the miserable or rather the abominable penny publications that prove the almost *licentious* liberty of the press, and that have been and continue to be sold of late. Even Newspapers have taken up the task. The GAZETTEER, at this moment comes to hand (Saturday the 16th September 1797), in the third page and fourth column, &c. of which I read

As a corroborative proof, let the reader recall to his mind what I said concerning that adept who was for a long time an unheeding Mason; was only initiated in the last mysteries when, on his recep-

in large letters, "We live in an age pregnant with the seeds of destruction to one *class of men*, and with the means of triumph to another. The energies of men are all actuated, they are embattled against ERROR, *and Superstition, along with its hideous train of Mitres, Diadems, and Sceptres, is* DESTINED TO VANISH, overwhelmed and exploded by the intrepid reasonings of all good, virtuous, independent friends." The writer then talks of *Scourges of Industry* and of friends of man; but, alluding to the French Revolution of the 4th of September, he continues: These "events will be found to be highly conducive to the promotion of the final success of those *schemes which have been conceived and arranged in the retreats sacred to Philosophy*, and to the description we thus allude to. *The* PROJECT *is the* EMANCIPATION *of a world*."

In the next column we find, that mankind are not only indebted to them (the French Government) for Liberty; but "they owe it to them, that the horrible reign of Priest-craft and MONARCHIC INSTITUTIONS have not been restored in one country and established for centuries in every quarter of the globe. To them we owe the re-newed guarantees of *ultimate victory in the struggle* TO PULL DOWN AND DESTROY THRONES. TO THEM ENGLISHMEN CAN ONLY LOOK WITH CONFIDENCE *for a redress of those grievances which have been* GENERATED IN THE LAP OF MONARCHY, and nourished and fostered from the cradle, to a state of manhood by wicked Ministers, and the *sycophant eulogists* OF A WORTHLESS COURT. *From them, Europe is yet destined to receive the* PALM OF LIBERTY, &c. &c. Glorious events! and glorious times, in which men five *only to witness the downfall of some pretender at* (probably misprinted for *as*) *the prelude to* THE OVERTHROW OF SOME THRONE."— Such are the doctrines forced upon that part of the public who support this Paper. They need no comment, but are such as should rouse the attention of every Englishman to oppose them. —Tr.

tion to the degree of *Kadosch*, he was judged a proper person to be admitted into the Propaganda; and who had it left to his choice to go to London, Bruxelles, or even to Constantinople; and, provided he would but propagate the principles of the French Revolution, was certain of repairing from the fund of the brotherhood the loss that his fortune had sustained.

It was thus that many new degrees had been added to Masonry, and even a new society, which the restless enthusiasm of the Sophisters of Impiety had invented to spread the ancient systems of disorganizing Equality and Liberty, and to ensure their triumph. It was to the Propaganda that they were indebted for the immense number of their adepts; or rather, in rendering impiety so common, the spirit of Philosophism had gained so much ground, that it was scarcely necessary to be initiated into the Occult mysteries to be a complete conspirator.

At that time few novices were to be found either in the Grand Lodges of the *Orient* or of the *Contrat Social*. The Revolution was so openly carried on there, that the Court could not be ignorant of it. Among the number, it was impossible that some should not look upon the Revolution as a most dreadful scourge, and in reality several were of this opinion. With certainty I may number among these latter the French nobleman who received the letter mentioned before, from Alfonse Leroy.

The Court and Louis XVI. informed of the Conspiracy, but to no purpose.

Being questioned, whether he had not observed something among the Masons tending towards the French Revolution, he made the following reply:

I have been the orator in many Lodges, and had got to a pretty high degree. As yet, however, I had observed nothing which in my opinion could threaten the state. I had not attended for a long time, when in 1786 I was met in Paris by one of the brethren, who reproached me for having abandoned the association; he pressed me to return, and particularly to attend a meeting which he told me would be very interesting. I agreed to attend on the day mentioned, and was extremely well received. I heard things which I cannot tell you; but they were of such a nature, that, full of indignation, I went immediately to the Minister. I said to him, *Sir, I am not entitled to question you; I am aware of the importance and of the consequences which may result from my intrusion; but were I to be sent to the Bastille, I must ask you (because I believe the safety of the King and of the State is at stake), whether the Free-masons are watched, and whether you are acquainted with what is contriving in their Lodges?* The Minister turned upon his heel, and answered, *Make yourself easy, Sir, you shall not go to the Bastille, nor will the Free-masons trouble the State.*

This Minister was not a man who could be suspected of having in any degree tampered in the Revolution; but he most certainly thought it chimerical even to surmise a plan of overthrowing monarchy, and concluded, like the *Comte de Ver-*

gennes, that, while he had the control of an army of two hundred thousand men, a revolution was little to be feared.

Louis XVI. was himself warned of the dangers which threatened his throne, but continued in that security which only ceased to delude him on his return from Varennes, when he said to a person in whom he confided, *Why did I not believe, eleven years since, what I so clearly see to-day! for I had been warned of it so long ago as that.*

If any one was entitled to disbelieve plots formed against his person or his throne, it was certainly the unfortunate Louis XVI. Seeking only the happiness of his subjects in all sincerity of his heart, never having committed a single act of injustice, perpetually sacrificing his own interest to that of his people, and ambitious of nothing so much as of the love of that same people, how was it possible for him to conceive that the conspirators could succeed in representing him as a tyrant? Louis XVI. had not one of those vices which draw down hatred on the Monarch's head. Publicly proclaimed the justest of Princes, and the most honest man of his empire, he was unfortunately the weakest of Kings—But if ever Ministers prepared a Revolution, it was certainly those in whom he placed his confidence. He began by entrusting himself to Mr. *De Maurepas*, whose inactive and careless disposition, dreading nothing so much as violent shocks or tempestuous broils, quietly permitted all those to gather which were only to burst forth when he was gone. The Sophister *Turgot* appeared but for a moment, as it were to make an essay of those systems which silently sapped the throne. The sordid œconomy of *Mr. de Saint-Germain* only served to deprive the Monarch of his bravest supporters. The quack *Necker* showed no talent but that of ruining the public treasury with his loans, and of accusing *Mr. de Calonne*'s profusion of the fact. Under Mr. de Vergennes, false policy fomented external Revolutions, but to infuse the spirit for, and prepare interior ones. Greedy courtiers disgust the Monarcy with their intrigues, alienate the people by their scandals, corrupt them by their impiety, and irritate them by their luxury. The assembly of the *Notables* convene with the apparent intention only of repairing great errors, at the sole expence of the Nobility and Clergy; and nothing guaranteed that great sacrifices would not prove a great source for new dilapidations. New dissentions threatened to break out between the King and the High Courts of judicature, when Brienne was on the eve of making his appearance to complete the ruin by turning on the Monarch all that contempt and hatred which should justly have been heaped upon himself. Not a single minister attempted to brook the torrent of Rebellion and Impiety; not one reflected on the inefficacy of the laws for a people who hated their chiefs, and had lost all tie of religion. The Sophisters of Holbach's club, those of Masonry, and all the mal-contents of all classes, whether noble or plebeian, had but little to do to create the desire of a Revolution; and that was the period which our conspirators waited for to consummate their plots; that was what the Propagandists called *creating want*. Every thing denoted that the time was come, and they applied themselves to muster up their forces for the completion of the catastrophe.

In the year 1787, about the same time that Mr. de Calonne, anxious to retrieve the finances from the disorder into which Necker had thrown them, was convening the *Notables*, a secret association, supposed of new invention, established itself at the Hôtel de Lussan in the street *Croix des Petits Champs*, under the name of *Amis des Noirs* (Friends of the Blacks). There was nothing new in this association but the name. All sectaries of Liberty, whether ancient or modern, every class of Sophisters, and all the Revolutionary Masons, had adopted this appellation only the better to conceal the grand object of their conspiracy under the specious pretext of humanity. While occupying all Europe with the question they had proposed, on the slavery of the Negroes in America, they never lost sight of that Revolution which they had so long meditated, and which was to liberate all Europe from the pretended slavery of the laws and of supposed tyrants. Their Lodges might become suspicious by their daily meetings, and they wished not to lose sight for a single hour of the grand object of their plots. The adepts did not agree as to the *method* of the Revolution, or as to the laws to be substi-

Friends of the Blacks.

tuted to those of the Monarchy. All however were unanimous on *Equality and Liberty*, the grand secret of their mysteries. They also agreed, that both Equality and Liberty were at an end, wherever the people were not sovereign, and did not make their own laws, wherever they could not revoke and change them at pleasure, and particularly where the people were subjected to a Monarch or Magistrates who governed in their own right, or who were not the agents and the executors of their will, and subject to be recalled whenever it might please the people. But among the adepts were many Sophisters who shaped out *Equality and Liberty* according to their own interests, their dispositions, their rank and their fortunes. They were in some sort the Aristocratic Jacobins. The adept Counts, Marquisses, Dukes, Knights, and wealthy Citizens, all these were perfectly of opinion that they were to lose nothing of their rank or fortune in this new system of Equality, but that, on the contrary, they were to share among them all the rights, authority, and influence which they were to wrest from their unfortunate Monarch. In a word, they wished for such a King as the first Jacobin Legislators dreamt of, a King whom they could domineer over, and who had no authority over them. Others wished for an Equality of Liberty in the grandees or wealthy, counterpoised by an Equality of Liberty in the plebeians, and concentrating in a common chief the King. This was the Equality of the *Monarchists*, who thought themselves guiltless rebels because they were not sufficiently powerful to direct the course of the rebellion. As for the last class, they wished neither for a constitutional nor any other King. With them every king was a Tyrant, and every tyrant was to be overthrown; all Aristocracy was to be exploded; all titles, rank, or power was to be levelled; and this last class alone was initiated in the profound secrets of the Revolution. They conceived that they could only proceed by degrees; that it was necessary to unite in order to compass the overthrow of the existing order of things; and, that accomplished, to wait the favourable moment for accomplishing their ultimate designs.

It was with this view that Brissot, Condorcet, and Sieyès proposed to form a general union of all the adepts, whatever might be their Revolutionary Systems, under the title of *Friends of the Blacks*; it was even agreed, that every man who had any serious cause of complaint against the court should be invited to join them. This was the reason why they invited the *Marquis de Beaupoil de Saint-Aulaire*, whom they supposed to be imbued with their principles through desire of revenge. But they were grossly mistaken. The Marquis had great reason to complain of the Ministry; but no one could better distinguish the cause of the Monarch from the injustice of his Ministers.

This, however, proved a fortunate error for history. What I am about to present to the reader concerning this association is made public by permission of Mr. de Beaupoil. He was kind (and I will say patriotic) enough to favor me with an account of what he had been eye-witness to in that secret society; and in vain would the historian seek a better authority.

Consonant with the wishes of its projectors, the association of the *Friends of the Blacks* was composed of all the adepts who had imbibed the principles of modern Philosophism, and they were generally initiated in the mysteries of Free-masonry. In the multitude of brethren were many thousands of dupes, all ardent for, all ready to second the Revolution, and all promoting it with their utmost exertions. Each member subscribed two guineas, and was entitled to attend the deliberations. That the plans might be better digested, a *regulating committee* was formed of the following persons, viz. Condorcet, Mirabeau the elder, Sieyès, Brissot, Carra, the Duc de La Rochefoucault, Clavière, Pelletier de Saint-Fargeau, Valady, La Fayette, and some others.

Conspirators under the name of *Friends of the Blacks.*

Had I not even mentioned the French Revolution, this list of its prime movers must naturally make it occur. And what could be the object of such a society, which begins by giving itself a *regulating committee* composed precisely of all those men who, in the course of the Revolution, have shewn themselves its greatest abettors? A Condorcet, who would have smiled at the conflagration of the universe, provided neither Priest nor King could spring from its ashes![9] A Mirabeau, who to the im-

---

9   He murdered himself. —Tr.

410

piety, the ambition, and all the other crimes of a Cataline, had nothing of his own to add but cowardice, and still retained all the daring profligacy of his patron.[10]

When the historian shall depict a Sieyès, let him begin with the visage of a snake; for it is solely to the art of hiding his venom that that abominable character is indebted for his reputation of a profound genius. Like Mirabeau, he had long studied the Revolutionary arts; he left to the latter the more striking features of crime, reserving to himself those luxuries of obscure criminals, who point out to the ruffians the crimes to be committed, and then sculk behind their blood-thirsty cohorts.[11]

With all the desire of operating a Philosophical Revolution, and of conducting it with profound policy, Brissot only dared appear on the second rank: But he had already formed the plan of his Republic, and his Philosophism only shrunk from the horrors of the Revolution, when the axe, with which he had himself assailed the throne, was suspended over his own head.[12]

Clavière, a greedy and frigid stock-jobber, comes from Necker's own country to sell to the Parisians the Revolutionary arts which he had practised there. Moderate in his expressions, even when he insinuated the most treacherous and ferocious

---

10 Died in great agonies of pain, 3d April 1791, supposed to have been poisoned by the Jacobins. —Tr.

11 Still exists, 20th September, 1797. —Tr.

12 Was guillotined 31st of October 1793. —Tr.

means, he seemed to have secretly watched Sieyès to learn the art of forming disciples.[13]

After having kissed the gallows, Carra appears to revenge himself on those laws which had not punished him for his thefts, and he seems to enjoy the liberty to which he is restored only to blaspheme like a demoniac both God and King.[14]

He that is ignorant of the effect of flattery on a weak mind, will be surprized to see the name of Rochefoucault among beings of this species.—Condorcet wanted a tool; as long as he could direct this unfortunate Duke he led him every where, to the Lodges, to the Clubs, to the National Assembly; he even persuaded him that he was leading him through the paths of virtue and honour.[15]

As to La Fayette, on his white horse at the head of the Revolutionary bands, he thought himself the favorite child of Mars; seated near the Sophisters, he believed himself a Philosopher; and the Hero of the Fish-market, he affects to rival Washington. Happy for him if his misfortunes have inspired him with a due sense of shame and sorrow for having been so long a time the puppet of the Sophisters and incendiary firebrands.

Lastly, the Advocate Bergasse was called to this regulating committee. This man had neither

---

13 Murdered himself the 1st of December 1793. —Tr.

14 Guillotined the 31st of October 1793. —Tr.

15 When he could lead him no longer he sent assassins to murder the Duke, who was torn to pieces by the mob, September 2, 1792. —Tr.

the folly of La Fayette nor the wickedness of Condorcet, but he believed in Revolutionary Equality and Liberty as he did in the *Somnambules*, who had persuaded him that he was their Messiah. He even expected to act the part. When, in the first days of that Assembly which was called National, he was entrusted with the care of framing the code of Equality and Liberty, he was quite surprized to find himself coupled with Mounier and several other co-deputies. He meant alone to restore the people to Equality and Liberty, and to triumph over Despotism. It was not the superiority of talents nor his high repute for honesty that acquired him his seat in this committee, but the wild enthusiasm of his ideas and his thirst after a new order of things. Happily for him, what made him quit the new Legislators, made him also abandon the Conspirators. His secession only left Condorcet, Sieyès, Mirabeau, and the other rebels, more at liberty to act.

When the Marquis de Beaupoil was invited to inscribe his name on the list of this association, he candidly believed that its object was the consideration of those questions, so worthy a generous soul, on the means to be proposed to the King of alleviating or perhaps abolishing the slavery of the Negroes. He did not however remain long in his error. The establishment of Equality and Liberty, and the compiling of the Rights of Man, were the leading features of all their deliberations, and consequences of the most alarming nature to Sovereigns were drawn and debated without the least hesitation.

Object of their committee.

"Notwithstanding my professed aversion for such opinions," says the Marquis,

I had the constancy to attend the meetings of the regulating committe till I was perfectly master of their plans. I remarked that all the members of the association were also members of the Masonic Lodges, and particularly of that society actuated by the same principles called *Philantropes*. I also observed, that there already existed a close correspondence with the other associations of the same sort both in Europe and America, and the general talk was on the certainty of a Revolution which was nigh at hand. Those brethren who did not belong to the committee came to bring their money, and repeat their most ardent wishes for the success of its arduous undertakings. They then mixed in the different Lodges and Clubs, which in fact professed the same principles, and the regulating committe maintained its primacy over these various Clubs, merely by being a selection of the most wicked members from them all.

Their grand object known, I might have pryed into their most secret mysteries; but I disdained dissimulation; and had I remained longer in this haunt of Conspirators I must have adopted it. Full of indignation, I declaimed vehemently against their plots; I required that my name should be erased from the list; I blotted it out myself, and left their den forever.

I ought certainly to have hastened to inform Government of the doctrines and plans of this Association;[16] but to denounce a society which

---

16　This is a most awful example of the fatal consequences of oaths

had admitted me to its mysteries, bears a face of
perfidy which I should have rejected had the idea
occurred. I confined myself therefore to printing a sort of antidote under the title of *Unity of
the Monarchical power*. Some time after that, I
printed a work called *Of the Republic and of the
Monarchy*, with a view to warn the King, and the
nation at large, of the consequences pending on
the Revolution. This was more than necessary to
expose me to all the vengeance of the Conspirators. I was acquainted that the very day after
my erazure, the whole sitting was spent in sug-
gesting means of punishing what they called my
treachery; many violent opinions were broached;
but Mirabeau only voted for calumny and other
means of representing me as a dangerous man,
and one to whom no credit was due. Carra and
Gorsas were entrusted with the commission,
and it was from their pens that flowed the most
violent declamations against me; and when the
proscriptions began, my name was to be found
foremost upon the list.

If the candour and loyalty of the Marquis hindered him from staying any longer among these
Conspirators, his account at least demonstrates that
he had remained long enough to remove all doubt as
to the grand object of their mysteries. I really believe
myself entitled to announce to the public, that a day
will come when even all the most secret deliberations of this den of Conspirators will be made public.

When the Revolution rendered it unnecessary
for the prime agents to wear the mask any longer,

of secrecy. —Tr.

the name of *Friends of the Blacks* was thrown aside and the association appeared to be dissolved. *The regulating committee* remained, and only enveloped itself in greater darkness the more surely to direct all the Parisian Clubs, the Sections, the Revolutionary Societies, and even the Jacobins themselves. If Gobel,[17] the too famous intruded Archbishop of Paris, was not a member of this committee, he knew their plans; he must even have been present at their meetings more than once. He would not otherwise have spoken so emphatically of what was contriving there at the time this unhappy apostate requested some secret conferences with me, concerning his reconciliation with the church.—I am at present perfectly persuaded, that it was the fear of the Regulating Committee which hindered him from keeping his word, and in some sort atoning for the horrible scandal he had given. It is true, that he never spoke to me of the commit-

---

17 I may now declare it, since this unhappy Gobel has fallen a victim to his vain terrors and mean apostasy. It was he whom I would not name when speaking (in my *History of the French Clergy during the Revolution*) of the Constitutional Bishops that wished to retract. Gobet was at their head. He requested several conferences with me, and we had three, which lasted two hours each. Every thing was prepared. Rome had answered with all the tenderness imaginable to Gobet's promises. His retraction was comprised in six letters, which were already written and directed to the Pope, the King, the Archbishops, the Clergy, the Department, and the Municipality of Paris.

But the unfortunate man wished first to quit France, to be out of the reach of the Jacobins. The report of his departure was whispered about, he was frightened, he remained, and Robespierre ordered him to be guillotined on the 9th of April 1794.

tee but in general terms, yet it was always with so much terror that I could easily surmise the atrocity of their plans: "No," said he, "no, you cannot conceive, you could not give credit to the lengths they mean to go, what plans, what means, they have in agitation. You have seen nothing as yet." We were, nevertheless, in April of the third year of the Revolution, and I had witnessed many horrid scenes.

Long before this period I was acquainted with an adept, a great Mason and Deist, but an enemy to carnage and plunder. He wished for a *Philosophical Revolution* conducted with more order and less violence, and was a member of the regulating committee. I shall never forget what he told me one day, when speaking of the committee, in nearly the same terms as Gobet had done. I could have foretold all that has since been done against the Nobility, the Clergy, and the King. "I go there," said he, "but with horror, and to oppose their frightful projects. Hereafter shall be known all that is carried on there, and how those savage minds add to the horrors of the Revolution. It shall be known, but after my death. I am too wise to publish it during my life. I know too well what they are."

I will not attempt to supply from my imagination what might be surmised from such a speech, respecting a committee entirely composed of the most inveterate enemies of the Altar and of the Throne which Masonry or the Sophisters could produce. But I will lay before my readers what I have learned from various adepts concerning that part of the Conspiracy to which this volume has naturally led us.

Of all the means adopted by the regulating committee, that which contributed the most to form the immense multitude of armed men which they wanted, was their correspondence with the Masonic Lodges dispersed at that time all over France in great numbers. In Paris alone there were one hundred and fifty, and as many in proportion, if not more, in the other towns and even in the villages.

Deliberations taken at the *regulating committee were transmitted to the central committee of the Grand Orient*; thence they were sent to the *Venerables* or Masters of the different Lodges in the Provinces. The very year in which this regulating committee was established, a great many of the Venerables received instructions accompanied by the following letter:

> As soon as you shall receive the enclosed packet you will acknowledge the receipt of it. You will subjoin the oath of punctually and faithfully executing all orders which you shall receive in the same form, without making any inquiry whence they come or by whom they shall be sent. If you refuse this oath, or if you are not true to it, you will be looked upon as having violated the oath[18] which you took at your initiation. Remember the *Aqua Tophana* (the most subtle of poisons).— Remember the *poignards* that will start from their sheaths to pierce the heart of the traitor.

---

18   This is another example of the fatal consequences of binding

Such nearly were the contents of a letter received by a man formerly a most zealous Mason, and of whom I learned that similar orders had been sent to the other Masters of Lodges. For nearly these two years past I have been in possession of a memorial which names several of the *Venerables* who received these instructions and faithfully complied with them. Such was the conduct of La Coste, a Physician of Montignac-le-Comte, in Perigord, originally the founder of the Lodge in that town, a Deputy at the second Assembly, and finally voting the King's death in the third. I can also name the Attorney Gairaux, who did not show less zeal for the Revolution. He was not the Master of the Lodge when these first instructions were sent. The packet was delivered to the Chevalier de la Calprade, at that time intrusted with the hammer at the Lodge at Sarlat; but, surmising to what lengths these first letters might lead him, he very providently resigned his place to Gairaux.[19]

---

oneself by oaths of the tendency of which we are ignorant. It may also serve to explain the question before noticed in page 249, as being put at the initiation of the Fellow-craft to the degree of Master: *Brother, are you disposed to execute all the orders of the Grand Master, though you were to receive contrary orders from a King, an Emperor, or any other Sovereign whatever?*—The danger of such oaths will receive a still stronger demonstration in the Third Part of this Work, when we come to treat of the dark and iniquitous Cabals and menacing Conspiracies of the *Illuminées.* —Tr.

19   I was in possession of another memorial which I am sorry to say has been mislaid. It was the account of a gendeman, who,

I am thus minute in my accounts, because it is essential that history be informed how so deep a plot was carried on, and how those millions of armed men appeared to second it at the same instant in every part of France.

Lest their numbers should not be sufficiently great, *the regulating committee* resoved on admitting a class of men, which had long since been excluded, to the lesser mysteries of Masonry. It was that of the day labourers, and all the lower classes of mechanics, even vagabonds and ruffians. With these men *Equality and Liberty* needed no farther explanation. It was easy for the adepts to infuse the revolutionary enthusiasm into them by the power of these words alone.

The Masons of a higher rank in Paris did not like to fraternize with such brethren. It was necessary to call some from the Provinces, and in a short time the suburbs of *Saint-Antoine* and *Saint-Marceau* were entirely Masonized.

Many years before the formation of this Regulating Committee, the well-informed adepts would

---

having refused to continue the correspondence with the Masonic Central Committee, was punished for it by him to whom he delivered it over. At the first dawn of the Revolution he was thrown into prison as an Aristocrate. Orders were sent for his delivery. The master, now become a Municipal Officer, changed the order for that of letting him walk upon a very high terrace. At the same time orders were given to the sentry to throw him off it, and these latter orders were executed. He did not die however of the fall, and I believe he is at present living in Spain.

write that the number of Free-masons was *incomparably* greater in France than in England; that the hair-dressers and valets, and every sort of profession flocked to the Lodges.[20] It will not be an exaggeration therefore to calculate the number of Free-masons at six hundred thousand; and at that period it could not be supposed that the generality of this immense number were averse to the plans of the Occult Lodges. Impiety and the declamations of the Sophisters supplied the last mysteries. The greatest novices were enthusiastically wedded to the ideas of Equality and Liberty. Let a hundred thousand of the brethren be subtracted as untainted with these principles, it will be the most the historian can do in favour of our youth who remained faithful to the spirit of their forefathers. Thus the *Regulating Club* could rely upon the support of five hundred thousand brethren, at that time spread all over France, all zealous for the Revolution, all ready to rise at the first signal and to impart the shock to all other classes of the people. The Sophisters already boasted that it was not such an easy thing to triumph over three millions of men.

This was the plan adopted by the Committee to organize the Revolutionary bands. The Sophisters had cleared the way by perverting the public opinion. The hiding places and dens of a Sect, the sworn enemies to Christianity and Sovereigns, had opened and expanded themselves. The adepts of

---

20   *Uber die Alten und Newen Mysterien* bey Frederich Maurer, 1782.

Occult Masonry had multiplied; their ancient tenets of Impiety and Rebellion had identified them in the new Lodges with that of modern Philosophism. Opinion had gained the heart; but plots, cunning, and secret artifice, had mustered up the forces. Had *Necker*, *Briennes*, the *Deficit* or the *Notables* never been mentioned in France, had Louis XIV. been upon the throne when the *Regulating Committe* and the *Central Club* of Masonry should have completed the organization of their skulking adherents, Louis XIV. himself would not have stopped the Revolution. It would have found chiefs. Public opinion would have named them, and the banners of truth would have been deserted. At the sound of *Equality and Liberty* he would have seen his legions disband, and rally under the standard of revolt. Had Louis XVI. refused to convoke the States-General, the Regulating Committee would have convened them; five hundred thousand adepts under arms would have supported the convocation, and the people would have flocked to the elections.

Philip d'Orléans elected Chief of the Conspirators.
Such was the progress of this twofold Conspiracy at the time of the convocation of the States-General. The skulking Sophisters of Masonry and the barefaced Sophisters of Holbach's Club perceived that it would be necessary to choose a chief who might be made the stalking-horse, and give them a sanction by his name. He was to be powerful, that he might forward the crimes which they had planned; he was to be cruel, lest he should flinch at

the sight of the numerous victims that were to be sacrificed to their horrid plots.—He needed not the talents, but the vices of a Cromwell. The conspirators soon cast their eyes on *Philip d'Orléans*, the pupil of some evil Genius.

D'Orléans, for his part, was conspiring as well as the combined Sophisters. More wicked than ambitious, he aspired at the Throne; but, like the evil genius, he delighted in ruin and devastation, even though he should not thereby exalt himself; Philip had sworn to seat himself on the Throne, or to overturn it though he were to be crushed under the ruins. For a long time had this unparalleled monster been callous to honor or remorse; a brazen front repelled the shafts of contempt or of disdain, nor was he to be affected by the hatred of man or of heaven. A youth spent in debauchery had deadened every honorable sentiment of his heart, and by the blackest deeds he sought to ensure his expectations of fortune. At an age when the love for riches is scarcely known, public report accused him of having enticed the young Prince of Lamballe into debauchery merely to secure to himself the immense fortune of this young Prince, who fell a victim to his cunning, while in quest of pleasure. Nor is there an action of his life which could render at all improbable such atrocious perfidy. Time only more and more developed a heart capable of such designs; he was cowardly and revengeful; ambitious and cringing; prodigal and avaricious. Proud of his name and the rank of Prince, he was the humble servant of the vilest populace; choleric and impetuous before his friends, cool and dissembling before those whom he wished to rain, callous to all good actions if he saw no direct means of directing them to evil purposes, and never meditating such dark and hideous plots as when he assumed the character of sensibility and benevolence. Little capable (from cowardice) of daring crimes, he was wicked enough to dedicate his riches to the completion of them. His heart, in a word, was the common sewer of every baleful passion, and of every vice. He needed but the opportunity to discover his bias to evil; and such was the chief with which Lucifer presented the Conspirators.

During the contentions which subsisted betweeen the Court and the Parliaments *Philip* had leagued with several of those Magistrates who were more worthy of being seated in the Regulating Club of the Conspirators than in the first Tribunal of the kingdom. He was much more employed as their tool to insult the Royal Majesty in the very sanctuary of the laws, than as a leader against the encroachments of Brienne.[21]

Louis XVI. for the first time showed his resentment, and Philip was exiled to Villers-Coterêts. This was the spark that fired d'Orléans heart with vengeance. He already hated Louis XVI. because he was King; he hated Marie Antoinette because she was Queen; he swore their ruin; he swore it in the transports of rage and fury; nor did his agita-

---

21   *History of the Conspiracy of the Duke of Orléans.*

tion cease but to leave him at liberty to meditate the means of vengeance. His first step was to call to his councils the greatest villains France could produce. That Laclos whose fable genius seemed to rise from the Stygian Lakes to guide the venemous and tortuous course of the blackest crimes.

Mirabeau and Sieyès flocked thither, nor was it difficult for them to point out the great helps to be acquired from the Masonic Lodges, of which he had been chosen the honorary chief. The Legions of Hell are bound by the bonds of friendship when evil is their object, and the grand plan was combined during the short period that Philip remained in exile. At that time he was initiated in the Occult Mysteries, but not as men of his rank formerly were; for it is certain that the brethren had considered him as sufficiently wicked to be admitted to their deepest mysteries. It is certain that the King-killing trial of the Vault in the degree of *Kadosch* was a voluptuous one for him.— In pronouncing those words, *Hatred to all Worship, Hatred to all Kings*, he must have seen all his hopes vanish of seating himself on the throne of the unfortunate Louis XVI., but he breathed vengeance; and, though he were to expend his life and fortune in the pursuit, he would not relent. He renounces the throne under the penalty of perjury, and was overjoyed at having associated with men who had sworn to destroy all thrones, provided they would first strike that of his own relative and King.

This oath discovered to him an ocean of crimes, but he did not shrink at their sight; they only served to stimulate him to the perpetration of them. Brissot declared that he subscribed to them all at that period, but that the *Court was too strong* as yet, and that he only retired to England to gain time, and to let the Revolution ripen. The Marquis de Beaupoil attests this fact, in his memorial, as having heard Brissot himself declare it.

The time was not yet come upon which the Regulting Committees had decided. They waited for the States-General; their artifices, their clubs, and a cloud of writers had nearly made the demand general. The Parliament of Paris called for them. France looked up to them as the regenerating power; but I have not as yet enumerated all the plots nor all the Sects which clamorously called for them to entomb the Monarchy and all its laws.

In these divers plots the Sophisters of the Encyclopedia, opposing the rights of Equality and Liberty to the Altar, had thrown themselves headlong into the gulph of hatred to Royalty.—The Tenebrious and Occult Lodges of Masonry, the antique mysteries of the adopted slave, had received the disciples of Voltaire and Diderot into their bosom, but to connect and more secretly invigorate that hatred of Christ and of Kings. The Sophisters of Impiety and of Rebellion had only intermixed their plots with those of the Lodges, or rather dens, ready to cast forth their Legions of adepts and firebrands enthusiastically armed to establishy their

Equality and Liberty on the ruins of the Altar and the Throne. The frightful Propaganda appeared with its treasures and its apostles.—The *Central and the Regulating Committees* could boast of their Secret Correspondences, their council, and their chief—all the forces of Rebellion and of Impiety were organized—still those were not the only scourges that were to desolate France.

Under the name of ILLUMINÉES a band of Conspirators had coalesced with the Encyclopedists and Masons, far more dangerous in their tenets, more artful in their plots, and more extensive in their plans of devastation. They more silently prepared the explosions of the Revolutionary volcano, not merely swearing hatred to the Altar of Christ and the Throne of Kings, but swearing at once hatred to every God, to every Law, to every Government, to all society and social compact; and in order to destroy every plea and every foundation of the social compact; they proscribed the terms MINE *and* THINE, acknowledging neither Equality nor Liberty but in the *entire, absolute and universal overthrow of all* PROPERTY *whatever.*

That such a Sect could have existed; that it could have acquired power; that it does exist; and that it is to this Sect that the most terrible scourges of the Revolution are to be traced, are without doubt among those extraordinary phenomena, of the reality of which the most incontrovertible proofs alone can convince the reader. Such will be the object of the third Part of these Memoirs.

After having successively developed the Conspiracy of the *Sophisters of Impiety*, that of the *Sophisters of Rebellion*, and that of the *Sophisters of Anarchy*, it will be easy for us to apply the different disastrous consequences of each of these conspiring sects to the French Revolution, and to prove that the Monster called Jacobin is no other than the aggregate of the triple conspiracy and of the triple sect.

END OF THE SECOND PART.

Index.

A

Abiram 267
Abrud-Banga 235
Adamites 288
Addas (disciple of Manes) 371
Adoniram 262, 263, 270, 272, 285, 286, 289, 327, 368, 369, 370
Albigeois 328, 358, 359, 361, 362, 363, 365, 373, 395
Alembert, Jean-Baptiste le Rond d' xvii, 1, 4, 14, 15, 17, 22, 23, 24, 25, 26, 27, 28, 31, 40, 77, 78, 82, 84, 113, 116, 126, 140, 145, 146, 157, 166, 167, 168, 180, 181, 182, 185, 193, 314

Alençon, John II, Duke of 69
America 129, 130, 153, 196, 407, 414
Amiens 234
Amis des Noirs 407, 409, 410, 416
Anabaptists 381
Anckarström, Jacob Johan 345
Anglican Church 362
Antichristian Conspiracy xviii, 78, 134, 143
Antimonarchical writings 144, 146
Antoninus of Florence 360
Archives of Free-masonry 322
Archives of the Free-masons

M

R

Rabaut Saint-Étienne, Jean-
Paul 156
Raphael (archangel) 275, 347
Ravaillac, Francis 4
Ravenna 335, 338
Raynal, Guillaume-Thom-
as-François 154, 155, 156,
157, 158, 197, 328
Rebiezi (brothers) 229
Regulating Committe 422
Reinerius Saccho 360, 362
Republican Ideas (Idées répub-
licaines; Voltaire) 189
Republicanism 12, 13, 24, 25
Rights of Man 413
Rights of Man, The (Paine) 401
Robespierre, Maximilien 5
Romans 39, 41, 56, 151, 202
Rosæ Crucis 272, 274, 276,
277, 280, 286, 328, 370
Rosenkreuz, Christian 349
Rosicrucian Lodges 322
Rosicrucians 272, 291, 296,
316, 322, 348, 349, 364,
369, 370
Rouen, Parliament of 211
Rousseau, Jean-Jacques 28,
54, 56, 85, 87, 88, 89, 90,
91, 92, 93, 94, 95, 96, 98,
100, 101, 102, 103, 104, 106,
107, 109, 113, 114, 115, 116,
121, 131, 136, 137, 140, 145,
146, 147, 148, 149, 150, 151,
157, 188, 190, 201
Royal Prerogative 21, 35, 113,
145

S

Saint-Antoine (suburb) 96
Saint-Antoine, suburbs of 420
Saint-Cloud, Park of 133
Saint-Domingue 237
Saint-Fargeau, Louis-Michel le
Peletier, marquis de 410
Saint-Germain 341, 406
Saint-Germain, Claude Louis,
Comte de 406
Saint-Marceau (suburb) 96,
420
Saint-Martin, Louis Claude de
300, 301, 305, 314
Sallak 297
Salmon, Thomas 74
Saluces, Jean-Ludovic de.
See Saluzzo, Giovanni Lu-
dovico of
Saluzzo, Giovanni Ludovico
of 69
Saracens 331, 337
Sarlat 419
Saturn (planet) 298
Saxe, Maurice de 76
Scotch degrees 265, 268, 269,
271, 273, 286, 291, 294
Scotch Masters 271
Scotland 270, 319
Sect, the xiv, xvi, 6, 10, 27, 31,
32, 33, 124, 126, 128, 133,
137, 141, 155, 168, 170, 173,
174, 180, 182, 183, 185, 186,
187, 192, 194, 198, 199, 210,
212, 213, 216, 231, 234, 237,
240, 241, 244, 247, 258,
259, 261, 272, 273, 275,
279, 285, 286, 287, 288,

www.ingramcontent.com/pod-product-compliance
Lightning Source LLC
Chambersburg PA
CBHW030807100426
42814CB00018B/434/J